Neighbours of Passage

The book is a sociocultural microhistory of migrants. From the 1880s to the 1930s, it traces the lives of the occupants of a housing complex located just north of the French capital, in the heart of the Plaine-Saint-Denis. Starting in the 1870s, that industrial suburb became a magnet for working-class migrants of diverse origins, from within France and abroad. The author examines how the inhabitants of that particular place identified themselves and others. The study looks at the role played, in the construction of social difference, by interpersonal contacts, institutional interactions and migration.

The objective of the book is to carry out an original experiment: applying microhistorical methods to the history of modern migrations. Beyond its own material history, the tenement is an observation point: it was deliberately selected for its high degree of demographic diversity, which contrasts with the typical objects of the traditional, ethnicity-based scholarship on migration. The micro lens allows for the reconstruction of the itineraries, interactions and representations of the tenement's occupants, in both their singularity and their structural context. Through its many individual stories, the book restores a degree of complexity that is often overlooked by historical accounts at broader levels.

Fabrice Langrognet, Ph.D. (Cambridge, History, 2019), is a Leverhulme EC research fellow at the University of Oxford, an associate researcher at the Centre d'histoire sociale des mondes contemporains (University of Paris 1/CNRS) and a fellow at the Institut Convergences Migrations. He specialises in migration history.

Microhistories
Series editors: Sigurður Gylfi Magnússon and István M. Szijártó

The *Microhistories* series is open to books employing different microhistorical approaches, including global microhistories aimed at grasping world-wide connections in local research, social history trying to find determining historical structures through a micro-analysis, and cultural history in the form of microhistories that relate directly to large or small scale historical contexts. They are interesting stories, that bring the everyday life and culture of common people of the past close to the readers, without the aspiration of finding answers to general "big questions" or relating them to the grand narratives of history. The series is open to publishing both theoretical and empirical works, but with a focus on empirical monographs which can communicate stories from the past and capture the imagination of our readers.

Published

Who Killed Panayot?
Reforming Ottoman Legal Culture in the 19th Century
Omri Paz

A Humanist on the Frontier
The Life Story of a Sixteenth-Century Central European Pastor
Marcell Sebők

The Rise of National Socialism in the Bavarian Highlands
A Microhistory of Murnau, 1919–1933
Edith Raim

Neighbours of Passage
A Microhistory of Migrants in a Paris Tenement, 1882–1932
Fabrice Langrognet

For more information about this series, please visit: https://www.routledge.com/Microhistories/book-series/MICRO

Neighbours of Passage
A Microhistory of Migrants in a Paris Tenement, 1882–1932

Fabrice Langrognet

LONDON AND NEW YORK

First published 2022
by Routledge
4 Park Square, Milton Park, Abingdon, Oxon OX14 4RN

and by Routledge
605 Third Avenue, New York, NY 10158

Routledge is an imprint of the Taylor & Francis Group, an informa business

© 2022 Fabrice Langrognet

The right of Fabrice Langrognet to be identified as author of this work has been asserted in accordance with sections 77 and 78 of the Copyright, Designs and Patents Act 1988.

All rights reserved. No part of this book may be reprinted or reproduced or utilised in any form or by any electronic, mechanical, or other means, now known or hereafter invented, including photocopying and recording, or in any information storage or retrieval system, without permission in writing from the publishers.

Trademark notice: Product or corporate names may be trademarks or registered trademarks, and are used only for identification and explanation without intent to infringe.

British Library Cataloguing-in-Publication Data
A catalogue record for this book is available from the British Library

Library of Congress Cataloging-in-Publication Data
Names: Langrognet, Fabrice, author.
Title: Neighbours of passage : a microhistory of migrants in a Paris tenement, 1882-1932 / Fabrice Langrognet.
Description: London ; New York, NY : Routledge, Taylor & Francis Group, 2022. | Series: Microhistories | Includes bibliographical references and index. |
Identifiers: LCCN 2021046852 | ISBN 9780367862350 (hardcover) | ISBN 9781032196046 (paperback) | ISBN 9781003017820 (ebook)
Subjects: LCSH: Immigrants--France--Saint-Denis--Social conditions--19th century. | Immigrants--France--Saint-Denis--Social conditions--20th century. | Tenement houses--France--Saint-Denis. | Saint-Denis-la-Plaine, France--History--19th century. | Saint-Denis-la-Plaine, France--History--20th century.
Classification: LCC DC34 .L352 2022 | DDC 305.9/06912044361--dc23/eng/20211022
LC record available at https://lccn.loc.gov/2021046852

ISBN: 978-0-367-86235-0 (hbk)
ISBN: 978-1-032-19604-6 (pbk)
ISBN: 978-1-003-01782-0 (ebk)

DOI: 10.4324/9781003017820

Typeset in Times New Roman
by MPS Limited, Dehradun

Printed in the United Kingdom
by Henry Ling Limited

To the memory of my mother,

Agnès Mathieu

Contents

List of figures ix
Acknowledgements xi
Abbreviations and acronyms xiii

Introduction 1

PART I
Changing places 17

1 Setting the scene 19
2 A carousel of neighbours 36
3 Consequential crossings 52
4 Chains of migration 71

PART II
Interactions and allegiances 91

5 Positive relationships 93
6 Confrontations 110

| 7 | Of states and tenants | 125 |
| 8 | A war-torn tenement | 143 |

Conclusion 159

Sources 166
Bibliography 177
Glossary 196
Index 199

Figures

1.1	The structural evolution of the *cités*, 1897–1929	25
1.2	The tenement's façade, viewed from the north, 1914	27
1.3	The *cités* viewed from the south, before 1914	30
2.1	Workers by Legras's entrance, 1904–1906	42
2.2	Workers by Mouton's entrance, 1905–1908	43
3.1	Distance between the tenement and the tenants' previous addresses	57
3.2	Distance between the tenement and the tenants' next addresses	58
3.3	Internal movements in the *cités*, 1891–1898	59
3.4	Luigi Pirolli among his fellow workers in the early 1900s	63
3.5	Louis Pirolli among his fellow workers around 1910	64
4.1	The livret an underage glassmaker from No. 100, seized during the 1901 investigation at Legras	75
5.1	Origin differential between spouses in marriages featuring at least one tenant, 1882–1931	95
5.2	Origin differential between tenement residents and their "filtered" witnesses at marriages, birth declarations and death declarations	100
5.3	Real Patronato Español de Santa Teresa de Jesús, Plaine-Saint-Denis, around 1930	103
6.1	The Avenue de Paris and rue Proudhon, no date	114
8.1	Giacinto Pirolli's passport, issued in Isernia, 1915	146
8.2	No. 96's porter Barbe Sommer in her apartment, late 1914	148
9.1	The glass factory after the bombing of April 1944	160

"We should take George Perec's Life: A User's Manual *seriously by writing the monography of a building ... the object of study would consist in looking at the manner in which the occupants of a building live together, in better understanding, in other words, the coexistence. It would be the biography of a street number."*

–Philippe Artières

Acknowledgements

In many ways, this book is the result of a collective effort. My gratitude goes to all the people who offered their time and skills at various stages of the project. For many months, my mother and role model, Agnès Mathieu, lent me her eyes and her patience to transcribe thousands of census registers and newspaper records. Pierre-Édouard Chaix turned the idea of an interactive map into reality and assisted me with statistical calculations. Laura Fregonese accepted to convert photographs of old notary records into neat and clean architectural plans, which are reproduced in Chapter 1. Maria Rosa Protasi shared precious information about the little glassworkers from Ciociaria. Romy Sánchez and Juliette Roussin both carefully proofread parts of the manuscript. Cillian Ó Fathaigh and Reagan Schweppe greatly helped me with language and style.

To say that I received invaluable help from some archivists is an understatement. Without Jean-Louis Bourry, Nadine Marié (Seine-Saint-Denis Archives) and Céline Delétang (French National Archives), this volume would simply not exist. I also want to thank Dorina Salim (Archives of the Préfecture de police) who generously facilitated my research. I do not forget the personnel at other institutions, especially the teams of Fanny Cam (Saint-Denis Archives) and Boris Dubouis (Paris Archives).

This book is the result of many discussions with smarter and more experienced scholars. Robert Tombs, Nancy Green, Arthur Asseraf, Emmanuel Bellanger, Charlotte Vorms, Gary Gerstle, Andrew Arsan, Manuela Martini and Muriel Cohen all provided me with useful feedback and suggestions.

I also direct my heartfelt thanks to all the people who accepted to share their family memories with me for this project. This added an invaluable warmth to the otherwise austere nature of archival work. Their generosity was humbling and inspiring.

Research is also a matter of financial resources. I appreciate the Gates Cambridge Trust and the UK Arts and Humanities Research Council for investing in my research, as well as the Fung Global Programme at Princeton University for giving me a chance to complete the manuscript in the best conditions possible. I also acknowledge the French government, which let me leave my previous job to pursue academic research.

I am also thankful to the Microhistories series' editors Sigurður Gylfi Magnússon and István Szijártó for their trust and patience, and to all the team at Routledge.

Lastly, Alexa Piccolo's unwavering support and encouragement have been invaluable throughout the process. I cannot thank her enough.

Abbreviations and acronyms

ACS *Archivio centrale dello Stato* (Rome, Italy)
AD *Archives départementales* (France), followed by the department number (ex.: 93 for the Seine-Saint-Denis)
AGA *Archivo general de la Administración* (Alcalá de Henares, Spain)
AHN *Archivo historico nacional* (Madrid, Spain)
AHP *Archivo histórico provincial* (Spain)
ANOM *Archives nationales d'Outre-mer* (Aix-en-Provence, France)
APP Archives of the *Préfecture de police* (Pré-Saint-Gervais, France)
APSD *Archives paroissiales de Saint-Denis*
arr. *Arrondissement*
AS *Archivio di Stato* (Italy)
ASC *Archivio storico comunale* (Italy)
ASD *Archivio storico diplomatico* (Rome, Italy)
AVP *Archives de la Ville de Paris* (Paris, France)
BG *Brigade de gendarmerie*
BMOSD *Bulletin municipal officiel de la Ville de Saint-Denis* (Saint-Denis, France)
BNF *Bibliothèque nationale de France* (Paris, France)
c. *Contre* (in a judicial context)
CA *Cour d'appel*
Cass. *Cour de cassation*
CDEE *Centro de Documentación de la Emigración española* (Madrid, Spain)
CDP *Commissariat de police*
FNA French national archives (Pierrefitte-sur-Seine and Paris, France)
Int. Interview (numbered interviews were those carried out for the study)
JORF *Journal official de la République française*
JSD *Le Journal de Saint-Denis*
M. Monsieur
MA Municipal archives
mar. Marriage
Mme. Madame

xiv *Abbreviations and acronyms*

PP *Préfecture de police*
PV *Procès-verbal*
SD Saint-Denis
SDMA Saint-Denis municipal archives (Saint-Denis, France)
SHD *Service historique de la Défense* (Vincennes, France)
T. corr. *Tribunal correctionnel*

In the following pages, a few shortcuts are used to make the reading easier. The French term *cités* (singular *cité*) will refer to the tenement block at No. 96–102 Av. de Paris in its entirety. Note that the term has acquired a different meaning in the context of the French banlieues after the construction of large public housing complexes in the 1960s. Nowadays, the word is more or less equivalent to the American "project." In the text, it will alternate with its imperfect translation "tenement," a historical term which refers to analogous realities in the US, Irish and Scottish contexts. A "tenant" or "resident" without further precision shall designate an occupant of the tenement under study. Addresses are frequently condensed into a simple civic number ("No. 98," "No. 96"), when no ambiguity is possible.

Some French expressions are marked with an asterisk (*); their definition can be found in the glossary at the end of this volume.

Introduction

By way of a pre-credit sequence, as it were, let us time-travel to April 1869.[1] That month, a few days and many miles apart from each other, four babies were born: Edmond, Ernest, Bernardo, and Lucie. Edmond's birthplace was a small village in Lorraine. His father was a shepherd and strolling basket-maker, his mother a *journalière** – that is, a daily worker who regularly changed jobs. At the same time, little Ernest was starting his life in the northeast of Paris, in the family of a coachman. His parents, both migrants from Normandy, had married just in time to make him a legitimate child. As for Bernardo he, too, was born into a newly-formed family, but one of farm-labourers. His family's house stood in a small settlement in the hills overlooking Cassino, in Southern Italy. Lastly, Lucie's life began in Franche-Comté, in a town of 2,000 inhabitants known for its century-old glassworks. There, Lucie's father – originally from a hamlet 40 miles further north – was employed as a carver.[2]

Little could these four families know that they would later become neighbours at the same unremarkable set of buildings in a Northern Parisian suburb called the Plaine-Saint-Denis. It would take a number of changes, at various levels, for their paths to cross. The first event was the Franco-Prussian war, which drove many Alsatians and Lorrainers east, such as Edmond's family. Their village was cut in half by the new border. Then, there were potent economic forces that made living conditions increasingly difficult in certain regions. Those were coupled with the rapid development of areas like the Plaine-Saint-Denis, a hitherto barren swathe of land near Paris where factories started popping up in record numbers from the 1870s. Among those factories was a glassworks known by the name of its founder, M. Legras. Not only did that plant play a major role in shaping the demography of the neighbourhood, but Edmond, Bernardo and Lucie's father all ended up holding jobs there for years.

Furthermore, housing for the four families in the "Plaine," as its denizens called it, still had to be erected. For now, the vast terrain where the buildings would stand was still all but empty. More importantly, those individuals would have to make a number of conscious life decisions which were not bound to happen. Some, as Edmond's and Bernardo's parents, left

DOI: 10.4324/9781003017820-101

agriculture for industrial jobs. In Lucie's case, both her father and her mother held on to their former occupations, only changing places. As far as Ernest was concerned, his immediate family would not join the ranks of factory workers. Instead, they would cater and provide lodging to others. This last part did not require a major material change; in the late 1860s, the hotel-restaurant which Ernest's family would come to control was already in operation. Upon walking through the front door, one would have found a migrant owner, migrant clients, and a pool table – three features that were to remain constant for a full century.[3]

It is there, in that specific environment, that this book anchors itself. The plot revolves around the residents at 96, 98, 100 and 102 Avenue de Paris – known as Avenue du Président-Wilson since 1919 – in the Plaine-Saint-Denis, a subsection of Saint-Denis. The action takes place between 1882 and 1932.

A microhistorical experiment

Far from arbitrary, this selection of place and time results from this study's design and is tailored to its main question: how did the people who lived there – most of whom happened to be migrants – experience sociocultural difference? This book contends that the answer has to include more variability across time, more intersectionality (broadly understood here as the combination of several parameters of difference[4]) and more agency than one would expect based on existing studies at the so-called "macro" level. The research presented in this volume was indeed planned as a nonconformist experiment. As such, it places the emphasis on the contingent dynamics of coexistence, rather than putatively natural separations between people. The aim is to deconstruct and historicise the forms of classification through which people differentiated themselves from each other and acted upon those differences. One of this study's main claims, in that respect, is that the explanatory value of ethnicity and nation, two of the usual objects of migration history when it seeks to understand migrants' social and cultural adjustments, should be scaled back to a more convincing historical position as "boundary-making" processes in competition, or synergy, with many others.[5] This case could be argued in a number of ways. The choice here is to use microhistory, for its characteristic blend of nuance, detail and vividness.

This monograph is also reflective of its times. Times, academically, marked by an aspiration to interdisciplinarity, combinations of qualitative and quantitative methods, multi-site and multi-source efforts. Times, politically, in which migrations are routinely misunderstood, caricatured and exploited for misguided purposes. This topicality constitutes, as it often does in migration history, the circumstantial incentive at the foundation of this project. It is only fitting, then, that this narrative should be rooted in the Plaine-Saint-Denis, which has had an immigrant-majority population for the past 150 years and counting.

As far as its theoretical components are concerned, this study does not take place in a vacuum. It results instead from the observation of several areas where academic scholarship could make progress. Let us briefly sketch them out in order to understand this book's major choices.

The academic literature

First, migration history has been affected by what sociologists would call "sample selection biases." That is to say that certain boundaries, certain delineations between people, have often been taken for granted by historians. They can be social in nature, like the ones that run between social groups framed in ethnic terms. Since the so-called ethnic turn effectively punctured the melting-pot model in the 1960s and 1970s, the core assumptions of the community study model have been left mostly unchallenged. To this day, the singularities of each type of migrants – meaning each ethnic, national or religious group – remain the focus of many historical studies. As a result, immigration societies come across as mosaics, made of side-by-side communities endowed by default with social autonomy. The problem is that presupposing by construction the existence of bounded ethnic units stands in the way of analysing the contingent processes of group formation. Calls to rethink ethnicity as "ethnicisation," i.e. something fundamentally negotiable and relational, have long remained unheeded.[6] Moreover, the bulk of ethnicity studies have tended to smooth over differences within each ethnic group, leading to "multichrome mosaics of monochrome identity groups."[7] Sometimes, even, the mosaic has only two colours. Over-determined by legal norms and political rhetoric, a number of studies assume a fundamental separation between immigrants on the one side and a "native" society on the other.

Presupposed separations are not limited to social groups; scholars can also unwittingly apply them to cultural notions. For one thing, the categories of difference that people use to position themselves and others are often isolated from each other. This reflects the cautious pace at which historians have taken advantage of the interconnections of categories such as nation, ethnicity, race and gender, not to mention their respective malleability.[8] Across disciplines, most scholars would now agree that as social constructs, ethnic, racial or gender boundaries undergo redefinition and displacement over time. Historical studies are key to document this; thus far, however, they have not fully embraced contingency, nor clearly repudiated essentialist presuppositions and teleological reasonings.[9] This old "fixist" perspective[10] is nowhere more palpable than in the enduring fortune of "identity." Two decades ago, Rogers Brubaker and Frederick Cooper powerfully warned against the shortcomings of this notion, suggesting that "identification" was more effective in conveying the contingent and provisional character of cultural dynamics taking place in the social.[11] Indeed, what is at stake should not be what an ethnic group, race or nation *is*, but rather how those categories actually *work,* and how they do so in connection with one another. This view has been increasingly vindicated by research examining differentiation mechanisms as cognitive practices.[12] The structures and singularities of those operational patterns, they have shown, are constantly reconfigured through the agents' lived experiences.

In line with those insights, the key notion of identification will be used throughout this volume. It should be understood in reference to never-ending cultural cognitive processes through which individuals classify themselves and others according to categories of difference. This does not mean that social boundaries are non-existent, or random; far from it. As contingent as they may be, the mental categories of identification have lay versions in the social world, and it is the performative character of those "enacted scripts" that triggers concrete individual and collective actions on a daily basis.[13] The difficulty is that these in-the-world, explicit manifestations – which are visible, through their traces, to the historian – often obfuscate as much as they reveal about what is happening in people's minds. Thought processes always retain a fundamentally ambiguous, mutable and idiosyncratic component.

The enduring essentialism of migration scholarship has been compounded by the insufficient connections between the institutional approach of difference and the studies of its grass-roots versions. The interest in the official, top-down categories of difference has been mainly rekindled by the popular concept of citizenship. To its promoters' credit, this concept allows for nuanced discussions of inclusion and exclusion based on official identifications.[14] It is also true that scholars are increasingly aware of the contingencies in the application of those categories, and of the bottom-up influence migrants have in shaping them.[15] However, the focus on the legal framework has had a significant side effect: perpetuating the national scope of migration studies. Migrants themselves often live their lives beyond, or beneath, nation-states; especially when and where the latter have a much weaker presence.

This has not gone unnoticed. A growing body of literature has attempted to take into account not-predominantly-national experiences and phenomena. Owing much to the context of post-structuralism, these "transnational studies," as they are generically labelled, are concerned with the interactions, exchanges, constructions and translations that occur whenever people, goods or ideas cross apparent boundaries. In that regard, historians of international migration – who, by definition, engage with such crossings – are not always prone to looking at relational dynamics taking place within or across ethnic boundaries in the society of immigration. They generally limit themselves to a more "vertical" sort of transnationalism, as it were – the one that ties the migrants to their homeland, which chronologically was the first focus of the transnational turn.[16]

All of this leaves ample space for innovative research. And this is also true of spatial and temporal choices. The historiography of migration traditionally operates in spatial compartments. This is due to at least three mutually reinforcing biases. The first is an administrative naturalism that leads researchers to handle legal and political denominations as immutable realities and apply them on to the past with little awareness of the "epistemological unconscious."[17] This stems in good part from the way archives are located, sorted and classified.[18] For instance, academic studies continue to treat the migrants of Paris and of the banlieues separately, skewing the assessment of the migrants' own lived geographies.[19] Administrative and archival divisions also contribute to setting apart "internal" and "foreign" migrants in the historiography, the former usually being left to demographers and demographic historians. The second bias is the much-decried "methodological nationalism," still prevalent in migration studies.[20] Scholars too often presume the existence and relevance of "national societies" at both ends of the migrating process, while assimilation and integration are only understood in national terms. The third unbecoming inclination is a positivist aspiration to historiographical legitimacy through demographics. The goal of the French historiography of migration, for example, has long consisted in restoring the importance of immigration in French history based on aggregate numbers of immigrants. Across the board, migration history remains haunted by the need to justify its own existence by such quantitative arguments.[21] While it has produced valuable results – thanks, in particular, to computer technologies[22] – this tendency has also contributed to the lack of microhistorical interest in the mobility experience.

This scientific context has left an imprint on the more specific historiography about Saint-Denis and the northern banlieues of Paris. For decades, that literature barely showed any interest in migration or migrants. Even Jean-Paul Brunet's major political history of Saint-Denis did not closely examine the living conditions of the working class, which concerned only 32 of his 1,647 pages.[23] Moreover, his otherwise nuanced narrative held onto a fixist vision of ethnicity in its sparse comments about foreigners and migrants.[24]

From the mid-1990s, the history of the suburban lower classes, long dominated by Marxist approaches, experienced a renewed interest, largely spurred by political controversies over immigration. This current initially left sociocultural questions to the side. Gradually, these were picked up by scholars who set out to revamp the history of the banlieues. In particular, Natacha Lillo's study of the "Petite Espagne" – the name by which a vast and discontinuous area covering parts of Aubervilliers, the Plaine-Saint-Denis and Saint-Ouen came to be known – focused on the interwar era.[25] In addition to Spaniards, the area hosted many Italians, "Gypsies" and French Southerners. As insightful as it was on politicisation, transnationalism and social conditions, Lillo's effort remained hampered by several theoretical and methodological blind spots.

First, it embraced the classic mono-ethnic approach, never quite addressing why Spaniards made for a legitimate and exclusive category of analysis.

Second, the study was built on the unchallenged assumption of the existence of a Spanish neighbourhood in the Plaine-Saint-Denis. Lillo even qualified it as something close to a "ghetto in the American sense," without any solid evidence to support such a claim.[26] Unlike Brunet, whose concerns revolved mostly around city hall, Lillo did notice the buildings at 96–102 Avenue de Paris. Unsurprisingly, however, they failed to elicit her interest; the place was outside what she perceived as the ethnic core of the growing Spanish area. Instead of assessing the buildings' diverse population on its own terms, she remarked the absence of what she was looking for: Spaniards living together.[27]

By contrast, Leslie Page Moch's later study of the Bretons in Saint-Denis and the 14th arrondissement of Paris insisted clearly on the contingent construction of the Bretons' ethnic traits.[28] That work also had the merit to mine sources that had been neglected by both Brunet and Lillo – namely, local police registers. Yet it did not go far enough to escape some of the most inhibiting traits of community studies: the supposed relevance of ethnicity, a limited interest in interethnic interactions and a major reliance on ethnic sources.

Beyond the question of the banlieues, the existing scholarship has also been shaped by an insufficiently reflexive approach to periodisation. For one thing, the First World War is still widely construed as an unquestionable turning point, as well as an autonomous period in itself. The attempt to dig into the history of foreigners and colonial subjects in France during the war is still very much enclosed within the traditional dates of 1914 and 1918, as are the majority of social history publications about the period.[29] This carries the risk of excessively singularising the war experience. Second, the dependence on administrative sources when studying migration has led to a disproportionate interest in the interwar period, in which new requirements and procedures produced more abundant records than in previous years. Today, historical publications on migration after the First World War still outweigh the works that dare take a longer perspective.[30] As this book will illustrate, however, the migrants from the interwar period and their peers from the Belle Époque were often one and the same.

Lastly, migration history traditionally positions itself at the macro level of analysis and disregards certain types of source material. There are various reasons for the deficit of micro-analysis in migration history. The first is epistemological. Many migration specialists initially mistook this new set of methods, developed in the 1970s, for a *pis aller* instead of an alternative process to produce knowledge and meaning. Micro studies only appeared warranted when sources to write history at the presumably "normal" scale, i.e. the macro level, were missing – an argument that still undergirds a number of microhistories.[31] Later on, the transnational turn, with its emphasis on global, connected or shared history, appeared to call for larger scales, rather than smaller ones. Despite its popularity in theorising globalisation, Arjun Appadurai's concept of "multi-scalar scapes" initially had a little empirical echo in local settings.[32]

The lack of micro approaches in migration history is also due to political and ideological factors. Since the 1960s, the torchbearers of migration history – themselves often the descendants of immigrants – had shared the emancipatory preoccupations of the New Social History and its efforts to "historicise ordinary people."[33] In that sense, these scholars were less concerned with individual experiences than with the big historical picture and its perceived unfairness towards particular ethnic groups or immigrants more generally. Overarching narratives and aggregate numbers, therefore, appeared more effective than individual itineraries, deemed intrinsically inconclusive, hence politically weaker. Over the last few decades, however, progressive scholars have realised that stressing the agency of individuals could, in fact, wield some political influence. This was a way of debunking capitalist and nationalist teleology while answering the postmodern call for contingency. As a newfound enthusiasm for microhistory burgeoned across topics and periods, more historians of migration have been trying their luck at the microscope.[34]

The last series of obstacles, practical and methodological in nature, help explain why migration historians have long been wary of taking the plunge into microhistory. The first attempts at microhistory had mostly been based on serendipitous discoveries of document "treasure troves" – judicial records, diaries, correspondences – containing unusually rich information about one individual, one family or one community. Migration history is no stranger to such source-triggered projects.[35] But things have changed. This book intends to show that a microhistory from scratch, so to speak, is now within the realm of possibility: new digital tools and databases make it easier to track specific individuals in the sources.

The prowess of digital tools is only one resource for microhistorians. There is also much to be retrieved from more traditional sites of excavation, some of which are routinely ignored by migration specialists. In particular, judicial and police records have not received enough scrutiny. They are an all-important material when it comes to reconstructing the past of those who did not leave direct, first-person traces.[36] The unparalleled collection of Paris "analytical registers," completed by the police every night in each neighbourhood, is a mine of information. Before this study, it had yet to be used by microhistorical investigations into particular families and individuals. Archives of local courts (*justices de paix**) and precious cross-references to judicial proceedings found in police records, military registers and the press, have also mostly stayed under the radar. As for the entire collection of French naturalisation files, perfectly preserved since the mid-19th century, scholars long considered them impenetrable, despite their immense potential for both quantitative and qualitative analysis.

Lastly, migration histories of Europe could rely more on oral history, which is an important tool to "grasp the infra-ordinary."[37] Despite valuable projects meant to retrieve and preserve migrant memories,[38] few historians of migration in France have attempted to interweave oral and written histories of migration.

The choice of an unorthodox framework

The research presented in this book is an attempt at connecting the promising concepts, sources and methods outlined above. This seemed indispensable to test a series of unconventional hypotheses.

First, the existence and relevance of ethnic groups ought to be a question, not a starting point. In this book, individuals will be the sole axiomatic social units. As Jacques Revel puts it, "in place of systems of classification based on explicit (general or local) criteria, microanalysis focuses on the behaviours that define and reshape social identities."[39] To reconstruct people's behaviours and interactions, methods will be borrowed from network studies, not only when it comes to the migrating process, but also in the society of arrival. As for transnationalism, this study adds a "horizontal" version to the customary "vertical" one; it looks at migrants' connections to each other, irrespective, at the outset, of national and ethnic lines that may or may not distinguish them. This is why internal and international migrants will not be set apart up front – they might have found themselves in more similar situations than we think. Likewise, foreigners and colonial subjects should not necessarily be treated separately.[40] In addition, the traditional approach to migration from the dominant standpoint of nationality and citizenship will be displaced and repurposed within a larger matrix of identifications. This study will give mutual interactions between migrants and public authorities a fair, yet not disproportionate place.

How and why did people migrate? How did the dynamics of sociocultural difference change over time as people moved across space? The main questions of migration history are at the heart of this study. In order to assess whether or not, and to which extent, geographic origin, gender, class and other criteria of difference had an effect on people's lives, the cohort of subjects under scrutiny needed to include people from many walks of life. In that regard, a single housing unit makes for a propitious field of experiment. As a "topographical community," it is not dependent on predefined ethnonational communities.[41] Choosing such a setting substitutes an artificial and non-reflexive way of sampling people with a similarly arbitrary, yet self-conscious, delineation. This has the advantage of not tampering, from the outset, with the issues under scrutiny.[42]

Amazingly, the history of a building has rarely, if ever, been attempted by historians, as opposed to ethnographers, sociologists, or even novelists and film directors. Many saw the biography of a building as an elusive "dream of history."[43] An exception is Jerry White's unparalleled historical observation of Jewish immigrants in a London East End block, which offered an inspiring model of investigation, thanks in part to its use of oral history.[44]

Here, the selection of buildings had little to do with their potential in terms of material and semiotic history. This was particularly difficult due to the constructions' almost entire levelling in the 1960s. The main factor was the search for suitable experimental conditions. A sufficient diversity in the population's characteristics – what anthropologists call "super-diversity" – was necessary in order to have any chance of assessing their respective relevance over time.[45] To the naked eye, census records were quick to show that the Plaine-Saint-Denis, in general, and the buildings at Nos. 96–102 Av. de Paris, in particular, provided ample measure of these variations. Second, the housing unit needed to be large enough for its inhabitants to have left a significant number of traces in the archives. The sheer size and turnover rate visible in census records appeared to clear that bar, as we will see in the first chapter. Third, a preliminary full-text search of the addresses in question in digitised newspaper collections proved promising. It turned up mentions of residents in both national scandals – which in that sense made the buildings quite exceptional and augured richer-than-average sources – and a number of small events, an expected consequence of their demographic and sociological magnitude. The presence of a bar-hotel and other shops at the front of the tenement also looked like an auspicious feature. This heralded meeting spaces, go-between characters and a wider array of social encounters than just neighbour-to-neighbour interactions. Lastly, Saint-Denis stood out as a welcoming field of investigation. Its macro and meso histories had already been laid out in detail, and the publicly available sources pertaining to its history were well kept, correctly structured and increasingly digitised.[46]

The book's time selection also results from various contingencies. First, it is meant to allow for 50 years of serial data, whether those were extracted from censuses, civil registries or naturalisation records. The beginning of the period corresponds to Saint-Denis first detailed population registers in the second half of the 19th century.[47] Its final mark matches the most recent year of civil registers that were legally accessible at the time of research. Second, as outlined above, the period had to span across the Great War in order to assess the extent to which the conflict had been a moment of change for the residents and their identifications. Additionally, the inclusion of the 1920s was critical to the analysis of the residents' naturalisations – the number of which swelled after 1927. A third element is related to macro, socio-economic considerations. Both ends of that half-century saw sweeping changes in the Plaine, with the rapid industrialisation and immigration in the early 1880s on one side and the start of the Great Depression on the other. These transformations were certainly felt in the micro-context, as we shall see in the first two chapters. Other important evolutions occurred at these two moments, with regard to transportation, hygiene, education and welfare.

Both time boundaries also refer to events that are more specific to the tenement block and its inhabitants. 1882 is the year in which civic

10 *Introduction*

numbers on the Avenue de Paris were modified; in that sense, it saw the official birth of Nos. 96, 98, 100 and 102.[48] 1932 was also a pivotal year in the *cités*. It is at that date that tenants from Southern Europe enlisted for the first time in the main benefit society of the Plaine, an important sign of their integration.[49] It is also in 1932 that Louis Pirolli, one of the protagonists of this volume and, hitherto, one of the most successful and well-regarded of the tenement's occupants, lost his managing job at the glass factory over misappropriation of the company's funds. His pristine reputation was consequently tarnished, highlighting the precariousness of those same integration trajectories.[50]

Sources and methods

This book is also the product of options made in the use of sources. In order to collect as much data as possible about the tenement's occupants, I thoroughly examined 300 volumes of birth, marriage and death registries, mostly at the Seine-Saint-Denis departmental archives and Saint-Denis municipal archives. This was supplemented by an exhaustive examination of marriage and baptism records kept at Saint-Denis parish archives. In four regions of origin of the tenants – Alsace-Lorraine, Caserta-Campobasso, Burgos, and Cáceres, I also hunted for civil and religious records. At the time of the research, only a fraction of these records had been digitised, and more importantly, nowhere were these manuscript documents searchable through full-text queries.

Seeking both context and precise information about the selected addresses and their residents, I explored about 150 boxes of municipal archives, mostly in Saint-Denis. I also unearthed precious information about the buildings' evolution and the financial situation of the residents in fiscal archives. This in turn allowed me to track down notary records, which I was then able to consult in public archives or obtain from notary offices. Diplomatic correspondence on high-profile scandals happening in the tenement yielded precious material, as well. The most fruitful trails of all, however, were those leading to hundreds of naturalisation files and over a thousand police registers, judicial files and military transcripts. I investigated those sources as methodically and comprehensively as possible, either by looking at every single document pertaining to the period, or by checking all the residents' names in individual collections and trying to track down as many of them as possible. To my knowledge, such sources had never been used before to document the lives of particular individuals.

Possibilities of full-text digital search in vast newspaper collections proved of great help, too. Newspapers were an important starting point for unearthing interesting episodes in the tenants' lives, but also the only source for periods at which other archives were missing. When press records could be combined with other accounts, they also helped me understand the discrepancy between the public narrative on the *faits divers*, influenced by the rhetoric prevailing at the macro level, and what actually happened to the inhabitants – as will become apparent in Chapter 6.

Lastly, this inquiry included a patient research of some of the tenants' descendants. I was able to collect over 75 testimonies of direct descendants, now scattered across five countries. Their indirect recollections needed to be handled with caution, especially for the majority of families who had not kept private documents from that period. Yet the bits of information retrieved were often the only access to several aspects of the migrants' living conditions and their own interpretation of major life events.

This research has been tailored to make the most of these sources. Beyond a common premise consisting in reducing the "scale of observation," microhistories often have shared methodological features.[51] It is their respective proportions that usually bear the singular mark of each project. In this study, a significant role is played by contextualisation. As much as this book contributes to challenging overzealous and somewhat deceptive beliefs in the supremacy of structures, it acknowledges the role played by the environment, in the broad sense of the word. People's circumstances inescapably exerted some degree of influence over their decisions, interactions and movements. Sustained attention will thus be paid not only to the material conditions, but also the demographic, social or cultural patterns, whether individuals acted in conformity or in contrast to those trends.

As far as source analysis is concerned, the critical examination will be both endogenous, focused on the document or the interview itself, and exogenous, through meticulous source crossing. From this inward and outward-looking effort, I will then derive inferences on individuals, their actions and their motives – sometimes venturing into a biographical approach, and in other instances offering more ethnographic snapshots. Whatever the hypotheses, however, they all obviously retain a measure of speculation; I will make sure to highlight the gaps and limitations of the record from which I have tried to piece things together.[52]

The presence in this research of serial data and quantitative tools is also worth noting. As will become apparent in Chapter 5, both the construction and the processing of the data could not be achieved without a deep dive into the sources at the individual level. In this sense, the statistical effort here is, to a large extent, a by-product of the gathering of qualitative information. Still, it has its own explanatory force. As much as averages and medians sound foreign to the actor-centred epistemology at the heart of microhistory, I will argue that quantitative analysis can play a supporting part in small-scale investigations such as this one.

As in any microhistory, whether the observed social and cultural dynamics are representative shall remain an open question. Certainly, there were comparable buildings at the time with comparable populations, both in the Plaine-Saint-Denis and elsewhere. Future studies may prove that some stories or patterns found in this tenement had, in fact, run counter to the norm. Were it the case, it would certainly not be a problem from a

12 *Introduction*

microhistorical perspective. As underlined by Edoardo Grendi's oxymoron "the exceptional normal," the anomaly is richer than the norm from a knowledge standpoint, for it gives access at once to the sociocultural standards and to their subversions.[53] The point here is to highlight the existence of one version of the migrant experience; one among a plurality, to be sure, but one that puts hegemonic beliefs and mainstream narratives into question. In that sense, large issues are definitely at stake here, as in many other microhistories.[54]

The book's structure

Now let us move on to the story itself. The notion of place is the common theme of the first part. The first two chapters focus on the tenement. Both the buildings (Ch. 1) and their demographic make-up (Ch. 2), far from being mere micro-structural conditions, appear as fluid realities whose characteristics depend not only upon the residents' perceptions, but also on our analytical choices. The third and fourth chapters investigate the migrations of the tenement's occupants, demonstrating that the salience of categories of difference depended in part on spatial movements (Ch. 3) and exploring the workings of some migration schemes (Ch. 4).

People's categories of difference were also influenced by their interactions, which are the focus of the book's second half. Personal interactions are addressed in the fifth and sixth chapters, which centre on the residents' intricate, and ever-evolving, social relations. When identifications based on geographic origin had a certain relevance in people's affinities, local and micro-regional solidarity was generally more meaningful than a broadly conceived ethnicity (Ch. 5). As for antagonisms, they were often less contingent upon origin than upon other variables (Ch. 6). The final couple of chapters engage with the extent to which public institutions participated in the construction of difference and how, in turn, the inhabitants negotiated and altered the logics of national identifications – both in peace (Ch. 7) and in wartime (Ch. 8).

Notes

1 The epigraph on page x is drawn from Philippe Artières, *Rêves d'histoire. Pour une histoire de l'ordinaire* (Paris: Gallimard, 2014), 101. All translations are mine unless otherwise stated.
2 AD54, 5Mi472/R5, Sainte-Geneviève, mar., 1863, No. 2; AVP, V4E2353, Paris 19th, 1869, mar., No. 93; ASC Rocca d'Arce, 1869, birth, No. 36; SDMA, E252, SD, 1887, mar., No. 411; SDMA, 1K1/33–8, ER, 1888–94, Lucien Perrin.
3 AMSD, 1G87, 1869, av. de Paris 90 [old number for Nos. 100–2]; SDMA, E209, SD, deaths, 1874, No. 776; *Le Petit Journal*, 8.12.1869.
4 Sumi Cho, Kimberlé Williams Crenshaw, and Leslie McCall, "Toward a field of intersectionality studies: theory, applications, and praxis," *Signs* 38, No. 4 (2013): 785–810.

5 Andreas Wimmer, *Ethnic Boundary Making: Institutions, Power, Networks* (Oxford: Oxford University Press, 2013).
6 Rudolph Vecoli, "An inter-ethnic perspective on American immigration history," *Mid America* 75, No. 2 (1993): 224; Kathleen Neils Conzen et al., "The invention of ethnicity: a perspective from the USA," *Journal of American Ethnic History* 12, No. 1 (1992): 5.
7 Rogers Brubaker and Frederick Cooper, "Beyond 'identity'," *Theory and Society* 29, No. 1 (2000): 33. For an example of such homogenisation, see Marie-Claude Blanc-Chaléard, "Les immigrés et la banlieue parisienne. Histoire d'une aventure urbaine et sociale (XIXe–XXe siècles)," in *Banlieues populaires: territoires, sociétés, politiques*, ed. Marie-Hélène Bacqué, Emmanuel Bellanger, and Henri Rey (La Tour d'Aigues: L'Aube, 2018), 95–109.
8 It took scholars a long time, in particular, to get familiar with the interactionist model put forward by the anthropologist Frederik Barth, based on boundaries between an "us" and a "them," rather than on the "cultural stuff" within the group. See Frederik Barth, ed., *Ethnic Groups and Boundaries: The Social Organization of Cultural Difference* (London: Allen & Unwin, 1969), 15.
9 Some scholars like Richard Jenkins have even criticised the mere idea of boundaries as a surrender to the assumption of inevitable separations between groups. See Richard Jenkins, *Rethinking Ethnicity: Arguments and Explorations* (London: Sage, 1997), 21.
10 Jean-Frédéric Schaub, *Race Is about Politics: Lessons from History*, trans. Lara Vergnaud (Princeton: Princeton University Press, 2019), 38.
11 Brubaker and Cooper, "Beyond 'identity'," 14–17.
12 See e.g. Rogers Brubaker, Mara Loveman, and Peter Stamatov, "Ethnicity as cognition," *Theory and Society* 33 (2004): 31–64.
13 Pierre Bourdieu, "L'identité et la représentation: éléments pour une réflexion critique sur l'idée de région," *Actes de la recherche en sciences sociales* 35, No. 1 (1980), 63–72.
14 Mae Ngai, *Impossible Subjects: Illegal Aliens and the Making of Modern America* (Princeton: Princeton University Press, 2004); Dorothee Schneider, *Crossing Borders: Migration and Citizenship in the 20th-Century United States* (Cambridge: Harvard University Press, 2011).
15 Mary D. Lewis, *The Boundaries of the Republic: Migrant Rights and the Limits of Universalism in France, 1918–1940* (Palo Alto: Stanford University Press, 2007); Claire Zalc, *Denaturalised: How Thousands Lost Their Citizenship and Lives in Vichy France*, trans. Catherine Porter (Cambridge: Harvard University Press, 2020).
16 Nina Glick Schiller, Linda Basch, and Cristina Blanc-Szanton, "Transnationalism: a new analytic framework for understanding migration," *Annals of the New York Academy of Sciences* 645, No. 1 (1992): 1–24.
17 Pierre Bourdieu, *Esquisse d'une théorie de la pratique* (Paris: Droz, 1972), quoted in Paul-André Rosental, *Les Sentiers invisibles. Espaces, familles et migrations dans la France du XIXe siècle* (Paris: Éditions de l'EHESS 1999), 15.
18 Philippe Rygiel, "Archives et historiographie de l'immigration," *Migrance*, No. 33 (2009): 50–9.
19 For Paris, among hundreds of publications that keep the banlieue out of the Paris narrative, see Annie Benveniste, *Le Bosphore à la Roquette. La communauté judéo-espagnole à Paris (1914–1990)* (Paris: L'Harmattan, 1989); Marie-Claude Blanc-Chaléard, *Les Italiens dans l'Est parisien. Une histoire d'intégration (années 1880–1960)* (Rome: École française de Rome, 2000); Pascal Blanchard and Éric Deroo, *Le Paris Asie: 150 ans de présence de la Chine, de l'Indochine, du Japon, dans la capitale* (Paris: La Découverte, 2004). As for the banlieue without Paris,

14 *Introduction*

see e.g. Noëlle Gérôme, Danielle Tartakowsky, and Claude Willard, eds., *La Banlieue en fête: de la marginalité urbaine à l'identité culturelle* (Paris: Presses Universitaires de Vincennes, 1988).
20 Andreas Wimmer and Nina Glick Schiller, "Methodological nationalism and beyond: nation-state building, migration and the social sciences," *Global Networks* 2, No. 4 (2002): 301–34.
21 See e.g. Gérard Noiriel, *Le Creuset français* (Paris: Seuil, 1992 [1st ed. 1988]), 45–8. Also, Paola Diaz and Guido Nicolosi, "Corps, identités et technologies 'par les nombres' dans l'imaginaire migratoire," *Socio-anthropologie* 40, No. 1 (2019): 9–28.
22 Geneviève Massard-Guilbaud and Philippe Rygiel, eds., *Siècles*, No. 6 (1997), issue entitled "Chiffres et histoire."
23 Jean-Paul Brunet, "Une banlieue ouvrière: Saint-Denis (1890–1939). Problèmes d'implantation du socialisme et du communisme" (state diss. in history, University of Lille, 1978), 434–47, 1110–27. Significantly, the socio-demographic side of the research was left out of the published version of the thesis: Jean-Paul Brunet, *Saint-Denis, la ville rouge: socialisme et communisme en banlieue ouvrière, 1890–1939* (Paris: Hachette, 1980).
24 Brunet, "Une banlieue ouvrière," 107–47; 172–6; 792–806.
25 Natacha Lillo, "Espagnols en 'banlieue rouge'. Histoire comparée des trois principales vagues migratoires à Saint-Denis et dans sa région au XXe siècle" (doctoral diss. in history, IEP Paris, 2001).
26 Lillo, "Espagnols en 'banlieue rouge'," 133–7. In addition, some of the key concepts used in the dissertation were left undefined: not only ghetto, but also integration, identity, networks.
27 Natacha Lillo, "Coexistence des migrants," *Projet*, Special Issue, April 2, 2008, last accessed July 27, 2021, https://www.revue-projet.com/articles/2008-04-lillo-coexistence-des-migrants/8012. See in particular the sentence on the *"immeubles de rapport"* of the Avenue du Président-Wilson, which clearly designate Nos. 96–102, and note the paradox with the article's title, "Coexistence des migrants."
28 Leslie Page Moch, *The Pariahs of Yesterday: Breton Migrants in Paris* (Durham: Duke University Press, 2012).
29 John Horne, "Immigrant workers during World War I," *French Historical Studies* 14, No. 1 (1985): 57–88; Tyler Stovall, "Colour-blind France? Colonial workers during the First World War," *Race and Class* 35, No. 2 (1993): 35–55; Li Ma, ed., *Les Travailleurs chinois en France dans la Première Guerre mondiale* (Paris: CNRS, 2012); Mireille Le Van Ho, *Des Vietnamiens dans la Grande Guerre. 50 000 recrues dans les usines françaises* (Paris: Vendémiaire, 2014); Laurent Dornel, *Les Étrangers dans la Grande Guerre* (Paris: La Documentation française, 2014).
30 See e.g. Stéphane Kronenberger, "Des temps de paix aux temps de guerre: les parcours des travailleurs étrangers de l'Est et du Sud-Est de la France (1871–1918)" (doctoral diss. in history, University of Nice, 2014) and Nimisha Barton, *Reproductive Citizens: Gender, Immigration, and the State in Modern France, 1880–1945* (Ithaca: Cornell University Press, 2020).
31 For instance, Claire Zalc and Nicolas Mariot, *Face à la persécution. 991 Juifs dans la guerre,* (Paris: Odile Jacob, 2010).
32 Arjun Appadurai, *Modernity at Large: Cultural Dimensions of Globalization* (Minneapolis: University of Minnesota Press, 1996).
33 Paul E. Johnson, "Reflections: looking back at social history," *Reviews in American History* 39, No. 2 (2011): 380.
34 Lara Putnam, *The Company They Kept: Migrants and the Politics of Gender in Caribbean Costa Rica, 1870–1960* (Chapel Hill: University of North Carolina

Press, 2002); Rebecca J. Scott and Jean Hébrard, *Freedom Papers: An Atlantic Odyssey in the Age of Emancipation* (Cambridge: Harvard University Press, 2012); Sydney Nathans, *To Free a Family: The Journey of Mary Walker* (Cambridge: Harvard University Press, 2012); Mae Ngai, *The Lucky Ones: One Family and the Extraordinary Invention of Chinese America* (Princeton: Princeton University Press, 2012); Karl Jacoby, *The Strange Career of William Ellis: The Texas Slave Who Became a Mexican Millionaire* (New York: W. W. Norton, 2016); Claire Zalc and Tal Bruttmann, eds., *Microhistories of the Holocaust* (New York: Berghahn, 2017); Rudolph Vecoli and Francesco Durante, *Oh Capitano! Celso Cesare Moreno-Adventurer, Cheater, and Scoundrel on Four Continents* (New York: Fordham University Press, 2018); Konstantina Zanou, *Transnational Patriotism in the Mediterranean, 1800–1850: Stammering the Nation* (Oxford: Oxford University Press, 2018); John-Paul Ghobrial, "Moving stories and what they tell us: Early Modern mobility between microhistory and global history," *Past & Present* 242, No. 14 (2019): 243–80; Emma Rothschild, *An Infinite History: The Story of a Family in France Over Three Centuries* (Princeton: Princeton University Press, 2021).

35 Martha Hodes, *The Sea Captain's Wife: A True Story of Love, Race, and War in the 19th Century* (New York: Norton, 2006).

36 Arlette Farge, "Les archives du singulier. Quelques réflexions à propos des archives judiciaires comme matériau de l'histoire sociale," in *Histoire sociale, histoire globale*, ed. Christophe Charle (Paris: Éditions de la MSH, 1993), 183–9.

37 Philippe Artières and Dominique Kalifa, "L'historien et les archives personnelles: pas à pas?," *Sociétés et Représentations* 13 (2002), 8.

38 In 2012, a number of academic and archival institutions joined forces on a project which led to interviews of former Nanterre inhabitants in the Oued Souf region in Algeria: see Rosa Olmos, "Mémoire de l'immigration algérienne, Oued Souf (Algérie) – Hauts-de-Seine (France): projet de collecte, conservation et traitement de sources orales," *Bulletin de l'AFAS* 38 (2012): 16–7. The Musée national de l'histoire de l'immigration also funds archival initiatives, often in close co-operation with various non-profit organisations such as *Génériques* – see e.g. CNHI, GIS Ipapic, "Collecter des témoignages ou récits de l'immigration: nouveaux fournisseurs, nouveaux usages, nouvelles compréhensions," proceedings of a seminar held in Bordeaux on April 26, 2012, last accessed July 27, 2021, https://www.culture.gouv.fr/content/download/72921/file/seminaire_GIS_CNHI_Bordeaux_avril_2012.pdf?inLanguage=fre-FR.

39 Jacques Revel, "Microanalysis and the construction of the social," in *Histories: French Constructions of The Past*, eds. Jacques Revel and Lynn Hunt (New York: New Press, 1995), 499.

40 Nancy Green and Marie Poinsot, eds., *Histoire de l'immigration et question coloniale en France* (Paris: La Documentation française/CNHI, 2008).

41 Michael Esch, "Sozialmorphologie und Netwerkanalyse: Die Osteuropäische Einwanderung in Paris, 1895–1928," in *Deutsche Handwerker, Arbeiter und Dienstmädchen in Paris: eine vergessene Migration im 19. Jahrhundert*, ed. Mareike König (Munich: Oldenburg, 2003), 98.

42 Only a few ethnologists and sociologists have attempted to sidestep ethnicity in the framing of their study, by launching investigations from non-ethnicised platforms. See Gerd Baumann, *Contesting Culture: Discourses of Identity in Multi-ethnic London* (Cambridge: Cambridge University Press, 1996); Andreas Wimmer, "Does ethnicity matter? Everyday group formation in three Swiss immigrant neighbourhoods," *Ethnic and Racial Studies* 27, No. 1 (2004): 1–36; Susanne Wessendorf, "Settling in a super-diverse context: Recent migrants' experiences of conviviality," *Journal of Intercultural Studies* 37, No. 5 (2016):

16 *Introduction*

449–63. For a rare attempt from a historian, see Jozefien De Bock, *Parallel Lives Revisited: Mediterranean Guest Workers and their Families at Work and in the Neighbourhood, 1960–1980* (New York: Berghahn, 2018).
43 See the epigraph above, page x.
44 Jerry White, *Rothschild Buildings: Life in an East-End Tenement Block, 1887–1920* (London: Pimlico, 2003 [1st ed. 1980]). For other examples of building histories, see Jean-Luc Pinol, *Les Mobilités de la grande ville. Lyon, fin XIXe–début XXe* (Paris: F.N.S.P., 1991); Florence Bourillon, "Un immeuble dans Paris," *Cahiers d'histoire* 44, No. 4 (1999): 701–15; John Foot, "Micro-history of a house: memory and place in a Milanese neighbourhood, 1890–2000," *Urban History* 34, No. 3 (2007): 431–52; David Lepoutre, "Histoire d'un immeuble haussmannien. Catégories d'habitants et rapports d'habitation en milieu bourgeois," *Revue française de sociologie* 51, No. 2 (2010): 321–58; Mahmoud Yazbak and Yfaat Weiss, "A tale of two houses," in *Haifa before and after 1948: Narratives of a Mixed City*, eds. Yazbak and Weiss (Dordrecht: IHJR, 2011), 11–42.
45 Steven Vertovec, "Super-diversity and its implications," *Ethnic and Racial Studies* 30, No. 6 (2007): 1024–54.
46 The SDMA have been pioneer in digitising material from censuses, civil registries and other sources and providing access to them on the internet. By contrast, the AD93 were one of the trailing departmental archives in that respect, but they have been rapidly catching up since 2018.
47 Lists of population do not exist between the 1803 and 1881 censuses. The latter, however, proved impossible to exploit with enough certainty, as it does not follow a regular order in the house numbers. See Chapter 1.
48 See Chapter 1, note 8.
49 SDMA, 5Q61, Société de secours "la Mutualité" de la Plaine-Saint-Denis.
50 Fabrice Langrognet, "The crossings of Louis Pirolli, a migrant among others (1886–1953)," *Quaderni Storici* 54, No. 3 (2019): 831–57.
51 Giovanni Levi, "On microhistory," in *New Perspectives on Historical Writing*, ed. Peter Burke (University Park: Pennsylvania State University Press, 1991), 95.
52 On this point, see Tom Cohen, *Roman Tales: A Reader's Guide to the Art of Microhistory* (Abingdon: Routledge, 2019), 1–15.
53 Edoardo Grendi, "Microanalisi e storia sociale," *Quaderni Storici* 12, No. 35 (1972): 506–20.
54 Arguments in favor of a microhistory unmoored from these "bigger-questions" concerns can be found in Sigurður Gylfi Magnússon, "The singularization of history: social history and microhistory within the postmodern state of knowledge," *Journal of Social History* 36 (2003): 701–35.

Part I
Changing places

1 Setting the scene

In the 1860s, Louise Versigny and her sister decided to rent a small house on a bare plot of farmland just outside Paris. It was located on the right-hand side, going north, of the millennium-old road connecting the capital to Saint-Denis through the vast and level Plaine de France. The swathe of territory immediately surrounding that "route de Paris" had just been absorbed by the city of Saint-Denis. That area was thus starting its official existence as the "Plaine-Saint-Denis."

The setting around the house was overwhelmingly rural. On all sides, fields alternated with grasslands and kitchen gardens. On the Versignys' one-acre plot, where milk cows had been seen grazing for years, a strip was covered with marsh. Water had to be fetched from stone wells. This was before the road was paved and lit; before horse-drawn tramways came that far north; before trains from Paris stopped in the neighbourhood.[1]

At least the route de Paris already had a double row of plane trees on each side. This soon prompted its new appellation as "Avenue de Paris," and provided the foundation for a grandiose elegance that would impress visitors for decades to come. "It was a magnificent avenue, a little like the Champs-Élysées," a tenant would recall many decades later.[2]

Cattle, alfalfa and lettuce were not the only sights on the horizon. Due to the Plaine's optimal positioning just outside the capital, and its propitious natural characteristics – flat lands protected from floodwaters, chalky terrain able to withstand heavy constructions, abundant underground water–, industry had thrived since the 1820s, when the local canal was inaugurated. Under Napoleon III's Second Empire, the Plaine's few active companies were still small in size, with warehouses more common than workshops. Across the Avenue from the Versignys', the new glass factory employed just a handful of workers, who went around with the factory's name embroidered on their caps.[3] The Plaine was still semi-desert.

Things would be different a few years hence. Louise, who soon inherited the leases after her sister's death, realised that housing was a rare commodity in the area. At a time of increased traffic and surging demography, she was persuaded – like many of her tenants would later be – to offer cheap

DOI: 10.4324/9781003017820-1

lodgings for rent.[4] This decision marked the foundation of the tenement at 96–102 Avenue de Paris.

This particular property, extending over less than one acre, would provide evolving spatial and material conditions to its inhabitants. More than just a space, the constructions, staircases, porches, courtyards and gardens created what Michel de Certeau called a "place;" that is, a configuration of positions emerging from social practice.[5] As such, the tenement evolved in conjunction with the experiences of its residents, who were "never rats in a housing maze" but rather the co-producers of their environment.[6]

The objective of this first chapter is to understand how the tenement's life as an inhabited thing intersected with its occupants' representations. The classic boundary between objective and subjective dimensions of a lived building is not so clear-cut; we are now well aware that places are above all mental constructs.[7] Here, space and time were not mere conditions under which the tenants' identifications were being enacted and negotiated. These dimensions were, themselves, in motion.

Place names

Toponymy is one of the first lenses through which the sense of place can be measured. In the Plaine, name changes could be imposed by public authorities. For a start, civic numbers were modified at the beginning of the period under study.[8] Then, soon after the socialists took control of Saint-Denis's city hall in 1892, the street immediately south of the buildings was renamed rue Proudhon after the famous French anarchist. This could have left an ideological mark on people's minds, if only they had shared the political culture of the city council. For decades, the street was commonly called "Prudhon" by locals, who unwittingly traded the revolutionary for the Romantic painter.[9]

In early years, locals were quite unbothered by the straightforward name "Avenue de Paris," which had initially emerged as a geographic term. Many did not even use it; on their correspondence, they simply added a number to "Plaine-Saint-Denis."[10] Authorities themselves were still hesitant, sometimes preferring the name "Route numéro 1" (road No. 1).[11] Yet years before the Avenue was renamed "Président-Wilson" to honour the American peacemaker, locals had started complaining about the name "Avenue de Paris." It was routinely mistaken, they argued, for the rue de Paris in central Saint-Denis, or the rue Saint-Denis in Paris.[12] In the early 1880s, a group of inhabitants petitioned the city council to have it renamed after Garibaldi – to no avail.[13]

The Plaine-Saint-Denis itself, where about a fifth of the 60,000 Saint-Denis inhabitants lived at the turn of the century, was generally viewed by its inhabitants as well as outsiders as a distinct entity from Saint-Denis.[14] When *Plainards*, as they are still called today, would talk about "Saint-Denis," they meant the city centre up north. Differences between the Plaine and the centre of Saint-Denis went beyond a simple geographic separation, delineated by the city's canal. For decades, the Plaine remained deprived of roadworks, public lighting and a water system. As a consequence, Plaine's councilmen repeatedly filed requests for administrative independence.[15]

Autonomous or not, the administrative status of the Plaine was of little importance to the people living there. For one thing, they would never experience the area as a single territory. The reference points were neighbourhoods of much smaller proportions. Often named after familiar landmarks such as streets, factories or public buildings, their borders were uncertain and overlapping. To the north, where the Stade de France now stands, lay *"le Gaz,"* named after one – and later two – gigantic gas factories. South on the Avenue stood the *"Pont de Soissons,"* a metallic railway bridge visible from afar; the area around it was known as *"le Landy."* Heading further south, one entered the sectors of *"la Justice"* and *"la Montjoie,"* based on corresponding street names. If one kept moving towards Paris, the next area was the *"quartier de la verrerie"* (i.e. the glass factory's neighbourhood). There stood the tenement at Nos. 96–102.

Locals also had their own geographic designations. Whatever the names of their street or neighbourhood, some had no doubt they were living in Paris. A couple of tenants referred to their address as "Paris Plaine-Saint-Denis 96."[16] The evolution of the tenement's name is also remarkable in that regard. The term *cité* was primarily used, before the First World War, to refer to a courtyard with multiple housing units.[17] In the early years, all the houses at the back of the plot at Nos. 96–102 were referred to as *"cité Nicolas."*[18] This expression was used by residents themselves up until the early 1900s, and was occasionally picked up by outsiders.[19]

The courtyards were then sporadically labelled in ways that reflected the origin of their populations – a point we will come back to in Chapter 2. Residents seem to have always preferred *"le 100," "le 96," "le 98."* As for the bar-hotel at No. 102, no one in the Plaine ever referred to it by its official name – first, *hôtel de l'Oise*; then, *hôtel du Point du Jour*. Like every other shop, they called it by the name of its owner. *"Chez Poullain," "chez Delamotte," "chez Mandagot"* were the vernacular appellations that served as milestones in the residents' mental geographies.

Surroundings

In the last third of the 19th century, the chemical and metals sectors employed swelling numbers of workers in the Plaine.[20] The glassworks, which had started with ten people in 1859, grew to about 500 in 1890, 862 in 1902 and 1,250 in 1909, covering at that date 16,000 square metres.[21] The area soon became overcrowded. The Avenue was so large that the population density was not what newcomers first noticed. Rather, they set their eyes on the eclectic mix of constructions: "brutal, indiscrete structures" in the shape of "bald quadrilaterals," alternated with low, "limping" buildings and clusters of factory chimneys that looked like "lances, masts or vertical cannons."[22] Upon closer inspection, acrid emanations and awful stenches were hard to escape. These were a direct result of the high concentration of chemical factories processing guts, fertilizers, ink, tallow, grease, or sulphuric acid. Air pollution would reach unbearable highs during the Great War.[23]

For Louise Versigny, her tenants and their successors, the daily geography worked in different concentric perimeters. In the first were the essential retailers: the coal merchant, charcutier, grocer, fabric merchant, shoemaker, dairy shop and baker; these were all within a few metres of the tenement's entrance. An open-air market took place twice a week on the opposite side of the Avenue and fostered encounters between people of all origins, classes and genders.

Most of the residents' daily lives took place on the eastern part of the Avenue. "The odd-number [i.e. west] side was another village," a former tenant remembered.[24] Next-door from the *cités* at No. 104, was "La Famille," a cooperative founded in the late 1880s where members could purchase basic goods at a discount ranging from 5% to 10%.[25] Access to that institution enacted differences between residents. Despite the absence of surviving records, we can be certain that – as with regular shops – the cooperative was mostly the purview of women. And those women would not have belonged to the poorest families, who could hardly afford the membership fee.

Men's sociability revolved around the *débits*,* as bistros were called at the time. In the vicinity of the *cités*, the offer of drinking establishments soon became plentiful to a fault. Everyone had his favourite; to mention the nearest, there was one at No. 102, another at No. 96–98 and a third at No. 92. During the First World War, at a time of major restrictions on alcohol consumption, there were 466 bars in the Plaine, or about one per every 105 people.[26] Bars were generally open to everyone, and few displayed an ethnic character. Age was not the barrier it was supposed to be, except for girls. Housewives were never explicitly barred, and the bourgeois norms of not going out without their husband did not have much currency in the area. But most simply did not have enough time to go.[27]

The local place of worship was initially an old chapel of modest proportions, a few hundred steps to the north of the tenement. In 1899 and 1900, a new church was erected across from the old one in a neo-romanesque style, and is still visible today. Walking there and back on Sundays provided residents with an important opportunity to exchange information, forge bonds and display their affinity or disdain for others. The local schools, routinely referred to as *"le 120,"* lay at roughly the same distance as the church. Inside the school premises was the largest meeting room in the area; it was regularly booked by societies of all sorts and served as voting precinct on election days. Municipal library, public baths, police station and post office – where migrant workers would line up every other Saturday to send remittances back home – completed this first cluster of public services.[28]

The second circle roughly matched the limits of the Plaine itself. There were the gas factories to the north, where a few men from the *cités* started commuting from the 1900s; the walls of Paris to the South; and to the East and West, the canal and the railroad, respectively. It is inside those limits that the cinemas, the football pitch and the boxing ring, all popular with residents, would later appear.[29]

But these leisure-related perimeters, as with their work equivalents, would only expand with more infrastructure and free time – in part thanks to the 1919 law on the eight-hour workday. In the early decades, an after-work stroll and a call at the bar were almost all residents could hope for on weekdays.[30] Weekends allowed for card games, the care of one's *jardin ouvrier* (allotment garden), and longer nights at the bar – for men, that is – in the time left after family gatherings and religious duties.[31] Public entertainment in Saint-Denis generally took place on Saturday and Sunday evenings.[32] It is also in this second perimeter that local festivals would take place. In early June, the *fête du Landy* raged north of the *cités* for a fortnight; right in front of the tenement, on the Avenue, the *fête de la Plaine* took place in August.

The centre of Saint-Denis, with its city hall, *justice de paix*,* cemetery and hospital were included in the third and largest extension of ordinary mobilities. Almost all residents had to go to these places at some point, though not more than a couple of times per year. Likely tired of commuting back and forth to the centre, Louise Versigny herself (who had no paid job to take leave from) stopped attending hearings at the *justice de paix* in person and instead hired a representative to plead her cases.[33]

Bordering towns of Aubervilliers and Pantin to the East and the northern districts of Paris to the South were also part of that extended, potential roaming space.[34] In Paris one also found *les Halles* (central market), where market gardeners went on a regular basis to sell their produce. The capital also had public and private institutions that would one day prove critical: hospitals, charities, embassies and train stations. The city became more accessible with the expansion of transportation in the two decades before the Great War. In 1892, the electrification of the tramway line on the Avenue de Paris made passages more frequent and reliable. Bicycles were spotted in the area beginning in the 1900s, and an early cycling club had its headquarters at No. 102.[35] A new train station opened in the Plaine in 1913, which many residents would use over the years. In 1916, the metro reached Porte de la Chapelle, about one kilometre south of the *cités*.

People had other ways to experience their lived spaces. Inside the walls of the Legras glass factory, workspaces were juxtaposed and reflected labour divisions. The factory had four departments: fusion and glassmaking, cutting and carving, decoration, storage and expedition. The male-only personnel of fusion halls were grouped into teams, called *places*, where age and earnings distinguished workers along strict hierarchies. Around the *ouvriers verriers* (glassmakers) and the *souffleurs* (blowers), the most senior and geographically static positions, buzzed the younger *cueilleurs* (lit. pickers) and the little *gamins* (apprentices), who hurried from one spot to the next, carrying red-hot glass balls at the tip of long metal canes.[36] Each team was attached to a particular furnace. The factory had three of them in 1872, six by 1892, ten in the early 1900s, three in the 1920s and two in 1931.[37] Almost all were used day and night.

The signposts of people's daily lives were also the smells, noises and visual impressions. At the glassworks, odours were often haunting and intoxicating. Some, like the smell of paint, followed you all the way home.[38] Heat and noise were intense inside the fusion halls, and workers had to yell to be heard by one another. The sounds of the factory reached well beyond its walls. A strident siren called workers in the morning, after lunch and at six; at midnight, the factory howled through the mouth of the *crieurs* (lit. shouters) who went door to door rallying those assigned to the night shift.[39] Colour coding also structured the glassworkers' environment: "in the corner of a courtyard, a pile of intensely white sand; in basements or underground stores... other piles of yet another white substance, soda; along the way... piles of blue, green, multicoloured shards."[40] And by the railway tracks, at the back of the factory, was the intense darkness of coal, of which the factory swallowed 15,000 tons per year at the beginning of the 20th century.

The tenement itself

The general appearance of the tenement block itself was quite unsightly, to put it mildly. At the turn of the century, it was perceived as a mix of hideous hovels by outsiders.[41] A "miserable aggregate of low and filthy tuf houses...," said an Italian visitor in 1901, "with shutterless windows and crumbling walls; pathways reminding of the streets of Venice for the narrowness, and of those of Santa Lucia for their dirtiness. They are paved with few, disconnected and irregular stones, where fetid, blackish waters stagnate permanently."[42] Although this does not do justice to 50 years of the tenement's history, former occupants were quick to acknowledge the place's overall ugliness.[43]

Inside, the buildings evolved constantly, through largely anarchic architectural metamorphoses. One reason for this was that before 1902, construction and destruction permits were not required by law; even after that, the new rules were only loosely enforced. One of the surviving permit procedures concerns a new building at No. 98 that was commissioned by Louise Versigny's heirs in 1903 and is still standing today. It was a sound, if not especially graceful, construction. It had toilets on the upper floors and its one-bedroom apartments, at around 28 square metres, were twice as large as their equivalents at Nos. 96 and 100. They were immediately coveted by families who could afford the higher rents. From that moment on, No. 98 started to drift away – both materially and symbolically – from the rest of the *cités*.[44]

The earlier history of the property is rather complex. Suffice it to say that housing units were erected gradually in the last third of the 19th century. Initially, Louise Versigny was a "primary tenant" and would sublet the land to others. They built most of the houses which she eventually acquired for

Setting the scene 25

herself. By the mid-1890s, Louise had full ownership of both land and houses.[45] This explains in large part why at the turn of the century, the four addresses were still perceived as one. In countless instances, people technically living at one civic number would refer to another when giving their address. In late 1902, the split of ownership resulted in the division of the plot into three different units: Nos. 100 and 102 remained very much united; No. 98 stood apart, with its own courtyard; No. 96 gradually became a distinct tenement itself. The addresses then grew more and more different from each other in the minds of their inhabitants. The inside of No. 100 is remembered as being quite open and accessible to passers-by. By contrast, non-residents would almost never enter No. 96.[46]

The following plans (Figure 1.1), based on rare originals unearthed in notary records and land register archives, give a sense of the periodic modifications of the tenement's inner disposition.

In conjunction with written and oral sources, these cartographic documents yield precious information about the characteristics of the building complex. Deceptively narrow entrances, paved only on the first metres; gardens slowly giving way to trodden earth and patches of wild grass; wooden shacks and depots for various merchants.[48] Between the houses, clotheslines, rabbit hutches covered with sheet-metal roofs, henhouses and the odd rock, on which people could trip and hurt themselves.[49]

For years, Louise rented out a parcel of land at No. 100–102 to carters who kept their horses in a stable, and another to a milkman for his cows.[50] This, along with barking dogs and stomping horses, was surely quite noisy. But the inhabitants themselves were probably responsible for most of the tenement's soundtrack, so to speak. Courtyard shouts were common, either from disputes or friendly calls, layered over the steady beat of a shoemaker's hammer and never-ending baby cries. The wooden floor and stairs constantly creaked under people's clogs. At the back of No. 100's front

Figure 1.1 The structural evolution of the *cités*, from 1897 (left), to 1902 (middle) and 1929 (right). The façades on the Avenue are at the bottom, with the north and Saint-Denis to the left, and the south and Paris to the right.[47]

building, a wooden staircase led to an inward-looking passage on the first floor.[51] This "balcony," as the residents called it, provided them with a meeting space, from which they could also greet people traversing the entrance pathway (see Figure 1.1). The two bars at the front often closed later than permitted, filling the night with loud voices and, occasionally, accordion music. Nights were always short; the dairy shop at No. 96 and the charcuterie at No. 98 clanged ironware before workers even had to wake up. Only Sunday would bring relief. What locals remember most about Sundays was the silence, especially at mass time.[52]

Changes of ownership had other consequences than just structural rearrangements. Louise Versigny had very much been a hands-on owner, who relentlessly micromanaged her property.[53] Like most landlords of her era, she had lived on-site from the start. Tenants would come to her to ask for favours, especially delays and loans.[54] But after being robbed in the night, she found the situation untenable and left.[55] Following her accidental death in 1901, acts of demolition and reconstruction were carried out in the courtyards. Neither the head of a local lorry company who acquired the northern half on auction, nor Louise's great-niece, who inherited Nos. 96 and 98, had much time to spare with the tenants.[56] She even seemed to openly despise them for their poverty.[57] Efforts to recover outstanding rents or evict indelicate occupants became rare. The money-making days of the *cités* were over.

The most consequential evolution of the tenement can be put in one word: decay. This can be attributed to several factors. First, most of the constructions were built for a quick profit. These flimsy units were intended to be torn down at the expiration of the land leases; this never took place. Second, landlords failed to keep up with the necessary works and repairs. Louise herself would sometimes baulk at necessary expenses.[58] The situation only worsened after 1914 (Figure 1.2). The official moratorium on rents imposed at the outbreak of the war further reduced any incentive to maintain one's property.[59] And after 1918, many residents remained effectively exempt from rent, because of the extent of the damage suffered by their dwellings during the conflict.

Fortunately, the *cités* were spared – by a whisker – from bombs dropped by German planes and the Big Bertha.[61] But there was no escaping the explosion of 15 million grenades in La Courneuve on March 15, 1918.[62] In the Plaine, virtually all windows were blown out. So strong were the vibrations from the explosion that one of the houses in the courtyard at No. 96 was shaken to the point of collapse. The lavatory in the courtyard crumbled and stayed out of order for the next two years. Six families were forced to leave their apartments and find another place to live.[63]

No. 96 never quite recovered from that severe blow.[64] Along with the rubble of the collapsed buildings (which would not be cleared until they were joined by new bombing debris in 1944), the courtyard went on to host a pile of metalwork dumped by a nearby factory starting in the late 1920s. This displeasing sight served as a vivid reminder of a vicious circle: since tenants paid little to no

Figure 1.2 The tenement's façade, viewed from the north, 1914. Postcard, the author's own collection.[60]

rent, no one bothered to take care of the building. It also reinforced the building's inner divides. The pile of materials further isolated the families in the back, who had already been the poorest. On the other hand, children eventually appropriated that new spatial element and integrated it into their sense of belonging. While the courtyard at No. 100 was arranged as a football pitch, the metal heap at No. 96 became a treasured place for hide-and-seek.[65]

Deterioration could bond the tenants together, but it could also drive a wedge between them.[66] This ambivalence appears in the upset letters they addressed to the authorities. There is no explicit evidence, however, that those complaints ever translated into ethnonational or class-based resentment. When the residents at No. 98 protested, for instance, against a stench emanating from No. 100, they blamed it on the insufficient size of the chimneys at No. 100 – not on their poorer neighbours themselves.[67] According to a Spanish resident at No. 100 who complained about the state of his building in 1922, some of his fellow tenants were not beyond reproach, but he did not identify them further.[68] The people to blame were more often the landlords and the municipality who failed to enforce existing regulations.

Inside the apartments

So many years later, what lay behind the doors of the residents' lodgings is the hardest part to document. We do know that most residents lived in one or two-bedroom apartments.[69] They generally had little furniture of their own, and none of it was of particular value. Sources that traditionally inform on material possessions are of limited use. Less than 0.5% of deaths in the *cités* led to succession declarations and almost none to an inventory. Better clues can be found in judicial and police records. In August 1914, a family of six at No. 96 had "a full copper bed, a full folding bed, a child bed, a cradle, two square tables, seven chairs, a cask, a brand-new stove, a tub for washing clothes, two cooking pots, a lamp, a pot, two big dishes, four plates, six spoons, six forks, four one-metre boards of and two two-metre ones, two wool mattresses."[70] Their next-door neighbours had almost the same objects, with the addition of a cupboard.[71] At No. 100, another family possessed a small, white wooden table.[72]

The most common decorations were family photographs and crucifixes. Windows were usually sealed, and dampness was common.[73] Walls were supposed to be whitewashed, but their surface was frequently covered in patches of mildew. They were not cleaner in the apartments of tenants who sublet furnished rooms, despite the legal requirements to that effect.[74] Along with smells of humidity, the buildings were filled with cooking odours. Stews of vegetables and potatoes and thick bean soups were popular in every apartment. At times, residents purchased finer products.[75] At the charcuterie at No. 98 they could find ham, salami, bacon, lard, pâté, and sardines in oil.[76] In the mid-1920s, at a nearby grocery, dried pasta would be sold by the tens of kilos, along with tomato sauce, chickpeas, dried codfish, coffee and chocolate.[77]

And yet the most persisting smell came from the toilets on the ground floor. Although landlords were quick to place the blame on residents who kept clogging the pipes with various objects, the massive disproportion between the number of outhouses and the demography of the tenement was bound to create a hygiene problem. There were only three toilets for 50 families at No. 100 in the late 1910s; at No. 96, there were five, but three of them were out of order.[78] As for freshwater, things were not better. "There is only one water tap for all the residents," one tenant complained, "and the concierge only turns it on from 9 to 11 and in the afternoon from 4 to 6. But quite often she says that the tap is damaged and takes it away, and as a consequence we spend a few days without water."[79]

To outsiders, Nos. 100 and 96 long epitomised squalor, even though nearby tenements were hardly in better shape.[80] Moreover, this came to be associated with ethnonational representations. Referring to No. 100, the famous socialist MP Jean Allemane referred to "those poor Italians" who lived "in abnormal conditions."[81] Several years later, a conservative newspaper reported that at No. 96, little Spanish children were living "sordidly, in the most revolting filth." The article clearly conflated their foreignness and their slum-like dwellings.[82]

Yet many families refused to compromise on cleanliness. "My father was very particular about our hygiene," remembered one former resident.[83] At a minimum, people would take a footbath in a pot in the kitchen every few days. When it did run from the tap, water was spared, especially hot water, because of the time it took to heat on the coal-stove. As for washing clothes, it was such hard work for women that most would only change clothes on Sundays.[84] Residents were not passive victims of their conditions. The way they reacted against dirtiness and decay, even when they could not afford to live elsewhere, underlines as much.[85] And their perception of the *cités* never quite matched the resigned and condescending view of external observers.

On some counts, things did improve over time. In the last years of our period, building interiors started to look better.[86] By the 1930s, walls were hidden behind fabric coverings, and manual workers were making enough to own a cupboard, a chiffonier, sometimes a dresser on top of their iron beds. Oil lamps were replaced by light bulbs as gas and electricity became available on all floors.[87]

Sharing space and time

Residents did not experience their material environment in a vacuum; they had to share it with others. At each apartment's table, everyone had their spot. If it had a shorter side, it would be occupied by fathers, the most static members of the family.[88] As soon as dinner was over, living rooms often transformed into bedrooms by unfolding the children's and lodgers' camp beds.[89] A genuine yearning for intimacy proved hard to fulfil due to the limited room available.[90] Children would escape and meet their friends on the avenue, where cup-and-ball, tops, marbles, jacks or balls were played under the trees. Boys would go on the slide down the ditch of the *fortifs*, as Paris city walls were called; girls, subject to more parental restrictions, remained closer to home. All children would buy ice cream and chips in paper cones.[91] Until the early 1900s, there were no automobiles. But the traffic on the Avenue was heavy with horse-drawn trams and carts. Throughout the period under study, a shockingly high number of tenement's children were injured or killed by vehicles of all sorts.[92]

The space distribution of the *cités* left a distinctive mark on people's encounters. Passing through the pathway and front door of No. 96, for instance, and avoiding a neighbour standing in the way was impossible. Cases of a slapped child and of two slain adults confirm as much.[93] On the other hand, some structural features provided people with several options for circulation. The hotel at No. 102 had a double access, through the bar at the front, and from the side, through the passage that led to No. 100. It allowed people to escape or steal from others without being seen.[94]

Cellars could serve as hiding places.[95] In principle, no one would try to climb on the tin roofs, except perhaps murderers in a hurry to flee.[96] As for the sidewalk right outside the buildings, or the shade under the trees, elderly people became used to sitting on chairs for long hours. This tradition, which would last until the 1960s, is visible in the following photograph of the *cités* taken before World War I (Figure 1.3).[97]

30 *Changing places*

Figure 1.3 The *cités* viewed from the south, before 1914. Postcard, the author's own collection.[98]

Lastly, time was also a key parameter in the residents' sense of place. Times of encounters – around work, chores and leisure – were often simultaneous.[99] On a Thursday in 1890, after her shift at the packing service of the glass factory, 24-year-old Mathilde Garnier went down at 7 pm from her first-floor apartment at No. 100. She was holding clothes to wash in one hand, and a bucket in the other. A neighbour of hers met her on the stairs, a discussion erupted, and Mathilde was hit on the face with an iron. Their chore times, unsurprisingly, overlapped.[100] Buying groceries, cooking (twice a day), cleaning, sewing and doing the laundry was the work of mothers. When tasked with any of these, men complained.[101] On Thursdays, women who went to the local washhouse on the other side of the Avenue were helped by their daughters. Boys were not entirely exempt from chores – they were seen fetching water in the courtyard, but they were subject to lower expectations than their sisters.

In a social life marked by a "rhythmic structure," times of leisure often coincided as well.[102] Saturdays and Sunday nights were for balls; Sunday afternoons for sport competitions; June, August and October for the local fairs. In the Plaine's *débits*,* people constantly ran into colleagues and neighbours. But the "layers of time" also diverged.[103] Inside the buildings, periods of joy and grief alternated for residents in similar yet asynchronous rhythms. These periods contributed to spatialising the different parts of the *cités*, fragmenting them with fleeting, yet significant, symbolic boundaries.

All in all, tenants were likely to share the same times and spaces, but their personal circumstances also led them to experience them differently. Their sense of place evolved depending on their own roaming perimeters and rhythms of activity. But these representations were also influenced by another set of circumstances: who they were, and who lived alongside them. The answers to these questions changed so frequently that a shifting make-up became one of the most persistent traits of the *cités*.

Notes

1 AD93, 2E7 300, Minutes Me Leclerc, 12.07.1862, Cottret-Blanchard; Versigny-Saudet, 23.02.1864, in FNA, MC/ET/XXXVIII/1224, Minutes Me Gamard, "Cahier des charges," av. de Paris 96, 12.10.1883; SDMA, E179, SD, 1865, deaths, No. 542, 18.06.1865, Louise Adélaïde Versigny; AD93, 4Q5, vol. 4994, 12, 1.09.1880, sale Trézel-Versigny.
2 *"C'était une très belle avenue, un peu comme les Champs-Élysées."* Int. No. 32, 19.04.2016.
3 *La Céramique et la verrerie*, 1893: 1376–9; *Bulletin de la Société de protection des apprentis et des enfants des manufactures*, 1867: 264. The glass factory was founded in 1859. M. Legras was recruited as head of manufacturing in 1864, became director the next year, and assumed ownership in 1866.
4 SDMA, 1G86, Matrices, 1865, 55.
5 Michel de Certeau, *The Practice of Everyday Life* (Berkeley: University of California Press, 1984), 117.
6 Donna Gabaccia, *From Sicily to Elizabeth Street: Housing and Social Change Among Italian Immigrants, 1880–1930* (Albany: SUNY Press, 1984), xviii.
7 Henri Lefèbvre, *Le Droit à la ville* (Paris: Anthropos, 1968).
8 See AD93, 4Q5, Acte 27, 19.12.1883, Lévêque-Versigny; also, compare *Annuaire-almanach*, Firmin Didot et Bottin, 1882, 2342, with 1883, 1283. The old 84, 86, and 88 became the new 96 and 98 av. de Paris, and the old 90 became the new 100 and 102.
9 See for an example among many AD93, 4U7/958, CDP SD-Sud, PV 4.02.1897 c. Beaudouin, 100 av. de Paris.
10 See SDMA, CT81, Petition, 4.06.1892. Also, FNA, BB/11/11050, 66799x28, Pezza.
11 SDMA, CT83, Letter from SD Mayor, 14.02.1892.
12 *BMOSD*, 29.11.1881, 204–5.
13 *BMOSD*, 1883, 157, 22.06.1883.
14 *BMOSD*, 18.05.1901, 20.
15 Musée d'art et d'histoire de Saint Denis, *Des cheminées dans la Plaine: cent ans d'industrie à Saint-Denis, 1830–1930* (Paris: Créaphis, 1998), 16–21.
16 Letter from M. and Mme. Moser to the Justice Minister, 7.10.1883, in FNA, BB/11/1710, 4521x83, Moser.
17 See e.g. AD93, 4U7/915, CDP SD-Sud, 20.09.1891, Report by officer Vincent about Nos. 2–4 av. de Paris (*"une cour, espèce de cité"*).
18 The name is probably related to a man named Nicolas Jacman who first erected the houses behind that of Louise Versigny, in 1868.
19 *Le Petit Journal*, 6.12.1869; AD93, 4U7/450, 21.04.1880, mandate signed by Mme Vachée; AD93, 4U7/453, 18.11.1881, Billion c. Maire; AD93, 4L2, Sainte-

Geneviève-de-la-Plaine, baptisms, 1884, No. 30, 24.02.1884; AVP, D4R1 490, 1887, No. 2875, Philippe Dimnet; *La Justice*, 23.08.1900.
20 Jean-Paul Brunet, "Aux origines de l'industrialisation de Saint-Denis," *Études de la région parisienne* 22 (1969): 16–22.
21 *Le Soir*, 16.05.1890; Centre de documentation et d'histoire des techniques, *Évolution de la géographie industrielle de Paris et sa proche banlieue au XIXe siècle*, vol. II: *Vers la maturité de l'industrie parisienne, 1872–1914* (Paris: CDHT, 1976), 469; FNA, F/12/8649, Légion d'honneur, Charles Legras.
22 Jules Romains, *Paris des hommes de bonne volonté* (Paris: Flammarion, 1949), 61.
23 *JSD*, 12.04.1916, 23.04.1916, 3.05.1916. On this topic, see, André Guillerme, Anne-Cécile Lefort, and Gérard Jigaudon, *Dangereux, insalubres et incommodes. Paysages industriels en banlieue parisienne, XIXe–XXe siècles* (Seyssel: Champ Vallon, 2004), 214, 282.
24 Int. No. 32, 19.04.2016.
25 Achille Daudé-Bancel, "Une coopérative de consommation, 'La Famille', société coopérative de consommation, d'épargne et de Prévoyance sociale, 104, avenue de Paris, La Plaine-Saint-Denis (Seine)," *L'Action populaire*, No. 88 (1905): 3–28.
26 APP, CB 92.11, 1915/388, 22.06.1915; CB 92.17,1921/23, 13.12.1920-08.01.1921. As a point of comparison, a 1941 provision still in force in 2021 forbids new openings of alcohol-serving establishments when the density rate reaches one per 450 people.
27 Int. No. 39, 4.09.2016.
28 Initially, a gendarmerie unit was stationed for two decades right next to the *cités*, in the courtyard of No. 92. After it left, the only police station was a little further up the avenue, at No. 120 until 1893. See Jean Lemoine, "L'émigration bretonne à Paris," *Science sociale* 14, No. 1 (1892), 177; Brunet, "Une banlieue ouvrière," 316–9.
29 A cinema opened at No. 217 av. de Paris in the late 1900s, another in the rue du Landy shortly thereafter (SDMA, 1Q6, 26.01.1911; 1Q7, 26.05.1914). Until the 1930s, screenings only ran from Friday to Sunday.
30 Brunet, "Une banlieue ouvrière," 1120–25. At Legras, people had in theory some free time between shifts. Until 1900, workdays were discontinuous: one shift worked from 6 to 11 am and from 6 pm to 11 pm, and another from 12 to 6 pm and from midnight to 6 am. But work was so strenuous that workers usually rested in their spare time (see *Le Soleil*, 10.05.1900; AD93, 4U7/997, Letter from M. Legras, 27.11.1901).
31 Many descendants of tenants stressed the importance of the "*jardins ouvriers*" in the interwar period, which could be located in the Plaine or in nearby banlieues. Int. No. 21, 1.08.2016; int. No. 38, 2.08.2016; int. No. 47, 23.11.2016; int. No. 71, 25.07.2018.
32 Lenard Berlanstein, *The Working People of Paris, 1871–1914* (Baltimore: Johns Hopkins University Press, 1984), 126.
33 A hearing of August 1894 was the last time she appeared in court in person (AD93, 4U7/507, 10.08.1894, Versigny c. Martens). Although she would initially supplement her income by working home as a seamstress (see SDMA, 1F17, 1886 census, 100 av. de Paris), the rental business quickly proved profitable enough for Louise to cease working entirely.
34 APP, CB 82.4, 1904/521–3, 29.05.1904; 1904/615, 30.06.1904; CB 89.48, 1914/1332, 23.10.1914; CB 92.14, 1917/1996, 8.12.1917; CB 92.24,1927/880, 30.04.1927.
35 SDMA, CT401, Letter from the Head of the PP's 2nd Bureau to the Mayor of SD, 24.08.1899.

Setting the scene   33

36 Charles Benoist, "Le travail dans la grande industrie," *Revue des deux mondes* 5/ 18, November 1st, 1903, 179–83.
37 SDMA, CT1136, "Verreries de Saint-Denis," No. 9049, 2°; AVP, D1U10 729, Conseil de prud'hommes de la Seine, Produits Chimiques, 18.11.1930, 29.12.1930, Nos. 49231, 49348, François Moreau.
38 Int. No. 16, 17.04.2016.
39 AD93, 4U7/940, BG SD, PV 19.04.1894 c. Klein.
40 Benoist, "Le travail dans la grande industrie," 178.
41 *Le Journal des débats politiques et littéraires,* 9.11.1912; *La Liberté,* 9.11.1912; APP, CB 92.14, 1918/207, 24.02.1918. Residents could also use the term (*taudis* in French): see Letter from M. Alvarez, 100 av. Wilson, to the Mayor of SD, 20.07.1922. The expression or its equivalents endured until after the Second World War.
42 Galeazzo Sommi-Picenardi, "La tratta dei piccoli italiani in Francia," *Nuova antologia. Rivista di lettere, scienze ed arti* 37, No. 723 (1902), 471.
43 Int. No. 56, 1.12.2016 (tenant at No. 100 from 1940 to 1944).
44 By the 1930s, the contrast had become starker. A tenant born at No. 100 in 1933 recalled: *"Le 98, c'était luxe par rapport au 96 et au 100. Il y avait des tapis, c'était un bel immeuble."* Int. No. 42, 23.04.2016. ("Compared with Nos. 96 and 100, No. 98 was a fine place. There were carpets, it was a beautiful building.")
45 *Affiches parisiennes et départementales,* vol. 51, No. 18, 438, 10.10.1868, No. 18135; FNA, MC/ET/XXXVIII/1224, Minutes Me Gamard, "Cahier des charges," 12.10.1883; AD93, 4Q5 7840, 21.06.1895, Bourges-Versigny.
46 Technically one could jump the wall between the two *cités,* but few did (int. No. 39, 4.09.2016).
47 Projections realised with the help of Laura Fregonese, based on plans found in AD77, 214E460, Minutes de Me Fauvel, "Cahier des charges ... av. de Paris 96, 98, 100 et 102," 30.05.1897; 214E482, Minutes de Me Fauvel, "Partage de la succession de Mlle Versigny," 15.12.1902; AD93, 2048W83, "Croquis d'arpentage," SD, September 1929 (139a).
48 FNA, MC/ET/XXXVIII/1224, Minutes Me Gamard, "Cahier des charges," 12.10.1883. Over the years, a painter, a shoemaker, a wine-merchant owned small workshops or storage shacks in the courtyard, made of wooden boards and roofed with cardboard coated with bitumen.
49 *Ibid.*; AD93, 4U7/533, 1896, 14.10.1896, Dion c. Robert; *Le Matin,* 13.09.1900; APP, CB 92.3, 1907/1087, 1102, 1121, 2002, 27.09.1907.
50 *La Presse,* 17.06.1874, Faillites, Léonard; SDMA, 25Fi280, 29.09.1880, Ayral; AD93, 4U7/494, 21.07.1893, Bantegnie c. Versigny (lease dated 15.04.1882).
51 AD93, 4Q5, vol. 6170, No. 6, 13.11.1886, Camus-Versigny.
52 APP, CB 92.17,1920/828, 3.10.1920; CB 92.20,1923/1227, 23.10.1923; CB 92.24,1927/479, 28.03.1927; int. No. 49, 6.07.2016.
53 See AD93, 4U7/450-542. Between 1880 and 1897, Louise went 23 times in person to the *justice de paix* for disputes over rents; 32 other times she was represented by a proxy.
54 AD93, 4U7/477, 11.09.1891, Versigny c. Borne.
55 AVP, D1U6 508, T. corr. Seine, 14.08.1894, Géring, Baudel, Sinnig.
56 On the auction, see Service de la propriété foncière (SPF), Auxerre 1, 5e bureau des hypothèques de la Seine, vol. 343, No. 3, 7.01.1908, Adjudication du 14.11.1907 portant sur les immeubles des 100 et 102 avenue de Paris à la Plaine-Saint-Denis, "Cahier des charges." The husband of Louise's great-niece, Ernest Barillier, was a butcher turned influential councilman in Paris. A notorious *antidreyfusard,* he served time in jail when he was suspected of plotting a coup against the Republic (see i. a. *Le Petit Parisien,* 4.01.1900).

57 *JSD*, 1.04.1920.
58 AD93, 4U7/540, 21.05.1897, Versigny c. Billotte.
59 Loïc Bonneval et al., *Les Politiques publiques de contrôle des loyers, comparaisons internationales et enseignements historiques (1914–2014)* (Lyon: Ministère de l'égalité des territoires et du logement, 2015), 15–34.
60 On the left side of the picture, the hôtel de l'Oise is M. Poullain's bar-hotel at No. 102; he is very probably the tall figure standing on the doorstep. He was the brother of the little Ernest mentioned in the introduction. The entrance pathway immediately to the left of the tree is No. 100, while the door of No. 98 is visible between the two horse carts, and that of No. 96 right after the load of casks.
61 See SDMA, CT352, CT930.
62 André Savoye, "La vie quotidienne dans la banlieue Nord et Nord-Ouest de Paris pendant la Grande Guerre" (doctoral diss., University of Paris IV, 2007), 67–71.
63 SDMA, 2ACW9, "96 av. Wilson"; SDMA, 1F27, 1911 census, vol. 1, 301–6; AD93, DR7 76, Dommages de guerre, SD, Note, 13.10.1924.
64 Because it was in partial ruins, it was bought for next to nothing by M. Prieur, the founder and head of a local company, who sought cheap solutions of lodging for his workers. See FNA, MC/RE/CXIX/27, Me Faÿ, 1920-28, No. 508, 12.05.1925.
65 Int. No. 42, 24.04.2016; int. No. 71, 25.07.2018.
66 Gérard Jacquemet, "Belleville ouvrier à la Belle Époque," *Le Mouvement social*, No. 118 (1982): 61–77.
67 SDMA, 16AC5, av. Wilson 100, Letter from the tenants at No. 98 to the Director of the Hygiene Service of SD, 7.12.1936.
68 *Id.*, Letter from M. Alvarez to the Mayor of SD, 20.07.1922.
69 This meant a surface of 15 to 20 square metres in total; see Alain Faure, "Comment se logeait le peuple parisien à la Belle Époque," *Vingtième siècle*, No. 64 (1999): 41–51. Hotel rooms at No. 102 had a surface of six square metres (see SDMA, 16AC5, Avenue Wilson 100-102).
70 AD93, 4U7/735-6, 1920, 6.02.1920, 9.04.1920, Damata ("Damoto") c. Barillier.
71 AD93, 4U7/735, 1920 (1), 6.02.1920, Pirollo c. Veuve Barillier; 4U7/736, 9.04.1920, Pirollo c. Barillier.
72 AD93, 4U7/723, 1916 (3), 27.10.1916, Gréco c. Lutel.
73 E.g. AD93, 4U7/635, 7.04.1905, 15.04.1905, Siméon c. Barillier.
74 AD93, 4U7/975, 981, 1009, 1020, CDP SD-Sud, PV c. Rodi (No. 102), Tedeschi (No. 100), Palma (No. 100), Pirolli (No. 100), 23.01.1899, 18.01.1900, 26.11.1903, 16.08.1905.
75 See e.g. AD93, 4U7/557, 7.10.1898, Delamotte c. Moutier.
76 "Inventaire des marchandises du fonds de charcuterie," in AD93, 1739W13, Bureau de l'enregistrement fiscal de Saint-Denis, *actes sous seings privés*, 15.01.1922, enr. 21.01.1922; "Inventaire des marchandises," in AD93, 1739W41, *actes sous seings privés*, 1930, 17.10.1930, enr. 21.10.1930.
77 "État des marchandises", in AD93, 1739W25, 1925, 1.04.1925, enr. 8.04.1925, Vacca-Pirolli.
78 SDMA, 16AC5, Av. Wilson 100, Letter from M. Duclermortier to the Préfet de la Seine, 3.05.1922; SDMA, 2ACW9, 96 av. Wilson, Report from the Bureau d'hygiène after an inspection on 21.05.1920.
79 SDMA, 16AC5, Letter from M. Duclermortier, *Id.*
80 See e.g. 2ACW9, 64 av. Wilson; 84 av. Wilson.
81 *JORF, Débats parlementaires, Chambre des députés*, 25.11.1901, 2332.
82 *La Liberté*, 2.11.1912.
83 Int. No. 50, 21.07.2016.

84 MA Saint-Ouen, LOC 75, H. Bertrand, "Souvenirs du début du siècle" [unpublished].
85 A 1904 poem about Saint-Denis illustrated this common tension between the aspiration to hygiene and an inescapable degree of soot and dirt: *"Pour moi, v'là la question sociale / Ça m'est égal de turbiner / Mais, j'veux pas avoir la gueul' sale / Malgré que j'soy' débarbouillé."* ("For me, here is the social problem / I don't care to slog away / But I don't want my face to remain dirty / Even when I've washed it."). Fabrice Delphi, "Saint-Denis-la-Suie," in *Outre-fortifs, impressions de la banlieue* (Paris: Malot, 1904), 7.
86 Int. No. 42, 23.04.2016; int. No. 54, 14.09.2016.
87 SDMA, 16AC5, Avenue Wilson 100–2; 40AC74, Av. Wilson 96, 98.
88 See Monique Eleb-Vidal and Anne Debarre, *L'Invention de l'habitation moderne: Paris, 1880–1914* (Paris: Hazan, 1995).
89 Int. No. 52, 28.10.2016.
90 Faure, "Comment se logeait le peuple parisien," 45.
91 SDMA, Tissot papers, 21 S 055 002, No. 1, 3.
92 APP, CB 92.6, 1910/812, 22.09.1910; CB 92.9, 1913/425, 8-9.05.1913; CB 92.9, 1913/529, 4.06.1913; CB 92.18,1922/88, 25-30.01.1922; CB 92.23,1926/1352, 10.08.1926-13.09.1926; 92.26, 1928/1443, 20.09.1928.
93 APP, CB 92.3, 1907/1042, 8.09.1907; CB 92.11, 1915/152, 8.04.1915; CB 92.21,1925/746, 2.06.1925.
94 APP, CB 92.2, 1905/826, 21.08.1905.
95 APP, CB 92.14, 1917/639, 19.06.1917-3.07.1917.
96 *Le Matin,* 29.09.1900; *Le Rappel*, 30.09.1900.
97 Int. No. 16, 17.04.2016; int. No. 32, 19.04.2016; int. No. 54, 4.09.2016.
98 The arrow pointing to No. 100 was drawn by the sender.
99 See Yves Lequin, "Les citadins et leur vie quotidienne," in *Histoire de la France urbaine*, ed. Georges Duby (Paris: Seuil, 1983), vol. IV, 344–5.
100 AD93, 4U7/909, BG SD Plaine, PV 25.09.1890 à 19h30 c. Euphrasie Hautefeuille.
101 APP, CB 92.14, 1918/207, 24.02.1918.
102 Eviatar Zerubavel, *Hidden Rhythms: Schedule and Calendars in Social Life* (Berkeley: University of California Press, 1985), 11.
103 Reinhart Koselleck, *Zeitschichten: Studien zur Historik* (Frankfurt: Suhrkamp, 2000).

2 A carousel of neighbours

"Boundaries between races and species seemed to be erased ... as in a pandemonium. Men, women, animals, sex, health, sickness, all seemed to be held in common by these people; everything went together, mingled, merged, superimposed...." This vivid depiction does not refer to the housing complex at 96–102 Avenue de Paris in Saint-Denis. It instead concerns the medieval court of miracles in Victor Hugo's famous rendition.[1] And yet tenants and observers alike routinely associated the two in a common evocation of density, diversity and poverty.[2]

How dense, how diverse and how poor exactly was the tenement's population? Where did the inhabitants come from? What did they do for a living? To understand both the migration experiences and sociocultural behaviours of this study's protagonists, the characteristics of the tenement's population provide indispensable context. They outline a group portrait, as it were, from which we will then be able to focus more closely on particular faces. Ethnographers have long used social surveys of their study communities to document population size, age and sex distribution, household structure and other basic sociodemographic variables. This is less frequent in microhistories. But some scholars engaging in mixed methods – combining qualitative with demographic and economic data – have provided encouraging examples.[3]

Here, the aggregate statistics are essential to further document the living conditions of the tenement population, in line with the previous considerations about the material conditions. More crucially, they provide background information on sex, income and geographic origins, which are key to understanding the dynamics of difference they are associated with: gender, class and ethnicity.

It must be acknowledged, however, that temporal, spatial and discursive biases affect any such demographic information.[4] In our case, all tenement inhabitants underwent multiple personal changes over the course of their lives; the same went for information collected about them. In the archives, a single piece of data (a person's town of birth, for instance) was subject to fluctuations over the years. People could modify their declarations, or the same statements could be understood and transcribed in different ways.

DOI: 10.4324/9781003017820-2

That being said, let us first take a look at the broad demographic picture. Then, we will get a sense of the tenement's socio-economic characteristics and its make-up by origins.

Major demographic figures

By collecting data from as many sources as possible, I was able to identify 4,845 people who were documented to have resided at 96–102 Av. de Paris/Av. Wilson in Saint-Denis between 1882 and 1932. This figure is obviously a low estimate of the actual number; many residents did not stay in the tenement long enough for their presence to be captured in written records. That number, however, is already significantly higher than what the censuses alone could reveal. Only 57% of all individuals identified as tenants had a line in at least one census register.

This is not to say that census lists should not be used – quite the contrary. They are the only comprehensive snapshots that allow for longitudinal analysis.[5] The first lesson we can draw from the census data is the quantitative evolution of the tenement's overall demography. The population peaked twice, at more than 500 inhabitants in the early 1890s and again before the First World War. The highest total was reached in 1911, with 549 inhabitants grouped in 141 households; the tenement's lowest numbers were in 1931, with 388 individuals divided between 113 households. While the constructions at No. 100 were initially the most populated, this changed in the 1920s in favour of No. 96.

Concerning the ratio of men to women, male residents were always a majority. In the early decades, tenants tended to live in couples and families; however, the arrival of single men in the late 1890s – sometimes accompanied by male children – perennially shifted the buildings' make-up. Single men also formed a majority of people renting rooms at No. 102's hotel. Between one-fourth and one-fifth of all heads of households in the tenement complex were single at census dates. And except for 1891, single male tenants outnumbered their (mostly widowed) female counterparts.

The tenants' average age remained low, increasing only slightly from around 25 in the early decades to 27 after the First World War. This was due in part to the falling birth rate entailed by the conflict. Another factor accounting for the increase in average age was the disappearance from the tenement of large groups of children living with "caretakers" (see Chapter 4).

Health

Overall health also improved over time, albeit gradually. The average age at death for tenement residents over the period stands at 24 years. High infant mortality diminished this number, with children under the age of one accounting for more than a fifth of all deaths. Archival records provide information on some of the contagious diseases that were regularly contracted

38 *Changing places*

in the *cités*: diphtheria, croup, dysentery, poliomyelitis, tuberculosis, meningitis, chronic bronchitis, typhoid fever and measles.[6] The military files of 205 one-time male inhabitants at Nos. 96–102 show that the list of conditions and disabilities extended even further. The most common of all was a general weakness, which speaks to the poor nutrition and harsh living and working conditions of most tenants.

Infectious diseases related to poor hygiene reinforced pre-existing disparities. When an epidemic of cholera-type diarrhoea struck in the summer of 1892, the five tenants who died lived in the humblest lodgings at the back of No. 100. One of the tenement children fell sick in front of his classmates and passed a few hours later.[7] The proximity of water wells to nearby cesspools exposed people to high risks, and their replacement with fountains likely dates to that year.[8] In addition to hygiene improvements, tenants could also rely on lucky breaks. Despite being widespread in the Plaine, the global influenza of 1918–1920 largely spared the *cités*.

Injuries sustained at work were even more common than diseases. They occasionally caused death but more often permanently disfigured tenants' bodies with missing limbs, burns and scars of all sorts.[9] In Saint-Denis as a whole, 15 work accidents were declared every day between 1901 and 1915; from 1916 to 1931, after the war effort dramatically expanded the heavy industry, this figure jumped to 43.[10] In three months of 1926, there were 137 work-related injuries at the Plaine glass factory alone.[11] Under the intense heat and fumes of chemical industries, strokes and respiratory diseases like emphysema were not rare.[12] At Legras, the use of minium as a glass component was bound to cause lead poisoning.[13] Male tenants were the most exposed to those work-related perils, but women were not immune, either.[14]

Depression and distress were also prevalent, leading some to contemplate suicide. I counted seven people living at Nos. 96–102 who were documented as having made such attempts over a half-century, two of whom survived.[15] As opposed to illness or frustrations with love, economic strife was rarely the main cause. Still, difficult material conditions did not help. Neither did alcohol, which remained a permanent scourge in the *cités*, as in all working-class banlieues. Not only did its widespread consumption precipitate illnesses, job losses, physical violence and numerous arrests, but it also prevented families from staying together and receiving public benefits.[16]

As hygiene in the tenement improved, the mortality rate declined. With time, residents started getting better access to healthcare, in particular by going to hospitals in Saint-Denis or Paris. After the Great War, childbirth in tenement's families was four times more likely to take place at the hospital compared to the period before. However, they still made up a small minority of the tenement's births (5.5%).

Birth rates remained high throughout the decades. This natural increase of around 1% at the beginning of the period – and again in 1901, 1911, 1921 and 1926 – partly explains the *cités*' constant overcrowding. In 1896, a family from Moselle lived with their five children; a neighbouring family had eight members, and another family had ten. All were living in one-bedroom apartments.[17] The influx of lodgers, which people took in to supplement their income, only increased the population density. Over the period, the number of people per household oscillated between 3.5 and 4.2.

Origins

It was not until 1911 that censuses started listing birthplaces. However, civil, electoral and military registers, as well as naturalisation files and genealogical databases, allowed me to fill in the blanks. I retrieved the exact town of birth of a large proportion of residents from earlier years – from two thirds in 1886, to more than 80% in 1891 and 1896, to three quarters in 1901.[18] What this reconstructed data points to, first and foremost, is diversity. Over 50 years, the inhabitants of the tenement hailed from at least 1,016 different localities, scattered across 172 administrative districts or provinces and 21 countries.

These figures bear witness to the intensity and variety of migration flows that regularly renewed the tenement's population. The percentage of tenants born in Saint-Denis never exceeded 25%, and those were mostly children of migrants. Apart from Saint-Denis, the most common birthplace of tenants across our period was Paris and its banlieue, which accounted for about 10% of the non-Saint-Denis-natives. This is consistent with broader calculations on the migrations between Paris and its surroundings.[19]

The proportion of other origins varied greatly over time. The half-century under scrutiny can be divided into five periods corresponding to as many immigration waves. From 1882 to 1898, people from the confines of France and the German countries made up the overwhelming majority of migrant residents, culminating at more than six out of ten non-Saint-Denis natives.[20] Their percentage declined with the arrival of the first Italians at No. 100 in 1898. Hailing from the provinces of Molise (administrative centre: Campobasso) and Terra di Lavoro* (Caserta), they upended the balance in favour of their contingent for a good ten years. In 1901, they accounted for more than 40% of those with a non-Saint-Denis origin. In 1908, Northern Spaniards from the Mountain of Burgos and southern Cantabria started arriving, as well. Along with individuals from Extremadura, their growing presence would characterise the third period of this half-century. World War I, with all the reshuffling it involved, stands out as another distinct moment. The ranks of people from the Nord and Pas-de-Calais, in particular, swelled during the conflict due to the presence of refugees from those parts. Finally, the interwar era saw the slow decline of previous immigration stocks, as well as the appearance of new ones – albeit of modest proportions – from Eastern Europe, in particular.

These trends give a limited view of the tenants' origins. A constant quarter of residents hailed from a variety of locations outside of those few regional clusters. For instance, the first Italians recorded in the *cités* were not from the Mezzogiorno but from the Duchy of Parma.[21] Families from Brittany, who made up an important subset of immigrants in Saint-Denis, were also a steady presence in the tenement, although in small numbers.

In order to provide a visual, and accessible, rendition of these evolutions, I have devised an interactive map based on the geographic coordinates of the tenants' birthplaces. This multi-scalar cartography displays the number of residents from every single location at each census year, while acknowledging the proportion of missing data each time. It can be found online.[22] The map highlights both the origin clusters and the faraway birthplaces of some residents, such as New York, Philadelphia, Buenos Aires, São Paulo, Stockholm and Saigon. These cities almost always corresponded to families' previous migrations. Likewise, many of the births in the Paris area coincided with temporary stops that families made before reaching the Plaine-Saint-Denis (see Chapter 3).

Let us now turn to the spatial distribution of origins within the tenement block. This largely depended on the material environment. At the turn of the century, newcomers had much less opportunity to settle at No. 96, as the housing capacity of that address had yet to be expanded. This is why Casertans and Molisans only lived at No. 100 in 1901 – so much so that it was temporarily dubbed a *"cité des Italiens"*[23] – before dispersing quite evenly throughout the block in subsequent census years. A few years hence the situation would be reversed. New rental space was mostly concentrated at No. 96 and some would view that southern part of the housing block as a *"cité espagnole"* (a Spanish tenement).[24] Whatever the reality, this type of ethnic shortcut was quite common in the area. For a while, it produced what sociologists call "social-urban boundaries."[25] These shapeshifting delineations were primarily the monopoly of outsiders, especially of those who lived in the vicinity. Despite the latter's own humble living standards, the real or fantasised misery of the disreputable tenement units at Nos. 96–102 served as a counter-model.[26]

Inside the *cités*, clusters of origin homogeneity could be found at various points in time. In the early 1880s, for example, the first two floors of the first building at No. 96 were inhabited almost exclusively by households from Lorraine. Those households had family ties to one another.[27] At No. 100 in 1907, apartments on the "balcony" and on the first floor of a house at the back of the courtyard were almost reserved to Casertans and Molisans. In 1929, residents of No. 96 were heterogeneously distributed, except for smaller constructions at the back where 12 out of 13 households hailed from Spain. It should be noted that those Spanish families were not distributed along provincial lines. All in all, most constructions remained fairly blended throughout the period.[28] In fact, the available evidence suggests that ethnic concentration, if present, was probably more operative at the scale of floors and corridors. This hypothesis has generally eluded the attention of historians, who rarely look further than the street or building level.[29]

Occupations and income

The tenants' occupations also underwent significant evolutions. An initial period of employment diversity in the 1880s was followed by a quarter-century dominated by the Legras glassworks. Although the factory did not shut down altogether during the First World War, the conflict had a negative impact on its production. Moreover, better wages were to be earned in armament factories. The heavier industry started to attract much of the workforce that had not been displaced by the conflict or had arrived since its outbreak. After the war, widespread progress in mechanisation led traditional factories of the Plaine to employ fewer workers than before. This trend explains the occupational diversity that took hold in the *cités* in the interwar period, with people commuting over greater distances – something made easier by the improvement of private and public transport. A peak in unemployment at the tail end of the period under scrutiny signalled the beginning of the Great Depression.[30]

Throughout the half-century, blue-collar jobs remained dominant among tenants. About three-quarters of male inhabitants whose professions were listed in the census were employed at factories and workshops. This was also the case of a significant number of women, but it is harder to gauge because housewives' profession fields were often left blank. In the tenement, the ranks of the *employés** (office workers) grew steadily from the 1910s onward, aided by the rapid expansion of feminised professions, such as secretaries and stenographers. In 1931, ten out of 50 female tenants whose profession was reported in the census were working desk jobs, while the remaining 40 held factory positions.

Still, we know that women's work was largely undercounted until the mid-20th century. Scholars have largely debunked the "optical illusion" created by official statistics, which left a wide range of female occupations in the shadows.[31] Social expectations shaped the questions of the census officials who would not take women's answers at face value, especially when married women reported occasional work. This "hidden-woman" effect could also be the consequence of under-reporting from women themselves, "for fear of tax collector following census taker."[32]

The micro focus can give a sense of the wide range of paid occupations performed by female tenants, and which mostly escaped the census. For instance, women like Marie Mor, from No. 96, and Clémentine Schwaller and Rosa Fraioli, from No. 100, had no jobs attached to their names in the census register. Yet they were compensated by Legras for sweeping the factory floors and allowed to resell specks of glass that they collected.[33] This was one of many ways for housewives to supplement their family's income. Some worked at home as part-time seamstresses; others, like a Spanish-born housewife at No. 96, would go to the wash house and do her neighbours' laundry for a fee. Another longstanding tenant at No. 100 would prepare oysters and snails to sell by the building's entrance.[34] As for shopkeepers' wives and daughters, they shouldered most of the retailing duties.

Figure 2.1 Workers by Legras's entrance, 1904–1906, Neurdein postcard (detail). AD93, ref. 49Fi/5907.

The ratio of skilled and unskilled workers is hard to measure statistically, as professions could either be described by their mode of payment (*journalier**) or by the nature of the work (*verrier,* for instance, i.e. glassworker). Daily workers could be foremen and managers; conversely, being listed as "*verrier*" by census officials did not mean that one was a qualified "*ouvrier verrier.*" What I was able to reconstruct by combining information is the unquestionable centrality of the glass factory in the early decades.

The factory grew steadily in the 1880s and 1890s, and the tenement was one of several with a high concentration of Legras employees.[35] In 1901, at least 71% of residents of both sexes aged 11 or over worked at the glass factory.[36] Based on photographs of the factory personnel in the 1900s, it is possible to identify the activities performed by women. They represented 38.5% of the labour force in the carving, cutting and wiping department. Their share was 53% in the decoration unit and 29% in shipping.[37] Women's careers were shorter, however, as demonstrated by their extremely low proportion among the 30-year-old employees.[38]

As far as professions were concerned, the importance of Mouton rose constantly as well. By 1911, this major wire-drawing plant was already the residents' second-largest employer, despite the significant distance between its site and the *cités* (600 metres against 100 for Legras). Mouton soon became an employer of choice for Spaniards; in 1911, they made up a third of the residents employed there. That proportion rose to 40% in 1921, before

Figure 2.2 Workers by Mouton's entrance, 1905–1908, Léon & Lévy postcard (detail). AD93, ref. 49Fi/5982.

receding to a quarter in 1926. At that last date, Mouton had become the primary employer at Nos. 96–102 in general, and of Spanish tenants in particular. In both cases, however, the percentages were now limited; it was nothing like the near-monopoly that Legras had enjoyed at the turn of the century. Of tenants whose employer was mentioned in the 1926 census, Mouton only employed 14.3%. In fact, after the Great War, residents were quite evenly divided between many factories.

Tenement newcomers who took industrial jobs were generally new to them. Some glassworkers or rail layers had previously worked as servants[39] or been born to parents who were domestic workers themselves.[40] A mason-turned-glassmaker had initially worked as a cloth-weaver.[41] Others included people who had worked as miners, millers and sawyers.[42] Some tenants, however, inherited their craft from their parents. This was the case of some – though not all – qualified *verriers*, as well as at least one laundry worker and one mason.[43] Since a vast majority of tenants came from rural areas, it is hardly surprising to discover that they had either been born into families of craftsmen – clog makers, cartwrights, blacksmiths, road menders – or families of farm labourers.[44] Almost all tenants from Italy and Spain had worked in agriculture before their emigration and had been born to land-working parents.[45]

Work in the Plaine was never hard to come by. In principle, unemployment was of no concern to healthy people. It only became a general problem at four moments: in the mid-1890s, in the second half of 1914, in 1919–1921 and after 1930. Nevertheless, employment by no means prevented misery. "People would find work, but it paid almost nothing," a Plainard remembered when asked about the Belle Époque.[46] At the turn of the century, most male occupants of the tenement would make around four and a half francs a day, either at the glass factory, the railroad or in new industries. Renault, the automobile company, had someone living at No. 100 among its very first employees.[47] Tenants on the city's payroll were compensated slightly better for menial jobs, but their pay remained low.[48]

Women were paid, at most, 50% of men's salaries.[49] Newcomers would earn less, on average, than their predecessors in the early years of each immigrant group's presence. Still, the gender pay gap was much more profound than any correlation between earnings and geographic origin. By the late 1900s, some tenants from Italy and Spain had become skilled workers and even foremen at Mouton and Legras; women never enjoyed similar opportunities. During and after the First World War, income inequality increased between factory workers and people living on benefits. The disparity also grew within factories themselves, due to the increasing division of labour and mechanisation. And while women were hired in record numbers during the war, the gender wage differential decreased only slightly.[50]

Economic hardship

Up until the First World War, the majority of tenants at Nos. 96–102 had a hard time making ends meet; the same could be said for a substantial proportion of the Parisian working class. An income of six francs for a family of five was barely sufficient. Food expenses, in particular, would consume two-thirds of the household's income.[51] Traces subsist of tenement residents taking out payday loans to cover current expenses – a luxury only available to the lucky few who had permanent jobs.[52]

Until the mid-1900s, overall inflation was either absent or negative.[53] This was not reflected, however, in the tenement's rent prices, which rose steadily. It is true that rents there were much more affordable than their equivalents in Paris proper; a number of people even moved to the *cités* precisely for that reason, such as a father of 17 who had gone bankrupt four times in the 1890s.[54] Still, rent prices in the *cités* picked up about 15% every ten years. This increase was not followed by an increase in wages, except for those who managed to remain in the same factory.[55] The rents' growth was apparently similar before and after the Great War, but that equivalence is misleading; crossing sources, I was able to reconstruct 21 precise measurements of the income percentage spent by tenant families on their rents. These measurements are clustered in the two periods for which we have more accurate data (thanks to naturalisation files): 1880–1900 and 1920–1932. After increasing to a share of 15–18% at the turn of the century, housing expenses in the tenants' budgets fell to an average of 6% after the war. In other words, in the interwar era, housing had become less of a burden.[56]

Limiting housing expenses long characterised the working class, who had low expectations of comfort and moved frequently between addresses.[57] What we often overlook, however, is that many people could not pay their rent on time and fell into debt spirals as a result. In the tenement, reasons for such predicaments were manifold. They often involved death, old age or adverse circumstances which few could afford to hedge against. "Allow me to write you this letter," a 35-year-old widow from No. 96 wrote to the Mayor in 1891, "because five months have passed since my husband died and I have received only five francs last month … there is no way I can feed my three children and me with my daily earnings of 1 fr. 50, my eldest who is 12 cannot be employed anywhere because of his disability … and on top of that I am late on my rent payments, the landlady wants to kick me out."[58] When people fell sick, they stopped earning money and had to pay for doctors and medicine. In such instances, "the great misery spread immediately in the families."[59]

Rent was due every three months. It was customary for landlords to grant short extensions. But when tenants were too deep in debt or left the buildings, landlords like Louise Versigny and the local shopkeepers would sue their debtors in court. Their goal was to eventually recover part of the outstanding rents via a sequester on the families' salaries, which kept the noose around people's necks.

In the last decades of the 19th century, Louise Versigny was a particularly active plaintiff. She obtained 61 court orders against her tenants between 1880 and 1900 – more than three times as many as her successors in the ensuing two decades.[60] People could gain her trust but quickly fall from grace. Sources show that she would extend credit to people she knew well, not only by delaying rents but also by lending them cash. But the moment they stopped paying entirely, she would go after them.[61] Concierges played a crucial mediatory role, in that respect. Employed by the landlords, they could obtain clemency for certain tenants. They also provided other key services: keeping a vacant accommodation for one's relatives; certifying the good morality of the residents' children when they were in danger of being placed in correctional institutions; and issuing precious certificates of residence, which were particularly critical in naturalisation procedures.[62]

Forced evictions were rare, with people generally moving of their own accord.[63] Still, being sued always meant bearing the extra burden of judicial fees on top of one's principal debt and interest. Debt would pile up fast at this rate. In 1898, for instance, a resident at No. 100 owed more than 1,700 francs – more than a year's worth of work – to a vast number of creditors including Louise Versigny, the butcher, the baker and two grocers. When he lost his job at the railway company, he became utterly insolvent, and the pugnacious landlady recovered a mere 2.5% of her rent money.[64]

Rarely in a position to afford to skip work – let alone afford an attorney, tenants could barely make their voices heard in court. When they did, they almost always secured extra time or rebates due to the poor state of their dwellings, to which the tenement's landlords generally admitted. The role of wives proved essential in this respect, as they often represented the family in court.[65]

Once a tenant was out, finding a new one was easy. There was a constant shortage of one or two-room dwellings in Saint-Denis, especially at the turn of the century.[66] This housing scarcity led to the expansion of both the hotel at No. 102 and the furnished rooms at No. 96 and 100.

Striving for a better life

Under these circumstances, families with two working parents were bound to fare better. A tenant who worked as a midwife, for instance, significantly supplemented her husband's income at Legras.[67] Truly better days, however, would only come at the later stages of people's careers. One resident of No. 100 started at Legras at age 14 in 1885. Twenty-five years later, he would finally earn the full salary of an *ouvrier verrier*, nine and a half francs per day.[68] M. Legras's treatment of his workers was a complex mix of exploitation and paternalism.[69] In 1881, he built new housing units that would accommodate 50 worker families in decent conditions.[70] The factory introduced compensation for the high costs of living; in the early 1920s, that indemnity would amount to 10% of the workers' basic income.[71] In addition, an in-house pension system, which included a profit-sharing component, was quite generous, kicking in at 55 years of age. Unions were quick to point out, however, that few reached that age, either for health reasons or because they were laid off. In 1903, only 19 out of 862 workers were 45 or older.[72] And when the owner announced better salaries to quell growing discontent, he could renege on his promises a few days later.[73]

To lift oneself out of poverty, a solution was the possibility of concurrently drawing income from an industrial job and a small business. Such businesses were nominally held by men but usually run by their wives. This widespread aspiration helps explain the record number of bars in the area. Tenants of the *cités* did not wait for the interwar period – with which this phenomenon is usually associated – to hold several jobs at once.[74] With the exception of those who ran a *garni** or worked as strolling merchants on their days off, running a shop and working in a factory was the most common combination. One of the grocers at the front of the *cités* was also a boilermaker;[75] his successor a mechanic;[76] yet another, a plumber.[77] For years, the owner of the bar at Nos. 96–98 spent his days packing glassware at Legras.[78] In the 1880s, an individual at No. 100 was at once a keeper at the cemetery, a rag-and-bone man and a cooper.[79] Most of the tenement's women also routinely accumulated jobs, not to mention the chores they did for their own family.

As we have seen, the population at Nos. 96–102 underwent significant evolutions over time: waves of migrants, health crises and improvements, socio-economic challenges, variations in job diversity, etc. These elements combined to create a human environment that was constantly shifting, a demographic carousel in the tenement. Despite – and partly because of – their turnover, the inhabitants of the *cités* regularly invested new symbolic meanings and boundaries into their habitat and its surroundings. Their cognitive maps changed as quickly, if not faster, than the material environment itself. Still, continuities are just as visible as inflexions. The *cités* always kept a demographic diversity in terms of gender, age and origins. Gender inequalities in terms of domestic and professional roles remained largely stable, for instance, despite the unique experience of the First World War.

The relation between physical space and cultural boundaries, however, was never static. It was fuelled by the kinetic energy of migrations. Migrations both shaped and were themselves shaped by the representations and decisions of the tenants throughout their lives.

Notes

1 Victor Hugo, *Notre-Dame de Paris*, trans. Alban Krailsheimer (Oxford: Oxford University Press, 1999 [1st ed. 1831]), 93–4.
2 François-Ignace Mouthon, "La traite des blancs," *Le Matin*, July 2, 1901. Visiting the area a few years earlier, an Italian diplomat had first heard locals use the expression to refer to a nearby building, at No. 87 Avenue de Paris (Raniero Paulucci di Calboli, "La traite des petits Italiens en France," *La Revue des Revues*, July 1st, 1897, 404). Former residents at No. 100 in the 1930s and 1940s employed that same phrase to describe the tenement: int. No. 39, 4.09.2016; int. No. 43, 23.04.2016.
3 Olivier Zunz, *The Changing Face of Inequality: Urbanization, Industrial Development, and Immigrants in Detroit, 1880–1920* (Chicago: University of Chicago Press, 1983); Joanne Vajda, *Paris, ville lumière: une transformation urbaine et sociale, 1855–1937* (Paris: L'Harmattan, 2015).
4 Peter Burke, *History and Social Theory* (Ithaca: Cornell University Press, 2005), 36–7.
5 From 1886 through 1931, they provide the name, first name, age, nationality, situation to the head of the household, profession and at times employer; from 1911, they included the tenants' town of birth. The 1881 census is not reliable, because numbers assigned to buildings do not correspond to the actual civic numbers.
6 SDMA, 1I227, PP, Bureau d'hygiène, "État des entrées," 5.10.1915; CT433, "Désinfections," 8.02.1916, 19.02.1916, 13.04.1918, 20.05.1918, 1.09.1918, 2.06.1919; CT551, "Nomenclature des maladies transmissibles," 2.08.1912; CT566, 1910–1913, "Inspections."

7 SDMA, CT560, CDP SD-Sud, "État nominatif des personnes atteintes du choléra-nostras ou de diarrhée cholériforme," 1892; CT58, Letter from the director of the boys' school, 26.07.1892; AD93, D4P4 57, "Documents préparatoires à l'établissement du cadastre," Nos. 42, 42 bis, 43, 98–100, 96, 102 av. de Paris [1880s–1890s].
8 Adrien Le Roy des Barres and Paul Louis Gastou, *Le Choléra à Saint-Denis en 1892, rôle des différents agents infectieux et des conditions hygiéniques dans l'invasion, la marche et la propagation du choléra* (Paris: Asselin et Houzeau, 1893).
9 For tenants at Nos. 96–102 who died from injuries sustained at the workplace, see *La Justice*, 19.02.1886 and APP, CB 92.3, 1907/1318, 26.11.1907, men crushed between wagons; APP, CB 92.7, 1911/133, 11.02.1911, a man incinerated after falling into a furnace. For tenants who had parts of their arms or legs amputated after work accidents: FNA, F/22/452, Report by M. Drancourt, 25.07.1901; *La Petite République socialiste*, 10.03.1900; APP, CB 92.13, 1917/74, 30.12.1916; for burns to the leg, *La Petite République socialiste*, 22.01.1898; to the feet, *JSD*, 8.09.1898; to the face: AVP, D4R1, 1018, 1899, No. 4683; to the entire body, *JSD*, 9.06.1907; for amputated fingers, *JSD*, 20.06.1897; crushed fingers, AVP, D4R1 1150, 1902, No. 2285 and D4R1 492, 1887, No. 3502; hand cuts, SDMA, CT768, 29.04.1902.
10 SDMA, 5Q29, Accidents du travail, 1926–8.
11 *Ibid.*
12 E.g. AVP, D4R1 732, 1893, No. 1505; D4R1 1058, 1900, No. 1710.
13 Étienne Auribault, "Note sur la protection contre les poussières dans l'atelier de mélange des matières premières d'une cristallerie," *Bulletin de l'Inspection du travail* 20 (1912): 97–9.
14 SDMA, CT768.
15 *Le Petit Parisien*, 29.07.1904; APP, CB 92.4, 1908/199, 20.02.1908; CB 92.6, 1910/266, 26.03.1910; *Le Journal*, 2.01.1912; APP, CB 92.10, 1914/12, 30.12.1913; CB 92.23,1926/1302, 5.09.1926; 92.28, 1932/1938, 14.09.1932.
16 Intemperance would flag parents as insufficiently "moral," as the term went at the time: APP, CB 92.21,1925/164, 28.01.1925-4.02.1925; 1925/170, 289 *bis*, 24.01.1925-6.02.1925.
17 AD93, D4P4 57, "Documents préparatoires...," *doc. cit.* As indicated in the previous chapter, one-bedroom apartments in the tenement had a floor area of 12–15 square metres, except at No. 98 after 1903, where they extended over 28 square metres.
18 Mistakes and misspellings in censuses from 1911 onwards did not allow for a complete recovery of origins either. I retrieved them with accuracy in 93.4% (1911), 89.8% (1921), 93.5% (1926) and 95.3 % (1931) of the cases.
19 Alain Faure, " L'invention des banlieusards. Les déplacements de travail entre Paris et sa banlieue (1880–1914): première approche," *Villes en parallèles*, No. 10 (1986): 233–48. It is estimated that 350,000 people were pushed out of Paris and into the banlieue by Haussmann's works alone: see John Merriman, *Aux marges de la ville. Faubourgs et banlieues en France, 1815–1870* (Paris: Seuil, 1994), 104.
20 What I refer to here are people from Bas-Rhin, Haut-Rhin, Moselle, Meurthe, and Vosges, and after the 1871 annexation, Oberelsass, Unterelsass, Lothringen, Meurthe-et-Moselle, Moselle, Belfort, and Vosges.
21 SDMA, CT928, No. 1178, 2.12.1888.
22 See www.paris-tenement.eu. Note that the red signs that do not bear a number denote just one individual.
23 *Le Rappel*, 22.08.1900; *Le Matin*, 29.09.1900; APP, CB 92.7, 1911/221, 3.08.1911.

24 Int. No. 71, 25.07.2018. Note that in 1911, No. 96 was still included among the "*cités italiennes*" (Italian tenements) by the police: APP, CB 92.7, 1911/221, 3.08.1911.
25 Brigitte Moulin, ed., *La ville et ses frontières. De la ségrégation sociale à l'ethnicisation des rapports sociaux* (Paris: Karthala, 2001), 13–4. Further south on the Avenue, at No. 30, the *cité Châtelain* had been known for a few years the "*cité des Bretons*" (Bretons' tenement) and then "*cité de l'Est*" (Easterners' tenement).
26 A similar process has been described by Alain Faure for a *cité* in the 13th arrondissement of Paris. See Alain Faure, "Aspects de la vie du quartier dans le Paris populaire de la fin du XIXe siècle," *Recherches contemporaines* 6 (2000–1), 292.
27 FNA, MC/ET/XXXVIII/1224, Minutes Me Gamard, "Cahier des charges," 12.10.1883.
28 Since census lists are useless in that regard, the information stems from scattered fiscal documents, notary records and health inspections: AD93, D4P457, "Documents préparatoires…," *doc. cit.*; FNA, MC/ET/XXXVIII/1224, *doc. cit.*; SPF Auxerre 1, *doc. cit.*, 7.01.1908; FNA, MC/ET/LVII/1637, Minutes Me Barillot, Barillier-Andrez, 31.07.1926; SDMA, 2ACW9, Av. Wilson 96, list of tenants, 20.03.1929.
29 Brunet, "Une banlieue ouvrière," 143; Annie Fourcaut and Mathieu Flonneau, eds., *Une histoire croisée de Paris et de ses banlieues à l'époque contemporaine. Bibliographie, bilan d'étape* (Paris: Ville de Paris, 2005), 13.
30 The crisis started being felt around the *cités* in late 1930. In October of that year, the glass factory put one furnace out of service and laid off 49 workers (see AVP, D1U10 729, Conseil de prud'hommes de la Seine, Produits chimiques, 18.11.1930, 29.12.1930, Nos. 49231, 49348). By mid-1931, six tenement residents were already unemployed (SDMA, 1F33, 1931 Census).
31 Margaret Maruani and Monique Meron, "Le travail des femmes dans la France du XXe siècle," *Regards croisés sur l'économie*, No. 13 (2013): 177–193.
32 Deborah Simonton, *A History of European Women's Work: 1700 to the Present* (Abingdon: Routledge, 1998), 156.
33 AD93, 4U7/1002, CDP SD-Sud, PV 22.12.1902, case against Legras Charles, int. M. Legras; AD93, 4U7/628, 9.09.1904, Dame Mor.
34 Int. No. 32, 19.04.2016; int. No. 71, 25.07.2018.
35 The first glassworkers had settled in the *cités* in the late 1870s, with three such families at No. 96 (at that time numbered 84) and two at No. 100 (then No. 90) in 1879 (SDMA, 1G91, Matrices, 1879, 391).
36 In 1901, 119 out of 329 residents aged 11 or older were explicitly listed as working at the glassworks, and that is without accounting for the other people listed as glassworkers or glass carvers whose employer's field was left blank.
37 SDMA, 1S21, Ernest Mesière, Album Legras, no date (ca. 1905–1910).
38 *Ibid.*
39 AD51, 2E 497/9, Passavant, mar., 1880, No. 6, 22.11.1880, Detante-Collinet (at No. 100 in 1901); AD56, Noyal-Pontivy, mar., 1875, No. 9, 21.01.1875, Dugué-Josselin (at. No. 100 in 1891).
40 AD14, 4E3289, Foulognes, mar., 1868, No. 2, 12.08.1868, Langlois-Mary. Mme. Langlois and her sons, employed at the glass factory, lived at No. 102 in the 1890s.
41 AD02, 5Mi0701, Wassigny, mar., 1863–1868, No. 52, 11.07.1864, Fontaine-Cahen (at No. 100 in the 1890s).
42 AD58, 2MiEC459, Saint-Léger-des-Vignes, mar., 1874, 24.10.1874, Gardet-Bonnot (at No. 96 in 1911); AD08, Bayel, 4E03511, mar., 1873, No. 5, 6.10.1873,

Robert-Lécuyer (at No. 100 in the 1880s and 1890s); AD51, Vanault-les-Dames, mar., 1887, No. 5, 21.05.1887, Burnécourt (at No. 100 in the 1890s).
43 Anne Marie Paton née Gaudé, laundry worker at No. 102 in 1891 (AM Nantes, 1E1726, 1er canton, 1887, No. 180); Jean-Claude Garnier, mason, at No. 100 around 1890 (AD88, 81E9-37797, Gruey, mar., No. 29, 2.03.1863).
44 For children of shoemakers, see Lucien Perrin, at No. 100 in the 1880–90s (AD88, 4E420/4-66262, Sainte-Barbe, 1838, No. 24, 3.05.1838); of clogmakers, Chrétien Doerflinger, at No. 100 in 1891 (FNA, BB/11/1464, 2256x78, mar. certificate, 1.07.1861); of boilermakers, Céleste Grandgérard, at No. 96 in the early 1880s (SDMA, E241, SD, mar., 1884, No. 327, 4.10.1884); of cartwrights, Fernand Brassart, at No. 98 in 1891 (AD59, 1MiEC 092 R001, Bouchain, mar., No. 36, 30.04.1872); of road menders, Alfred Brunet, at No. 100 in 1896 (AD59, Iwuy, M [1861–80], 1872, No. 21, 24.07.1872). Examples of tenants who were born to farm labourers are innumerable. For an example, see Joseph Dugué, in the tenement in the early 1890s (AD56, Noyal-Pontivy, mar., 1875, No. 9, 21.01.1875).
45 For only a few examples, see ASC Acquafondata, *Registro della popolazione*, 1911; MA Merindad de Valdeporres, births, 1885, No. 93, 26.04.1885, Marcelino Lopez Saíz; MA Mesas de Ibor, births, 1892, No. 38, 28.11.1892, Teófila Joséfa Trenado Gómez. This was not limited to migrants from those regions: see AD22, Plounévez, 1895, mar., 14.03.1895, Le Mignot-Garandel (at No. 100 in 1896).
46 Pierre de Peretti, *Saint-Denis 1870/1920. Les témoins parlent* (Saint-Denis: SDMA, 1981), 4–5.
47 AD93, 4U7/353, 5.12.1898, Bénard-Crosson.
48 See for a former glassmaker turned municipal street cleaner, SDMA, CT151, "Secours," 2.03.1910, Bour.
49 In the packing and shipping department at Legras, for instance, men earned an average of 130 fr. a month in 1903, and women only 50: see Benoist, "Le travail dans la grande industrie," 169–94.
50 Brunet, "Une banlieue ouvrière," 1111.
51 Marcel Lecoq, *La Crise du logement populaire* (Paris: Société immobilière de la région parisienne, 1912), 14.
52 SDMA, CT242, "Exploits d'huissier," 30.06.1905, Berdot, av. de Paris 96.
53 Jeanne Singer-Kérel, *Le Coût de la vie à Paris de 1840 à 1954* (Paris: Armand Colin, 1954); Brian Mitchell, *International Historical Statistics: Europe, 1750–1988* (New York: Stockton Press, 1992), 840–1.
54 SDMA, CT806, "Demandes de secours, 1890–1891," Letter from M. Leroy, 100 av. de Paris, no date [1890].
55 Based on 253 data points before 1914, and 25 after 1923, retrieved from judicial and notary records. Although information is often missing as to the characteristics of the apartment, I can rely on averages as the lodgings in the tenement were roughly similar in size.
56 The ratio in the early years remains in the lower tier of those that have been calculated at a broader scale. See Loïc Bonneval and François Robert, *L'Immeuble de rapport. L'immobilier entre gestion et spéculation, Lyon 1860–1990* (Rennes: Presses universitaires de Rennes, 2013), 139–40.
57 Maurice Halbwachs, *La Classe ouvrière et les niveaux de vie* (Paris: Alcan, 1913), 425.
58 SDMA, CT806, "Demandes de secours, 1890-1891," Letter from Mme. Cuny, 96 av. de Paris, no date [October 1891].
59 Peretti, *Saint-Denis 1870/1920,* 4–5.
60 AD93, 4U7/450–745.

61 AD93, 4U7/542, 16.07.1897, Versigny c. Maire; 4U7/353, 21.04.1898, Joigny et autres c. Maire. M. Maire had been a tenant of Louise Versigny's for about 15 years when she lent him money.
62 AD93, 4U7/723, 27.10.1916, Gréco c. Lutel; APP, CB 92.10, 1913/859, 11.09.1913; CB 92.21,1925/170, 289 *bis*, 24.01.1925-6.02.1925; FNA, BB/11/2654, 3500x92, Wymann.
63 SDMA, CT241, "Exploits d'huissiers," 10.09.1912, Victoor; 27.09.1912, Rose.
64 AD93, 4U7/354, 15.09.1898, Boucher et autres.
65 Installments granted by the court were not necessarily a much better prospect that the withholding of wages by the employer, usually capped at 10%. In the 1880s and 1890s, instalments granted to tenants at Nos. 96–102 ranged from 2 to 10 fr. every fortnight. For crucial interventions of tenement women on behalf of their husbands, see AD93, 4U7/467, 1.06.1888, Gautier; 4U7/472, 18.04.1890, Billon; 4U7/507, 10.08.1894, Versigny c. Martens, Gailland. Only rarely did women carry a formal power of attorney, but in practice their informal plea was allowed by the judge.
66 Claudine Fontanon, "La banlieue Nord-Est de Paris: structuration des espaces industriels et des zones de résidence," *Villes en parallèles* 1, No. 10 (1986), 19.
67 SDMA, 1Q2, 26.07.1898; 27.07.1900; 1Q3, 29.04.1901; 1Q4, 27.02.1904; 1Q9, 26.10.1918; CT69, Letter from Mme. Herholt, 28.05.1885. Along with the husband's income as a stoker at Legras and later the pension he started receiving from the factory from 1908, the couple was eventually able to buy a bistro and two houses (APP, CB 92.9, 1912/1086, 28.10.1912; AD93, 1729W73, No. 218, succession Herholt, 14.10.1913).
68 SDMA, CT96, Letter from the Préfet de la Seine to the Mayor of SD about Louis Racollier, 17.11.1921.
69 Michelle Perrot, "De la manufacture à l'usine en miettes," *Le Mouvement social*, No. 125 (1983): 3–12.
70 FNA, LH/1562/64, Legras.
71 FNA, BB/11/7863, 10084x22, Gabriele.
72 Benoist, "Le travail dans la grande industrie," 191.
73 *JSD*, 25.05.1890.
74 Claire Zalc, *Melting shops. Une histoire des commerçants étrangers en France* (Paris: Perrin, 2010), 112; 147.
75 See Étienne Billon, in AD93, 4U7/453, 18.11.1881, Billon c. Moriann, Cuny, Maire; AD93, 1E66/131, SD, mar., 1883, No. 14, 13.01.1883; 1E66/183, SD, deaths, 1883, No. 1088, 4.08.1883; SDMA, 1G95–6, Matrices, 1884–5.
76 See Louis Crosson, in AD93, 4U7/495, 18.08.1893, Crosson c. Letourneur; SDMA, E276, SD, births, 1893, No. 1343, 8.11.1893; AD93, 4U7/503, 27.04.1894, Crosson c. Thibaut; SDMA, 1F21, 1896 census, vol. 2, 98 av. de Paris.
77 See Albert Coipeau, in SDMA, 1 F 27, 1911 census, vol. 1, 31.05.1911; AVP, D4R1 1784, 1914, No. 5139.
78 See Eugène Péchié, in *Archives commerciales de la France*, 14.04.1909, 478; AD93, 1E66/318, SD, mar., 1909, vol. 1, No. 349, 19.06.1909; SDMA, 1F27, 1911 census, vol. 1, 98 av. de Paris.
79 AD93, D4P4 57, "Documents préparatoires…," *doc. cit.,* Jules Lelièvre.

3 Consequential crossings

Luigi Pirolli was born in 1886 in a mountainous region between Rome and Naples. His family lived in a hamlet of a few dozen farmers. At age 15, Luigi made his way to No. 100 Av. de Paris. By that time, his immediate family had already acquired a significant experience in migration.

Two of Luigi's paternal uncles had been on the move for several years. Like other highlanders before them, they had decided to work as strolling musicians.[1] Beginning in the 1880s, they performed in various regions of France, with a preference for Normandy where a number of their fellow villagers were already active.[2] When Luigi was still a boy, both uncles regularly returned to the village, and they could already speak French. For his part, Luigi's father Giacinto certainly knew some English; in 1890, he and his brother Antonio had embarked in Naples, for New York, only to return more than three years later. This second migration venture made transoceanic emigration another option for the family. But as far as Luigi was concerned, the first major migration in his life would be to the Plaine-Saint-Denis in 1901.

The tenants' migration culture and history merit a detailed analysis for at least two reasons. First, they are useful for what they reveal about the migratory process itself – its causes, its context and its actual logistics. These findings can contribute to the collective effort of dispelling some persistent myths about 19th and early 20th-century migrations: that they took place over long distances and along straight lines, and were bookended by immobility; that people travelled with all their possessions on their back; that geopolitical tensions severed ties between those who fell on different sides of international borders. Second, journeys across space are also interesting because they were moments of identification. Whether they left their place of residence, stayed behind, or saw other people arrive in their wake, people's sense of belonging underwent significant rearrangements. The same was true for their social status, both in the society of arrival and in the society of origin. In other words, crossed boundaries were not only natural and administrative but also cultural and cognitive. This dimension has been only partly addressed by cultural sociologists.[3] Their work has shed light on the interdependence of objective and subjective processes of social positioning in immigration societies, where the construction of social status hierarchies

DOI: 10.4324/9781003017820-3

results in movable boundaries between groups.[4] They have rarely examined this phenomenon in the context of the migratory process itself. On the other hand, insights from social psychology have shown that trajectories across space significantly depend on how migrants anticipate their future, and have the ability to transform the way people imagine their lives.[5] This chapter is an effort to apply these frameworks of analysis to the case in hand and nuance them depending on the empirical evidence. Paying attention to the ways in which social and cultural difference could be enacted or reconfigured through migrations is still quite unfamiliar in migration history. From close range, this interlocking of physical and symbolic mobility becomes visible.

The drivers of migration

Then as now, economic conditions were often crucial in triggering people's migrations. In Brittany, northern Spain and southern Italy, demographic pressure and stagnant agricultural wages combined to make life in rural areas harder. Mid-sized towns did not have enough industries to offer many replacement jobs.[6] On rare occasions, sources record emigration motives in the residents' own words – at least, as they were transcribed by police officers. In 1907, a resident at No. 100 left his native Cantabria "where he could not make a living, in order to work in France where he was almost sure of being able to subsist."[7] Two men who arrived at No. 96 in 1923 from their native Extremadura respectively declared that they had emigrated "for want of work," and because "life in Spain was hard."[8]

In Luigi Pirolli's native home region near Cassino, shrinking wood resources, crop prices brought down by foreign competition and declining revenues from domestic work had made emigration an appealing option by the early 1880s.[9] We know that neither of Luigi's two uncles earned enough to pay taxes, and both were officially regarded as "poor." But they were not the poorest in the village; the family owned a large, two-storey farmhouse.

On the mind of many emigration candidates was also the need to escape the perils of crime and reckless violence. From time to time, towns of the Castilian west were visited by *bandoleros* and Carlist rebels. In Italy, the Mezzogiorno had been plagued by banditism in the 1860s. The Pirollis were no exception; a cousin of theirs had fallen victim to a gruesome attack. In later decades, crime receded but did not vanish from the Italian South. In the mid-1900s, a few years before a migrant from the same region arrived at No. 96 after a detour to Germany, his mother had been killed in their village and his father had barely escaped the same fate.[10]

The migration decisions of the tenement's Alsatians and Lorrainers were often politically charged. Some of them had migrated early and "opted" in time for French citizenship – that is, in 1871 or 1872 – after their native provinces were absorbed by the German Empire. This was the case for a handful of tenant families.[11] Nevertheless, many tenement occupants who hailed from the annexed provinces emigrated more for economic than for political reasons. The majority only left their region in the 1880s, which runs counter to what broader accounts have perhaps too hastily suggested.[12] In small communities of the East, German rule barely changed anything.[13] There is little evidence that the Alsatian and Lorrainer tenants migrated because of a greater attachment to France than others in their community. A descendant of Lorrainer glassworkers at Legras recalled being told by her grandparents that their own forebears had emigrated "so as not to become German." However, this was probably a retrospective distortion, as the family had only moved to Paris a few years after the annexation.[14] More importantly, people from the new German provinces made no mystery that economic motives came before any other considerations. A father of seven from Lorraine who lived at No. 100 in the early 1890s candidly said that his resources had not allowed him to emigrate earlier.[15] Neighbours of his alluded to "interests" that had prevented them from leaving their region earlier. Others alleged, rather unconvincingly, that they had been ill during the entire option period.[16] Another tenant at No. 100 "had a job in Alsace and hoped that the province would not remain German for very long."[17] This mindset is likely to have been shared by a large number of tenement residents from the East. For them, the political situation was not entirely irrelevant, but it was clearly secondary to day-to-day concerns.

At the other end of the journey, opportunities in Paris and its suburban workshops acted as strong magnets. There, industrial wages were higher on average than elsewhere in France.[18] That reality was certainly tangible at the individual level, as evidenced by the case of three former shoemakers who lived at No. 100: one from Normandy who made leather clogs, another from Alsace who carved wooden ones, and a third from Romagna who made boots. Seeking new jobs in the Plaine – where they were respectively hired in metalworking, glassmaking, and construction – meant earning at least 25% more than in their original trade.[19] Tenants from the East who had already been working in the glass industry also increased their income. The size of the Parisian market and swelling domestic demand for glass allowed Legras and his peers in the Paris area to offer higher – if not generous – wages than their smaller competitors in Eastern France.[20]

Another draw of the Plaine-Saint-Denis was its high density of industries. The precariousness of daily contracts could only be offset by the ease of changing shops. During his years at No. 100, a migrant from southern Italy would work as a bottle-maker at Legras, a rolling mill operator at Mouton, a metalworker at another factory and a steel-caster at yet another one.[21] A neighbour of his from northern Spain changed employers eight times between 1918 and 1930.[22] As one Plainard would recall, "we would leave one company, the next morning we would join another."[23]

Besides economic motives, migration culture and experience were critical factors when deciding to make the journey either to the Plaine or away from it. Some had long been accustomed to moving within the rural context.[24] In southern Italy as in northern Spain, the migration culture combined traditions of transhumance, smuggling and inter-village connections. For instance, a Cantabrian tenant had first migrated to another village less than two miles away from his birthplace.[25] Documents show that many tenants from Lorraine had also been used to moving around their home region.[26] For occupants of Nos. 96–102, it was common to have made a long stop in the largest town near their place of origin.[27]

Long-distance migrations, however, generally required additional skills and knowledge. For one thing, formal education was instrumental in enabling aspiring migrants. Literacy would help with administrative controls, learning a new language and integrating into a new environment. As children, Luigi Pirolli, his father and his uncles had certainly attended their village school. Records consistently show that they were all able to read and write. This was a remarkable feat when assessed against the general population of the Mezzogiorno, but not exceptional at 96–102 Avenue de Paris.[28]

Despite being generally less educated and less mobile than men, women's own experiences with migration were also an important factor in making families' emigration possible. We do not know if Luigi Pirolli's aunt Teresa (Antonio's widow) ever left Pozzilli before emigrating to the Plaine-Saint-Denis in 1901. What is certain, however, is that while her husband was away in America, she had the opportunity to develop some of the skills that prepared her to move to the Plaine with her youngest son and provide for the two of them.

Journeys and itineraries

Some families had first-hand experience of long-distance travel. Glassworkers were used to relocating on a regular basis.[29] This was the case for others as well. Birthplaces recorded in the census show that at the turn of the 20th century, a growing number of French, Italian and Spanish tenants at Nos. 96–102 had already migrated to the Americas, Britain, Germany and even Sweden before settling in the Plaine.[30] In France alone, the map of iron-casting and mining towns overlapped with some of the tenants' trajectories.[31] Several had even spent time in Paris years before their migration to the Plaine-Saint-Denis.[32] For them, the journey was a familiar one. Sure enough, Paris and its suburbs were rapidly changing. But these returning migrants must have felt less foreign than their peers who arrived there for the first time. To many newcomers, the crammed buildings were synonymous with the discovery of urban life, Paris and even France altogether.

In order to reach the Plaine, all had to find ways to make the trip itself. In the 1880s, Luigi Pirolli's uncles had travelled to France on horse-drawn carts. It was not uncommon for migrants in the late 19th century to cover part of the distance to Paris on foot; this was the case of Luigi's parents and siblings in 1907.[33] An important turning point, however, happened towards the end of the century with the expansion of railway networks. In the span of a few years, the regions of origin of many future tenants, including Lorraine, northern Spain and southern Italy, became connected to main cities or ports for the first time.[34]

Not all were necessarily able, or willing, to take advantage of these new means of transportation. Train fares remained high; this was especially true for Southern Europeans on the French leg of their journey, due to the weakness of the peseta and the lira. In the 1900s, reaching Bilbao cost the equivalent of two to three days of work for a farm labourer from the Burgales highlands; from the border to Paris, it was about 20 times as much.[35] During the interwar period, trains would become ubiquitous, allowing for Spaniards, Romanians and Czechs to arrive much quicker and for much cheaper.

Luggage is another crucial component of travelling. Sources suggest that apart from administrative documents, most tenants first set foot in the Plaine with limited belongings: crucifixes, family photographs, articles of clothing, the odd cooking tool, a few coins.[36] Cliché images of migrants with suitcases are misleading; most travellers carried their belongings in bundles or, as one family from No. 96 recalled, in makeshift trunks made out of orange boxes.[37] In the interwar period, newcomers could be seen carrying mattresses on their backs.[38] Musical instruments, jewellery and dogs could be brought along, too. As for the concierge at No. 96, she kept an engraving of the lost provinces of Alsace and Lorraine in her kitchen. Whether her family had carried it along from their native Moselle or bought it in Paris, it bore testimony to both her longing for home, as well as the penetration of state propaganda in the late 19th century.[39]

Provenance and destination

In the broader arc of tenants' lives, the importance of their stay in the *cités* depended on where they had been before and where they were headed next. Certain documents such as military records, naturalisation files and judicial archives allowed me to retrieve many addresses of the tenants' immediate provenances and subsequent destinations. The following graphs record the distances between those addresses and the tenement block (Figures 3.1 and 3.2).[40]

These limited sets of data highlight, first, that the *cités* served as a gateway to the Paris area at various moments in time. In the early years, Alsatians and Lorrainers often settled directly in the buildings, as illustrated by the four dots at 300 kilometres around 1880. Thereafter, the data stresses the nearby origins of most residents; they usually moved from either other addresses in the Plaine or neighbouring suburbs.[41] In fact, itineraries were rarely linear; Paris was often a mere stop among others. For instance, a family of tenants from Belgian Flanders had moved to Somme, Nord, Aisne, Marne and again to Somme before making their way to the Plaine.[42] It was not until the turn of the century that people from afar started heading straight for the tenement again.

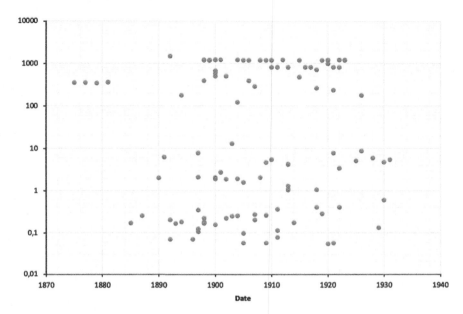

Figure 3.1 Distance between the tenement and the tenants' previous addresses (kilometres).

Destinations on the way out remained almost constant throughout the period. When they left the tenement, the overwhelming majority of residents would move to another address in Saint-Denis, Paris or another banlieue. The median distance between the tenement and the tenants' next addresses was less than 300 metres. Throughout their 50 years in the Plaine, the successive residences of Luigi Pirolli and his wife, Maria, we confined to a small radius around Nos. 96–102. Where people moved generally depended on their living standards. For most, the first move brought them to comparable lodgings nearby. There, they could benefit from lower rent, better hygiene, an extra room or simply a place of their own after getting married. People would also move if their new job was too far away, given the cost-cutting necessity of having lunch at home; this remained the case until factories opened canteens after the Great War.[43]

In the *cités* themselves, families could move from one building to the next, or even from one floor to another. Precious notes from land register inspectors in the 1880s and 1890s provide a glimpse into these movements, often overlooked by historians.[44] Source crossing shows that these moves could have been connected to deaths, births, weddings, disabilities that made it impossible to remain on the upper floors or even the demolition of one's house (Figure 3.3).[45]

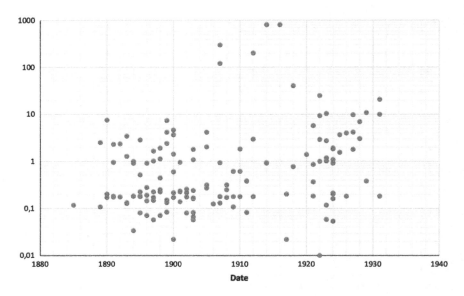

Figure 3.2 Distance between the tenement and the tenants' next addresses (kilometres).

Even when travelling short distances, spatial mobility could both result from and accelerate social transitions. When, in 1907, the Pirolli family was reunited in the Plaine, they did not move back to No. 100. Instead, they opted for a somewhat better building around the corner. At their new address lived a much smaller community: there were only two other families, from the Loire Valley and Lorraine. As close as it was to Nos. 96–102, the Pirollis were now the only Italian family on their street. This was a sign of their rapid integration.

Secondary journeys and return trips

Secondary movements and return trips were another important feature of the tenants' migration patterns. We know for instance that Maria Pirolli's father and brothers took secondary trips while living in the tenement. They spent two consecutive summers playing music in Normandy before coming back to the *cités*. This type of trip would become common among Italian and Spanish tenants.[46] Beyond those temporary sojourns, a significant number of tenants would eventually continue their journeys onto destinations all around the world: the Americas, Britain and Algeria, to name a few.[47]

Trips home were certainly not as rare as broader studies have suggested.[48] We should not conflate attachment to one's native region with national sentiment; nevertheless, these journeys home were of great significance to

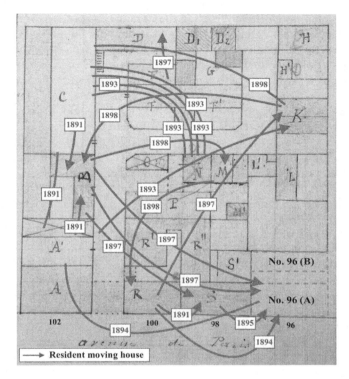

Figure 3.3 Internal movements in the cités, 1891–1898. AD93 ref. D4P4 57.

people's transnational ties and identifications.[49] Homecomings could be short and made for various purposes – including illicit ones.[50] But going home long remained expensive. This was due, in part, to the costs of transport, but also because of the need to impress other families and distribute lavish gifts. All the while, travellers received no income during the length of their trip. This is not to say that people could not return frequently and for extended periods of time. One Italian teenager arrived at No. 96 in 1912, returned to his hometown in 1913, came back to the tenement in 1915, went home again in 1917 and returned once more to the Plaine in 1919.[51]

Journeys back and forth could be frequent even across the Franco-German border. The border inherited from the war of 1870–1871 was much more permeable than what it seemed.[52] In one case, a glassworker from Alsace and his family arrived in the Plaine in 1877. Then, in 1888, he and his parents were back in their native village, where he got married. Three years later, he and his wife were in the Plaine-Saint-Denis again, at No. 96–102. His parents and siblings, meanwhile, had moved into another housing complex across the Avenue. His parents continued to go back and forth between the Plaine and Alsace until they died in their village in 1904.[53]

Conscription was one of the most common reasons for coming home. Immigrant men were often married in their village en route to, or right after, their military service.[54] But men were not the only ones to go back and forth across borders. A female tenant from the Mountain of Burgos made her way back to Spain with her husband and children in 1916. She came back to the tenement a year later with her children; her husband stayed behind in Spain.[55] Other women went home to give birth, where they could benefit from more extensive support systems.[56] Tenants would also send home children they could not afford to keep with them.[57]

Many tenants eventually returned to their region of origin for good. Returnees could then enjoy a noticeable improvement in their social status, provided they were "prepared" for that adjustment and had stayed abroad long enough to make a difference.[58] The standing of Maria Pirolli's parents grew after their stay in Paris, as evidenced by her father's election to his hometown's municipal council in 1913 and 1914.

Still, the tenants' mindset about their possible return was more ambivalent than meets the eye. Once again, Luigi and Maria Pirolli offer a case in point. In the early 1920s, after almost four years of war in Italy, Luigi recovered his position at the glass factory and had every chance to successfully integrate into French society, which he eventually did. He also clearly intended, however, to keep ties with Italy, as evidenced by the house he purchased in his village. In fact, the couple's options were even broader. They had relatives in Italy, Philadelphia, and later Algeria and South America. As their life in the Plaine improved in the interwar period, Luigi and Maria became less inclined to either go back or move elsewhere. Once they acquired citizenship and their daughter married a Parisian police officer, the possibility of re-emigration or return became even more remote. In the end, they never permanently returned to Italy.

All of these migration patterns conceal a wide range of individual experiences; family and personal histories mattered a lot. Scattered examples confirm that those who were higher in the migration chain were better able to cross their original group boundaries.[59] This did not mean that they severed their transnational ties – quite the opposite. Back-and-forth migrations, particularly those due to military duty, made identifications more intertwined. Nothing better symbolises this than an object that Luigi Pirolli crafted in 1931. To celebrate his 30-year presence at the Plaine-Saint-Denis glass factory, he made a glass cone filled with brightly-painted stones. According to the story passed to his grandson, these stones came from Luigi's native village.

Migrants and non-migrants

Migrations were also key in shaping relations between those who left and those who did not. Although many female tenants had emigrated to the Plaine with their families (or, in some instances, on their own), some stayed home temporarily. Others never came. "Partial societies" emerged in French, Spanish and Italian provinces where men were absent.[60] In the Mountain of Burgos, between 1910 and 1914, more than three times as many men emigrated as women.[61] All the same, many women developed the necessary know-how to run the farms on their own and support each other when needed. Such was the case of Luigi's mother and aunts. Their ascendancy enabled the migration of male members of the household.

In certain cases, children were left behind with neither of their parents. This points to the broader family circle's participation in the migration project. A tenant at No. 100 brought his wife and three of his sons with him to the Plaine; three others stayed in Italy. One of the latter had been born in Lyon but was now growing up in the village.[62] He may have reunited with his parents at a later point. In the meantime, migration played a central role in his childhood; his first memories were of travel, and his parents and some of his siblings lived far away. We can only speculate on the consequences of that situation for him. They might have been positive – more money, higher status and the freedom of being outside the direct control of his parents – or negative, due to his family members' absence and his own frustration at being left out.

At times, people planned to leave but never did. A tenant from Lorraine made plans to leave the Plaine for New Caledonia; three others were keen on Tahiti or Diego-Suárez. They may or may not have made it, but it certainly shows that the Plaine-Saint-Denis was not fulfilling their dreams of fortune.[63] Decades later, a resident at No. 100 was invited by his uncle, a rich farmer in the United States, to come and join him. He applied for an American visa before finally changing his mind.[64] Such hesitation might have been the consequence of stronger connections with people in the Plaine than those with relatives in other destinations. This process could have also worked the other way around, with people settling in because their projects of return or re-emigration did not pan out. It is, in fact, probable that a number of individuals kept their options open. Some likely never abandoned either the possibility of a return home or that of a secondary migration to other shores. Indications suggest that many stayed in-between. For instance, one longtime resident of No. 100 went back to Italy during the First World War after growing up in the tenement. He later returned to the Plaine in 1920 and dodged the Italian draft. A few years later, however, as he pursued a career in the metal industry and became increasingly involved in the Plaine's social life, he would periodically visit his Italian hometown; he kept an address there and occasionally leased his services as a carpenter.[65]

When others move

When people remained in the Plaine, the regular arrivals and exits of others brought their own set of challenges and possibilities, constantly redrawing sociocultural boundaries. Towards the end of the Great War, for instance, many of those who were temporarily brought to the Plaine by the conflict departed at last. This exodus disrupted the networks of many residents and altered their paths of integration. In a matter of months, a Greek tenant from Anatolia was deprived of the presence of many fellow nationals, who, like him, had been working at the local gas factories. Another Greek who had been owning No. 96's bistro also left. These departures, coupled with his native island's annexation by Turkey, made integration all the more necessary for this Greek tenant. His marriage to a French woman certainly helped, but settling in his new environment must have been challenging.[66]

Upon arrival, newcomers were thrust into an environment in which migrants like themselves fought for their social status.[67] Luigi Pirolli's position at the factory improved considerably in the early 1910s. As a senior glass-carver, he may well have enjoyed a less foreign – or, at least, less Italian – status at Legras. Now, those who were looked down upon for their dismal appearance and inability to speak French were not Italian but Spanish. For Luigi then, who started going by Louis and had some of the Spanish children as subordinates, a dynamic combining class distinction and inter-ethnicisation likely contributed to further "francise" him at that time (Figures 3.4 and 3.5).[68]

The young Spaniards were growing up in the same conditions that Louis Pirolli had, ten years earlier. They were to him what he had been to the factory's Bretons and Alsatians: a contrasting presence. Compared to these young migrants, he appeared all the more local and well-integrated.[69] This contrast worked both ways; the young workers and their families, initially wary of considering themselves Spanish,[70] were being turned into Spaniards, whether they liked it or not. For a while, this identification became synonymous with poor, exploited and foreign.

During the First World War, the new political and demographic context of the Plaine made ethnonational boundaries shift again. This was due, in particular, to the arrival of refugees from Belgium and Northern France. In February 1915, there were already about 900 registered refugees in the Plaine; by mid-May 1915, this number had doubled.[71] The *cités* at Nos. 96–102 housed a total of 57 people officially registered as wartime refugees.[72] Their interactions with neighbours often involved complex factors, of which individual stories can give a sense.

One Tuscany-born refugee in his 60s had settled in the north of France in 1880; there, he had worked for decades at a chemical factory and married two French women. When he arrived in the *cités*, the other inhabitants must have regarded him and his wife (technically Italian nationals) as refugees above all else. The benefits they received as such were likely to trigger jealousy. At any rate, that couple probably felt less foreign than their new neighbours from southern Italy and Spain. Given the woman's French origin, her husband's longtime presence in the country and the pair's experience as refugees, they had good reasons to identify more with others from northern regions than with their fellow Italian nationals.[73]

Figure 3.4 Luigi Pirolli among his fellow workers in the early 1900s. Postcard. AD93 ref. 49Fi/9223.

Another refugee who moved in at No. 96 had no trouble belonging; he had lived in the Plaine decades earlier.[74] But he was still a German national. This meant dealing with suspicious authorities until the end of the war, despite his long career in the French military and the military service of his male relatives. This combined with another issue to adversely affect his reputation. The younger woman he moved in with was often drunk and occasionally resorted to prostitution to supplement the couple's income. Situations like theirs may have cast a negative light on refugees. Other tenant families may have nurtured some level of self-importance and righteousness upon seeing this behaviour, even though many had migration histories themselves and it was not uncommon for housewives to engage in sex work during the war. Moreover, the men and women employed in armament factories enjoyed comfortable salaries of seven or eight francs a day – considerably more than what refugees received. This gap would have raised some of the tenants' relative class position and "indigenised" them compared to the refugees.

The First World War brought new types of newcomers to the Plaine. Like other foreigners before them, Chinese and colonial workers from Indochina and North Africa would provide points of comparison, desire and fascination

64 *Changing places*

Figure 3.5 Louis Pirolli among his fellow workers around 1910. Photograph by E. Mésière. SDMA ref. 1S21.

in the neighbourhood. The *coloniaux* (as the colonial subjects were known, including the Chinese although they were not from the French Empire) lived under poor conditions in military barracks, set up in various locations around the Plaine. This spatial segregation was bound to affect the Plainards' identifications as a result.[75] This is not to say that they couldn't mingle with each other (see Chapter 8). But racist prejudices were hard to overcome.

By contrast, members of a truck depot of the British army, stationed around the corner from the *cités* starting in March 1915, rapidly integrated into the neighbourhood. They were frequent customers at No. 102's bistro, and some of them had affairs with local women. This translated into pregnancies and marriages.[76] From 1918 onwards, American soldiers arrived in the Plaine, as well. Many of these servicemen were immigrants themselves, from Italy, Poland, Germany or Turkey. Some of the Italian-Americans may have even known the Plaine in their youth. Sources bear traces of former tenants who, after re-emigrating to America, came back to fight in France. They may have made their way back to the Plaine to reconnect with former acquaintances, as we know some of their successors from the Second World War would do.

In short, migration could be intimately related to the displacement of one's social status and identifications. Border-crossings, mobilisation of

Consequential crossings 65

resources, return trips, as well as the arrival or departures of others, were key in constructing sociocultural difference in people's daily lives. The evidence analysed in this chapter suggests that those factors would either enhance or diminish the salience of ethnonational, gender, or class distinctions, which depended partly on spatial movements. But those movements would not have happened without the connections that enabled people to migrate in the first place.

Notes

1 For all details and sources about Luigi Pirolli and his family, see Langrognet, "The crossings of Luigi Pirolli."
2 Historians who have specifically studied Italian migration in Normandy have paid little attention to travelling musicians. See Marielle Colin, ed., *L'Immigration italienne en Normandie de la Troisième République à nos jours: de la différence à la transparence* (Caen: Musée de Normandie, 1998); Marielle Colin and François Neveux, eds., *Les Italiens en Normandie: de l'étranger à l'immigré* (Caen: Musée de Normandie, 2000).
3 Michèle Lamont and Virág Molnár, "The study of boundaries across the social sciences," *Annual Review of Sociology* 28 (2002): 167–95; Wimmer, *Ethnic Boundary Making*.
4 Pierre Bourdieu, "The forms of capital," in *Handbook of Theory and Research for the Sociology of Education*, ed. John Richardson (New York: Greenwood Press, 1986), 241–58.
5 Saara Koikkalainen and David Kyle, "Imagining mobility: the prospective cognition question in migration research," *Journal of Ethnic and Migration Studies* 42, No. 5 (2016): 759–76; Tania Zittoun, "Imagination in people and societies on the move: a sociocultural psychology perspective," *Culture & Psychology* 26, No. 4 (2020), 654–75.
6 Abel Châtelain, "L'attraction des trois plus grandes agglomérations françaises: Paris-Lyon-Marseille en 1891. Migrations parties des départements français selon le lieu de naissance," *Annales de démographie historique,* 1971: 27–41; Abel Poitrineau, *Remues d'hommes: les migrations montagnardes en France au XVIIe–XVIIIe* (Paris: Aubier, 1983); Pascual Madoz, *Diccionario geográfico, estadístico y histórico de España y de sus posesiones de Ultramar* (Madrid: Madoz & Sagasti, 1984 [1st ed. 1849]); Page Moch, *The Pariahs*; Jesús-Ángel Redono Cardeñoso, "El turno de los campesinos: protesta social en la España rural del cambio de siglo (1898–1923)," *Revista de História da Sociedade e da Cultura* 12 (2012): 393–415; Marcel Le Moal, *L'Émigration bretonne* (Spézet: Coop Breizh, 2013).
7 FNA, 19780030/257, 3032x48, Barquin.
8 FNA, 19780007/234, 13409x46, Moreno; 19780314/237, 23223x48, Trenado.
9 On crop prices, see Ercole Sori, *L'emigrazione italiana dall'Unità alla Seconda guerra mondiale* (Bologna: Il Mulino, 1979), 115; on wood resources, Pietro Tino, "La montagna meridionale: boschi, uomini, economie tra Otto e Novecento," in *Storia dell'agricoltura italiana in età contemporanea,* ed. Piero Bevilacqua (Venice: Marsilio, 1989), vol. 1: *Spazi e paesaggi,* 677–754; on the textile industry, Monica Lautieri, *Industrie manifatturiere e mondo tessile nell'antica provincia di Terra di Lavoro* (Villanova di Guidonia: Aletti, 2017). On the broader economic situation and its impact on emigration, see i.a. Annalisa Carbone, *Le cento patrie dei Molisani nel mondo* (Isernia: Cosmo Iannone, 1998); Piero Bevilacqua, "Società

66 Changing places

rurale e emigrazione," in *Storia dell'emigrazione italiana*, eds. Piero Bevilacqua, Andreina De Clementi, and Emilio Franzina (Rome: Donzelli, 2001), 95–112; Maria Rosa Protasi, *Emigrazione ed immigrazione nella storia del Lazio* (Viterbo: Sette Città, 2010).
10 Int. No. 28, 21.07.2016.
11 SDMA, E43, 19.05.1872-17.06.1872, No. 384, 2.06.1872; E50, 23.09.1872, No. 1313; SDMA, 1I12, Letter from the Mayor of SD about Sommer François-Charles, 8.12.1897. We found seven other tenants who had opted, along with their respective families. On this topic, see Alfred Wahl, *L'Option et l'émigration des Alsaciens-Lorrains (1871–1872)* (Strasbourg: Presses universitaires de Strasbourg, 1973).
12 Benoît Vaillot, "L'exil des Alsaciens-Lorrains. Option et famille dans les années 1870," *Revue d'histoire du XIXe siècle*, No. 61 (2020), 121. The average point of immigration of 34 tenant families from Alsace-Lorraine – all those for whom we have been able to retrieve this information – was in the fall of 1881.
13 Alfred Wahl and Jean-Claude Richez, *La vie quotidienne en Alsace entre France et Allemagne, 1850–1950* (Paris: Hachette, 1993).
14 Int. No. 29, 21.10.2016; FNA, BB/11/1502, 2506x79, Clementz.
15 FNA, BB/11/2294, 5892x89, Bour.
16 FNA, BB/11/1981, 2472x87, Fixari; BB/11/1491, 1462x79, Diédat; BB/11/1464, 2263x78, Wernert.
17 FNA, BB/11/2033, 7604x87, Orth.
18 Jean-Marie Chanut et al., "Les disparités de salaires en France au XIXe siècle," *Histoire & Mesure* 10, Nos. 3–4 (1995): 381–409.
19 AD76, 4E05809, Réalcamp, 1872, No. 28, 23.05.1872 and SDMA, E298, mar., 02.01.1897-31.12.1897, No. 188, 22.05.1897, Alphonse; SDMA, 1F19, 1891 census, vol. 2, 100 av. de Paris and AD67, 4E413/1, Rosteig, 1830, No. 19, 28.10.1830, Doerflinger; AVP, V4E 4992, Paris 18th, births, 1879, No. 1334, 2.04.1879 and AVP, V4E 6800, Paris 12th arr., deaths, 1887, No. 3522, 23.09.1887, Vaccari. On the income comparison, see Yves Guyot, "Les industries, les salaires et les droits de douane," *Journal de la société statistique de Paris* 45 (1904): 132–44; *Les Temps nouveaux*, 5.08.1905, p. 3; Colette Laffond, "L'industrie de la chaussure à Izeaux (Bas-Dauphiné)," *Revue de géographie alpine* 34, No. 1 (1946): 69–85.
20 For the same job, in 1911, the average monthly earnings in Portieux (Vosges) were 65 francs, in Bayel (Aube), 120, and at Legras, 140. See Philippe Picoche, "Une entreprise vosgienne. La verrerie de Portieux (1850–1950)" (doctoral diss. in history, University of Lyon II, 2000), 161.
21 FNA, BB/11/11167, 72601x28, Puzzuoli.
22 FNA, 19770897/190, 41813x38, Martínez.
23 SDMA, 121ACW9, "Interviews expo 1870–1920," 2.
24 Abel Châtelain, "Les migrations temporaires françaises au XIXe siècle. Problèmes. Méthodes. Documentation," *Annales de démographie historique*, 1967: 9–28.
25 FNA, 19770897/190, 41813x38, Martínez (at No. 100 from 1917 to the 1940s).
26 Evidence of this is found in the geographic dispersion of family members attending their wedding. See e.g. FNA, BB/11/1491, Diédat.
27 See, for Brittany, the Dugués, at No. 100 in 1896, who first moved to Pontivy: AD Morbihan, Noyal-Pontivy, mar., 1875, No. 9, 21.01.1875. This case runs counter to what Jean-Paul Brunet affirmed: "The Breton immigration [into Saint-Denis], which was a collective immigration, worked without intermediary stops, neither in the towns and cities of Bretagne nor in Paris" (Brunet, "Une banlieue ouvrière," 134, my trans.). For Extremadura, see the

Matéos, from Serrejón and Peraleda, at No. 100 from the mid-1910s, who had first migrated to Navalmoral de la Mata (see AD93 D2M8205, SD, 1921 census), or the Rodríguez, from Cumbre and Belvís de Monroy, who settled in Saucedilla before heading to France and moving in at No. 96 in 1915 (FNA, 19770877/124, 1151x33).
28 On the literacy of residents, see Chapter 5.
29 See Corine Maitte, *Les Chemins de verre: les migrations des verriers d'Altare et de Venise (XVIe–XIXe siècles)* (Rennes: Presses universitaires de Rennes, 2009); Benoît Pinchard, "L'étude socio-généalogique des verriers. Problématiques, méthodes et perspectives," *Éclats de verres,* No. 18 (2011): 53–9.
30 Here are some of the destinations residents emigrated to before settling in the *cités*: New York City, Philadelphia, Buenos Aires, São Paulo, Mexico City, Stockholm, Edinburgh, Hamburg (see e.g. *Passenger Lists of Vessels Arriving at New York, New York, 1820–1897*, NARA Series M237, roll 561, Jan. 22, 1891, ship Maasdam, Bonaventura Pirolli; FNA, 19770898/81, 47492x38, Merucci; AD93 D2M8205, SD, 1921 census, 100 av. Wilson, Manuela Castaño née Lamy; FNA, 19780013/156, 21168x46, Carnevale; Saíz, 2001: 11–4; APP, 328W12, No. 850897, Gallaccio; FNA, 19770881/45, 25656x33, Verrecchia; int. No. 50, 21.07.2016).
31 Tenants had made stops in Montataire, Le Creusot, Châtillon-sur-Seine, Montceau-les-Mines.
32 Antoine Isz, at No. 100 in the 1880s and 1890s, had already lived in Paris with his wife in the mid-1860s before going back to Moselle (see SDMA, E252, mar., 1887, No. 63, 26.02.1887; AVP, D4R1 645, 1891, No. 658). A widow, Catherine Engelmann, had come for a first time to the Paris area in 1871, before going back to Lorraine and emigrating for good to Saint-Denis with her children a few months later (int. No. 27, 24.07.2016). Joseph Schiel, who left his native Moselle in 1890, had first come to the Paris area under the Second Empire, more than 30 years earlier (AD57, 7E19 5/7, Enchenberg, 1857, mar., 23.09.1857; FNA, BB/11/2561, 5782x91).
33 Luigi Einaudi, "Un traffico infame di carne umana," *La Stampa*, 26.05.1901; int. No. 76, 17.03.2021.
34 In 1886 Venafro, near Pozzilli, was connected to Rome and Naples, and from Naples, Molisan and Casertan migrants would go on to Marseilles or the Americas by boat; see Fernando Cefalogli, *Il Molise nell'Unità d'Italia* (Isernia: Cosmo Iannone, 2011), 139. As for the train known as the *Ziggel*, connecting Rosteig and Soucht in Lorraine, it opened in the 1890s; see André Schontz and Arsène Felten, *Le Chemin de fer en Lorraine* (Metz: Serpenoise, 1999), 240–1. The *ferrocarril de la Robla*, built in northern Spain to connect coal-mining areas and the industries of the Bilbao area, reached the Merindades area in the early 1900s; see Javier Fernández López and Carmelo Zaita, *El ferrocarril de la Robla* (Madrid: Agualarga, 1987). In Extremadura, Navalmoral de la Mata had been connected to Madrid by train in 1878; see José Bueno Rocha, *Navalmoral, 600 años de vida* (Navalmoral de la Mata: Ayuntamiento de Navalmoral de la Mata, 1985), 154–6.
35 The price on the French leg (Hendaye-Paris) was 60 fr. for 2 adults in 1909; children under 3 could travel for free and those aged three to seven paid half price; 30 kilograms of luggage were included per adult (*JORF*, 21.06.1909, p. 6735). 30 fr. were worth about 40 pesetas in the mid-1900s; see François Sauvaire-Jourdan, "La crise du change en Espagne," *Bulletin hispanique* 7, No. 3 (1905): 293–304. On the Spanish side, we can estimate the price per passenger between Villarcayo and Bilbao at roughly 2.5 pesetas in the mid-1900s. Peasants from the Mountain of Burgos would not have earned more than 1 peseta per day

68 *Changing places*

at the time; see Ricardo Robledo Hernández, "Crisis agraria y éxodo rural: la emigración española a Ultramar (1880–1920)," in *La crisis agraria europea de finales del siglo XIX*, ed. Ramón Garrabou (Barcelona: Crítica, 1988), 212–44.
36 Int. No. 39, 4.09.2016; int. No. 49, 6.07.2016.
37 APP, CB 92.5, 1909/665, 3.08.1909; int. No. 71, 24.07.2018.
38 Int. No. 71, 24.07.2018.
39 Int. No. 27, 24.07.2016.
40 These two graphs are based on cases in which we can know with reasonable accuracy (relying on people's own declarations) the tenants' address immediately before (125 instances) or immediately after (147 instances) their stay at Nos. 96–102.
41 In 1898, the arrival of the very first Italian residents, among whom Luigi's future wife Maria, had no visible impact on the graph, as they moved into No. 100 from another, overcrowded building across the street, which had to be evacuated due to its perilous conditions. See AD93, 4U7/966, PV Carlesimo, Vozza, 18.11.1897; AD93, 4U7/972, PV Polinier, 13.07.1898; CDP SD-Sud, int. Mathias Rodi, 16.08.1901, in AD93, 4U7/995, *Dossier d'instruction* No. 49750, 27.08.1901.
42 AD93, 1E66/397, SD, deaths, 1925, vol. 2, No. 1366, 25.10.1925, Vertenten ("Vertente"); AVP, D4R1 732, 1893, No. 1629; SDMA, E298, mar., 1897, No. 92, 20.03.1897; AD Somme, 2E71/22, Beauval, deaths 1887–1893, 1890, No. 83, 4.11.1890.
43 Brunet, "Une banlieue ouvrière," 1115.
44 AD93, D4P4 57, "Documents préparatoires à l'établissement du cadastre," Nos. 42, 42 bis, 43, 98-100, 96, 102 av. de Paris [1880s–1890s].
45 For illustrations, see Mapps (AD93, D4P4 57, *doc. cit.*; SDMA E269, SD, mar., 1891, No. 118, 11.04.1891); Peltier (AD93, D4P4 57, *doc. cit.* and SDMA, E299, deaths, 1897, No. 493, 7.06.1897), Sauvage (AD93, D4P4 57, *doc. cit.*; SDMA, 1F19, 1891 census; SDMA, 1I12, Letter from the Mayor of SD, 10.12.1895). Demolition is what prompted four households to move in 1893 from the house marked with an N to the one marked with a C on the figure.
46 See FNA, BB/11/7650, 13980x21, Saíz; AD93, 1E66/275, SD, births, 1915, vol. 1, No. 425, 14.04.1915; APP, CB 92.18,1921/1173, 15.12.1921-21.12.1921; int. No. 71, 25.07.2016.
47 SDMA, 1F24, 1901 census, 100 av. de Paris; FNA, F/22/452, Report by M. Drancourt, 25.07.1901; FNA, 19770876/18, 25377x32, Salvatore; AVP, D4R1 1295, 1905, No. 1897, Thomas; AVP, D4R1 688, 1892, No. 3870, Pollet; AD78, 1R/RM 397, 1908, No. 57, Pellé; FNA, 19770891/70, 42547x36, González; AD93 D2M8205, SD, 1921 census; FNA, 19770898/81, 47492x38, Merucci.
48 E.g. Marie-Claude Blanc-Chaléard, "Les Italiens à Paris au XIXe siècle," *Studi Emigrazione* 35, No. 130 (1998): 229–49.
49 Mark Wyman, *Round-Trip to America: The Immigrants Return to Europe, 1880–1930* (Ithaca: Cornell University Press, 1993); Nancy Green and Roger Waldinger, eds., *A Century of Transnationalism: Immigrants and Their Homeland Connections* (Urbana: University of Illinois Press, 2016), 11–2.
50 One tenant wanted for attempted murder in the Plaine-Saint-Denis fled to Italy, only to come back a few weeks later just to fire gunshots at the same man once again (AD93, 4U7/690, 2.06.1911, Toussaint c. Gabrielli; APP, CB 92.7, 1911/221, 3.08.1911). For a typology of return motives from a sociological standpoint, see Rosemarie Rogers, "Return migration, in comparative perspective," in *The Politics of Return. International Return Migration in Europe*, ed. Daniel Kubat (New York: Center for Migration Studies, 1984), 277–99.
51 FNA, 19770896/57, 24259x38, Caporuscio.

52 François Roth, "La frontière franco-allemande 1871–1918," in *Grenzen und Grenzregionen. Frontières et régions frontalières,* ed. Wolfgang Haubrichs and Reinhard Schneider (Saarbrücken: SDV, 1993), 131–45.
53 See AD93, 4U7/1024, CDP SD-Sud, int. Philippe Wernert, 25.08.1906; SDMA, 1F15, 1881 census, av. de Paris, Nos. 19 and 41 (sic); AD67, 4E413/10, Rosteig, 1888, mar., No. 5, 8.10.1888, Wernert-Schneider; SDMA, 1F19, 1891 census, 133 av. de Paris; AD67, 4E413/10, Rosteig, 1892, mar., 1.08.1892, Staub-Werner; FNA, BB/11/1464, 2263x78, Wernert; FNA, BB/11/2397, 1265x90, Wernert; SDMA, E277, SD, mar., 1893, No. 320, 19.08.1893; AD67, 4E413/12, Rosteig, 1896, mar., No. 9, 15.09.1896, Werner-Grussi; AD67, 4E413/12, Rosteig, 1901, mar., No. 1, 11.02.1901, Werner-Frank; AD67, Rosteig, 4E413/16, 1904, No. 8, 26.06.1904; AD93, 1E66/369, SD, deaths, 1909, No. 54; AVP, D4R1 565, 1889, No. 2847, Wernert; MA Aubervilliers, 1E184, births, 1898, 17.11.1898, Werner.
54 I came across at least seven cases of tenants from southern Italy who went home to marry between 1900 and 1915: FNA, BB/11/6172, 18503x14, Fraioli; BB/11/10742, 51385x28, Puzzuoli; BB/11/10387, 33613x27, Carbone; BB/11/13343, 26126x30, Tedeschi; BB/11/10371, 32806x27, Greco; BB/11/10700, 49272x28, Leo; BB/11/13376, 27779x30, Greco.
55 FNA, BB/11/12124, 11018x29, Varona.
56 FNA, BB/11/13343, 26126x30, Tedeschi.
57 Int. No. 71, 24.07.2018. Symmetrically, tenant families could take care of children whose parents could not afford to raise them: see SDMA, E257, SD, deaths, 1888, No. 364, 9.04.1888; 1F19, 1891 census, vol. 2, 96 av. de Paris, Bichler.
58 Jean-Pierre Cassarino, "Theorising return migration: the conceptual approach to return migrants revisited," *International Journal on Multicultural Societies* 6, No. 2 (2004): 253–79.
59 Peggy Levitt, "Social remittances: migration driven local-level forms of cultural diffusion," *International Migration Review* 32, No. 4 (1998), 926–48.
60 Dionigi Albera, Patrizia Audenino, and Paola Corti, "I percorsi dell'identità maschile nell'emigrazione. Dinamiche colettive e ciclo di vita individuale," *Rivista di storia contemporanea* 20, No. 1 (1991): 69–87.
61 Consejo provincial de fomento de Burgos, *Estadística emigratoria de la provincia: causas principales de la emigración y medios para que disminuya* (Burgos: Díez y Compañia, 1914).
62 CDP SD-Sud, PV 16.08.1901, int. Nicandro Forte, in AD93, 4U7/995, *Dossier d'instruction* No. 49750; ASC Pozzilli, lista di leva, classe 1888, Antonio Forte.
63 FNA, BB/11/1981, 2472x87, Fixari; SDMA CT84, Courriers à l'arrivée, 1887–1889, Letters from the Head of the First Division of the Administration of the Colonies, 26.12.1887.
64 FNA, BB/11/11264, 77542x28, Orsi.
65 APP, CB 92.4, 1908/611, 15.06.1908; SDMA, 1F27, 1911 census; AD93 D2M8205, SD, 1921 census; AD93 D2M891, SD census, 1926; SDMA, 1F33, 1931 census (all on 100 av. Wilson); ASC Pontecorvo, liste di leva, 1901, No. 178; SDMA, 5Q61, "La Mutualité" de la Plaine-Saint-Denis, No. 461.
66 FNA, 19770894/2, 28280x37, Scopelidis; int. No. 68, 24.07.2018; APP, CB 92.16, 1919/707, 2.10.1919.
67 Jeanne Gaillard 1980, "Les migrants à Paris au XIXe siècle. Insertion et marginalité," *Ethnologie française* 10, No. 2 (1980): 129–36; Alain Faure, "Une génération de Parisiens à l'épreuve de la ville," in *Bulletin du Centre d'histoire de la France contemporaine,* No. 7 (1986): 157–73.
68 On inter-ethnicisation, see Vecoli, "An inter-ethnic perspective."

69 Norbert Elias, "Introduction: a theoretical essay on established and outsider relations" [1976], in *The Established and the Outsiders,* ed. John Scotson (Thousand Oaks: Sage, 1994), xxx–xxxii.
70 Susan Freeman, *The Pasiegos: Spaniards in No Man's Land* (Chicago: University of Chicago Press, 1979).
71 APP, CB 92.11, 1915/51, 2.02.1915; APP, CB 92.11, 1915/273, 15.05.1915).
72 See SDMA, CT1328, "Belges. 1918-1919"; H 41, Military registers, 1918, Lancelon; CT1003, "Réfugiés du Pas-de-Calais," no date; CT223, List of refugees summoned to city hall for work, no date [1918]; CT1328, "Répertoire. Réfugiés. 1919"; AD93, D742–9, "Secours aux réfugiés," 1915–20.
73 AD93, 4U7/1037, PV 29.06.1921, Cavecchia; AD93 D2 M8205, SD, 1921 census, p. 295 *sqq.*; SDMA, CT1328, "Répertoire. Réfugiés. 1919"; AD02, 5Mi1709, Chauny, 1894, No. 253, birth, 5.06.1894; AD02, 5Mi1711, Chauny, 1901, mar., No. 374, 27.07.1901.
74 SDMA, CT145, Letter from the Préfet of the Seine, 15.01.1919, about M. Faath; CT1328, "Répertoire. Réfugiés. 1919"; MA Amiens, 2E931, mar., 1884, No. 442, 3.11.1884; SDMA, E307, SD, deaths, 1899, No. 993; E308, SD, births, 1900, No. 326; E312, SD, deaths, 1900, No. 631; SDMA, 1F24, 1901 census, 16 rue Trézel; AD93, 1E66/334, SD, mar., 1918, 2.02.1918; 1E66/395, SD, deaths, 1924, vol. 2, No. 1413; APP, CB 92.21,1925/170, 289 *bis*, 24.01.1925-6.02.1925; *JORF, Lois et décrets*, 21.11.1921, 3065, Augustin Hug.
75 On the colonial workers' living conditions, see *Bulletin des usines de guerre* 1, No. 44/346, 26.02.1917.
76 AD93, 1E66/330, SD, mar., 1915, No. 355, 24.11.1915; 1E66/332, mar., 1917, No. 153, 1.04.1917; 1E66/334, mar., 1918, No. 266, 23.05.1918; 1E66/334, mar., No. 517, 10.10.1918; 1E66/334, mar., 1918, No. 533, 26.10.1918; 1E66/334, mar., 1918, No. 557, 16.11.1918; 1E66/335, mar., 1919, No. 226, 7.04.1919; 1E66/337, mar., 1920, No. 223, 28.02.1920. APP, CB 92.11, 1915/605, 26-29.08.1915; SDMA, 4 H 3/58, Letter-petition from the shopkeepers of the Plaine-Saint-Denis to the Mayor of SD, 1.05.1916.

4 Chains of migration

Joaquín de Garate was one of the first Spanish migrants to settle in the Plaine-Saint-Denis. A cooper-turned-wine salesman from the Basque country, he arrived with his brother in 1879 after a year in southwestern France. Joachim, as the Plainards came to know him, was first put up by a French carter and boilermaker. This Frenchman had been living in the *cités* for years, and the two would remain close friends. Joachim's status kept rising; he became a French citizen in 1892 and married a local teacher a few years later. Once he founded his own wine-selling business at the turn of the century, he even amassed significant wealth. This was helped by a sizeable inheritance from his father-in-law, as well as large-scale tax evasion.

By the mid-1900s, Garate had become a central figure in the area. Through the cycling club he founded, as well as his vast network of clients (including residents at No. 96), he made many contacts. He was chosen to be honorary vice-president of a veterans' brass band society; this signalled his rapid integration. Among his closest friends were a city council member and the bar owner at No. 102. Thus, when a growing number of Spanish families began arriving in 1908 and 1909, the Garates were the ideal facilitators; they helped people find work and lodging and assisted with their administrative obligations. In subsequent years, the first people they had helped would play the same role for others.[1]

Social relations were often crucial in the tenants' migrations to and from the Plaine-Saint-Denis. Based on kindred, longstanding connections from their region of origin or more indirect recommendations, such ties helped migrants ponder, devise and execute their migration strategies. Sociologists are now familiar with the typology of those bonds of solidarity and the functions they perform with regard to migrants' selection and adaptation.[2] Across migration studies, scholars have largely embraced the concept of network to refer to people's relationships based on reciprocity, trust and social norms. This approach also conveys a degree of agency and rational choice among migration candidates. By mobilising social capital, people seek well-established pathways of movement. In organising the journey, finding a dwelling and securing a job upon arrival – all the while avoiding

DOI: 10.4324/9781003017820-4

the many pitfalls of settling in an alien environment – people have to make consequential decisions, and the assistance of others is critical.[3]

It is one thing to conjecture the existence of historical migration networks;[4] a whole other to actually reconstruct them from sources.[5] A number of microhistorians have started to map ego-centred networks to understand people's actions and representations.[6] In the particular context of Nos. 96–102 Av. de Paris, the archival record suggests that many tenants had relatives or points of contact to turn to upon arrival, thereby taking part in chain migrations. In other words, they relied on "networks, based on kin and kith, of information, mutual help, and emotional and material resources [which] provided guidance and sustenance to those undertaking the trip. Such networks determined timing and destinations, promised lodgings and jobs, and insured social integration into a community."[7] Few seem to have come entirely independently, although it has been rightly stressed that such cases should not be neglected.[8]

This chapter is meant to give a sense of the types of networks that brought people to the tenement over the years. It highlights common patterns, idiosyncrasies and, at times, circulations of practices. Through a few granular examples, the first half of the chapter reassesses some well-established hypotheses about family and regional migration chains. In particular, it stresses the key role played by intermediaries, as well as the overlap between networks of farm labourers, travelling merchants and factory workers. This overlap has heretofore eluded specialists' attention.[9] The chapter's second half addresses a more specific and intriguing type of migration scheme that affected the tenement's demography and the experience of its inhabitants: the import-export trade of underage glassmakers. In contrast to the existing scholarship on child labour, which has mostly remained enclosed within the ethnic boundaries of Italian emigration, the microhistorical focus allows for an exploration of that traffic's multiethnic dimension.

Mutual help

The tenants' migratory chains shared several characteristics over the years. First among them was an initial migrant selection by gender. Families from eastern regions had initially migrated *en masse*. Starting in the 1890s, however, many male tenants came alone. If they were married, they might send for their wives and/or mothers at a later stage. A man from the province of Toledo travelled twice without his wife to the Plaine, and twice she trailed him by a few months.[10] By contrast, a female neighbour of theirs from the province of Caserta arrived with her entire family. They all left at the outset of the First World War. But once the conflict was over, only her father and children returned to the Plaine; she would make her way back in the mid-1920s.[11] In only a few cases was it the other way around, with wives and adult children arriving first and the husband joining them later on.[12]

The second feature of migration chains was the help relatives provided in finding accommodation. Sources record examples of Italians and Lorrainers moving in with their siblings or cousins at Nos. 96 and 100.[13] Migrants could also pass on their lease to their kin. At the end of the First World War, a man from the Burgos area took over the apartment in the front building at No. 96 from a Spanish couple who had initially put him up as a lodger. He then hosted a cousin of his, before letting her become the tenant of the apartment while relocating with his family to the back of the courtyard.[14]

The third important aspect of migration chains was their encouragement by employers. Companies were regularly in need of fresh manpower, and they seem to have routinely committed to hiring their workers' relatives. One Lorrainer from No. 98 started at Legras in 1882, just one day after leaving his native village; we know his brother-in-law had been hired by Legras a few months earlier.[15] Relatives did not have to be currently employed by the factory to provide help. One former occupant of the tenement worked at Legras in the 1890s and then went back to Lorraine. He was gone by the time his son reached the Plaine in 1904, but he recommended him to his former boss all the same.[16] Lastly, employers also had their own regional network. Among his first workers, M. Legras had relied on former colleagues and neighbours from his own village in Lorraine. In the 1880s and 1890s, four glassworkers at No. 100 hailed from the same village as *"Monsieur le patron."*

These interpersonal connections relied on information sharing, either when people met in person or when they exchanged correspondence. The rare letter specimens that survive in private collections represent but a tiny fraction of those that came in and out of the tenement. As people promoted or discouraged the migrations of their relatives, we know that all sorts of misrepresentations, exaggerations and omissions were possible.[17] Illiteracy was limited and did not serve as a real barrier. Someone in the entourage, at both ends of the chain, would help those who could not read or write.[18] In any case, the most important part of correspondence was often the remittances enclosed in the envelope – that is, until banks and post offices developed alternative, more reliable options to move money across borders.[19]

In many migration networks, a few pioneers played a pivotal role. The case of one tenant from southern Italy illustrates this. By the late 19th century, Casertans and Molisans – which is not the same as saying Italians in general[20] – densely populated the northeastern district of Paris called La Villette. There, a man named Rosario Verrecchia had settled in the 1870s or early 1880s. He had taken a job at the major railway company called *Chemin de fer du Nord*.[21] Through his work, he made enough money to buy out a small, two-room hotel-restaurant in the heart of the neighbourhood. His wife worked there daily, while he continued his work at the railroad. The hotel was one of the few retreats for newcomers from his native region. In the mid-1880s, the Verrecchias' address was probably shared by emigration candidates in their native village as a primary point of contact.[22]

Initially, the Plaine-Saint-Denis served as an extension of La Villette for southern Italians. Rosario Verrecchia was one of the first to not only commute, but to settle in the Plaine-Saint-Denis; he did so with his family in 1896. At that time, only a handful of Italian families had been living in the tenement's vicinity. Sources only record, in fact, one other Southern Italian family before the Verrecchias: that of Luigi Salvatore. This was Rosario's own brother-in-law who, as early as 1893, had moved to the Plaine with his wife and children. After an injury had forced him to quit his railway job in Paris, Rosario and his wife reverted to the classic solution of singing and playing music in Normandy. But they had not spent a full year on the road before they heard about an opportunity at Legras. This news probably came through Salvatore, who did not take advantage of it himself and re-emigrated to London instead.[23]

By the 1890s, several cousins of Rosario Verrecchia had also settled in La Villette. After recently transitioning from music to industry, one of them worked in construction and another at a sugar refinery.[24] Sources suggest that the latter then secured a job at Legras and a dwelling at No. 100 through Verrecchia.[25] Other cousins of his were the Pirollis, featured in the previous chapter, to whom he would provide similar services when they arrived in the Plaine. Far from dismembering families, the migration process could actually reinforce ties of kinship.[26]

We also know that in those same years Verrecchia – who spoke fluent French – would help some Legras colleagues from his native region obtain the legally required work permits, or "*livrets*" (lit. booklets) for their underage children (see Figure 4.1). He would personally go to city hall and produce, on their behalf, their fake birth certificates in support of the applications.[27] It is likely that he would have taken a fee for those services. By the time he moved to No. 100 in 1898, he had become a prominent middleman for his *compaesani*. The centrality of Rosario's role would match the indirect recollection of Salvatore's great-grandson, who affirmed that the two brothers-in-law acted as "the emigration channel"[28] to Saint-Denis.

Verrecchia and his peers mostly assisted their relatives and acquaintances. But sources also point to the presence of go-between characters whose influence in the Plaine extended beyond their family and community of origin. Their help proved no less instrumental for a number of the tenement's occupants over the years.

For Spaniards, the main figure of this kind was the aforementioned Joachim de Garate. Just a few weeks after two Spanish couples arrived at No. 100, Joachim was already on friendly terms with them.[29] He and his wife forged bonds with a number of Spanish families from the tenement.[30] Although he had been living in France for decades, Joachim had kept strong ties with his home country. From the late 1870s onward, he went back to Spain regularly – first, for his three-year military service and later, in 1884, to marry a Basque woman. At least six children were born from that union over the next 15 years. Nevertheless, Joachim kept his family status secret from French authorities when he applied for citizenship and, of course,

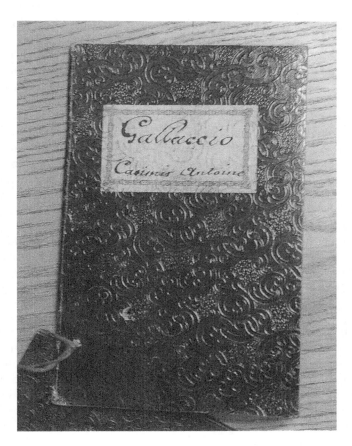

Figure 4.1 The livret an underage glassmaker from No. 100, seized during the 1901 investigation at Legras. AD93, ref. 4U7/995. Photograph by the author.

when he married his French wife.[31] Privately, however, his two lives were openly intertwined; at least two of his Spanish sons eventually came to live and work with him in the Plaine. Eventually separating from his French wife, Joachim retired to San Sebastián after the First World War, leaving his business to his brother.[32]

What matters is that in the 1900s, the Garates had become bona fide notables at both ends of the migration chain; their recommendations carried great weight, especially for Spanish newcomers.[33] In later years, the mantle would be assumed by other, similar figures. During the First World War, an Asturias-born tenant at No. 96 served his countrymen in various capacities; having lived in France since the early 1900s, he worked as interpreter, procurer of Spanish and French administrative documents, job purveyor and, to their dismay, occasional crook.[34]

For Italian residents, one of the people whose clout extended beyond their initial regional base was Louis Pirolli himself. After the Great War, he was simultaneously a decorated Italian veteran, a head of department at the glass factory, and the owner of an Italian grocery on the Avenue. At that point, his wife and daughter played a major role, as they were the ones running the shop on a daily basis; his daughter was certainly better equipped to offer all kinds of help to Italians, as she had completed primary education in both France and Italy.[35] In 1922, Louis alongside one of his brothers and a cousin, founded a mutual benefit society called *Stella meridionale* (lit. southern star). Records are otherwise missing about this organization. Still, this initiative indicates a consciousness, from Louis's part, of a role to play in assisting his fellow nationals (or at least his fellow southerners). It underscored his centrality among Italians in the area; they could rely on his knowledgeability with French institutions and his solid position in a major factory. At the same time, Louis Pirolli likely made use of his ethnic origin. Catering to Italians was a way to sustain his grocery business and increase the ranks of his benefit society, thereby cementing his financial and social standing at the local level.

Ties of indenture

In the Plaine-Saint-Denis of the late 19th century, family-based migration networks overlapped with another type of operation: the importation of child workers. The trade of young manpower had long been the preserve of wandering trades – playing music, shining shoes and selling food or statuettes. During the 19th century, the practice gradually evolved to satisfy industrial demand, especially in the mining and glass sectors.[36]

But beginning in the 1840s, cultural resistance and regulation increased across Europe in an attempt to rein in this exploitation of children – with limited initial success.[37] In 1892, a new French law prohibited the employment of anyone under 13 in factories. This outraged the glass industry, which claimed that children were indispensable to its business model.[38] After vainly lobbying the government for exemptions, French glass barons decided to circumvent this legislation by resorting to foreign children. Their ages were harder to check, and by 1900, 1,700 Italian minors were working in French glass factories.[39] The majority were accompanied by their parents, but dozens were under the supervision of caretakers.

Starting in 1896, Legras swiftly replaced the bulk of its youngest French manpower with Southern Italian children.[40] To find this new supply, he could tap into the networks that had been dispatching street vendors and young performers across Europe.[41] Boys – and less so, girls – had been routinely consigned by struggling parents to people, called *padroni** (singular *padrone*), who would employ them on the streets, provide for their food and clothing and send any extra income to the family.

Legras was a late-comer to the new system. One tenant from No. 100 had been accompanying minors to a glass factory near Lyon as soon as 1893.[42] Moreover, the *padrone* who supplied Legras with its first 12 Italian apprentices and soon moved with them to No. 100 turned out to be a toxic connection. His name was Donato Vozza, and he came from Casalvieri, a notorious hub of ruffians in the province of Caserta.

Infamous *padroni* and ordinary parents

A criminal past was not uncommon among the *padroni* at Legras. One of these child-suppliers had been part of a gang of burglars for years before bringing his young wards to the tenement at Nos. 96–102.[43] But no one was quite as tough as Vozza and his wife, whose charges were severely mistreated and undernourished. For months, in spite of anonymous complaints, Vozza received only slaps on the wrist; that is, dozens of fines for hosting the children without the proper authorisation for a furnished room business.[44] Three of the boys eventually died of illnesses; this triggered a general outcry that had echoes in France, Italy, Spain and even in the United States.[45] As a famous Italian diplomat and the former queen of Naples joined in the chorus, Vozza was arrested in Italy. For her part, his wife was prosecuted in France. But after all was said and done, the *padrone* only got six months in jail and an unpaid fine for his crimes; no charges were brought against the *padrona*. Archives of the Italian trial have not survived, but its lenient outcome was a testimony to the judges' unease with a practice that was generally consensual. And it further highlighted the difficulty of combatting the ruthlessness of traffickers with inadequate laws.[46]

This episode, which would capture imaginations to the point of inspiring a successful novel and a feature film,[47] initially prompted more scrutiny from labour inspectors into the Legras factory. In the summer of 1901, an inspection showed that of the 79 employment documents presented by Italian child workers, many did not correspond to their holder. Others had been established on the base of forged birth certificates.[48] This investigation was part of an increased effort by the labour inspection service to enforce the aforementioned 1892 law in glass factories; nationwide, 552 unlawful age offences were discovered in the industry in 1901, compared to 223 the year before.[49]

In the case of Legras, not all underage children were under the care of *padroni*. In fact, many were put to work illegally by their own parents. One of these parents was Giacinto Pirolli, Luigi's father. It seems that Giacinto and his sons barely escaped being caught red-handed by inspectors. The three of them were in Paris by January 1901.[50] At that point in time, Luigi was old enough to become an apprentice, unlike his younger brother Giustino. Giacinto obtained a regular booklet for his eldest son, and Luigi was officially hired in February. For Giustino, Giacinto could have secured a booklet based on a counterfeit birth certificate, something he would do for his other children in the years to come.[51] Instead, he had the boy pose as two different nephews of his: Augusto and Ferdinando. Each time, Giacinto ensured that the child was at least 13. These nephews of his had emigrated to America a year before, and Giacinto may have kept their original birth certificates. When asked about his age, the fake Ferdinando, unfortunately, revealed his real date of birth to the inspector.[52] The need for secrecy must have been drummed into Giustino by his father. Many decades later, he would still lie about his starting date at Legras and keep silent about his first years at No. 100.[53]

When the census operations took place in the spring of 1901, Giacinto Pirolli and his two sons were already working at Legras; Giustino's declared age was duly inflated.[54] It may well be that Giustino, as well as youngsters like Luigi who actually had the required age, were let go during the summer of 1901 to assuage labour inspectors. This would have marked one of the first episodes in Luigi and Giustino's lives in which a national identification as Italian translated into a tangible and, in that case, adverse consequence. Father and sons may have taken a summer trip to Italy at that point. But after a few months passed and the pressure decreased, Luigi and Guistino could be hired again at the glassworks.[55]

The scrutiny of labour inspectors receded in the following years. A total of eight procedures were opened over a decade against Legras. The resulting fines, which were negligible compared to the factory's turnover, concerned 24 underage labour cases.[56] This represented only the tip of the iceberg; most of the time, children were swiftly hidden upon the inspector's arrival. Giacinto Pirolli made sure his underage sons were assigned to the night shift, because as one of them later put it, "at night inspectors are asleep."[57] Even the latter were willing to look the other way when it came to certain violations, such as the absence of a weekly 24-hour rest that the law mandated for minors.[58] Nevertheless, a whiff of scandal stuck to Legras's reputation. The best way to put matters to rest was then to move away from Italian *padroni* and look for other sources of supply.

A child-supplying priest

Conveniently, a more reputable child-recruiter was becoming famous in Paris. Joseph Santol, a priest from the Pyrénées region, founded a charity in 1899 called *Le Placement familial*. Its aim was to match young children from all over France with demand for labour in industry, agriculture and domestic service. His activity escalated quickly; by 1905, his organisation had already placed over 14,000 boys and girls, aged six to 18, profiting from the indenture contracts signed with their families.

Just like his small-scale Italian competitors, Santol resorted to various illicit practices to maximise revenue. Not only did he provide underage children with fraudulent birth certificates, but the dwellings where he temporarily accommodated them before dispatch were "hideously dirty."[59] His other frauds included obtaining half-priced tickets from railway companies as a form of donation while making families pay full price. He also deducted food, dwelling and clothing from the child's salaries, despite being paid for this by employers.[60] Despite hundreds of complaints, recurrent vitriolic accounts in the press and numerous probes opened by prosecutors, the well-connected clergyman always managed to escape conviction.[61]

Santol's placement scheme allowed factory owners like M. Legras to formalise child-recruitment practices developed with Italian *padroni* and give them a veneer of respectability. With the blessing of glass and mining companies, Santol started to open boarding houses near major industrial sites. The one he opened in the Plaine-Saint-Denis in 1905, with a capacity of 30–45 children aged 13–18, exclusively supplied Legras. In theory, Santol's children were somewhat better compensated than other minors. In reality, Santol's organisation retained the apprentices' entire salary, leaving them with half a franc per week.[62]

The Spanish *padrones*

In the mid-1900s, Legras's production was still growing. The number of youngsters provided by Santol was not nearly enough, and these kids did not come cheap.[63] Securing child labour remained a challenge. According to labour inspectors, four factors explained the reluctance of most families to send their children to work in glass factories: the hard working conditions, the risks of burn wounds, the brutality of senior workers and the lack of career perspectives, since the proportion of children employed was too high for all of them to become glassmakers.[64] So the factory managers turned to another source: Spaniards.

The first few to be hired by Legras in 1908 moved in at Nos. 96 and 100 Av. de Paris. Those *padrones*, their wives and their young wards – some of whom were their own children – had been living with a few dozen compatriots in *garnis* in Levallois, another suburb to the northwest of the capital.[65] Originally cattle-herders from remote valleys of northern Spain, they had a long tradition of smuggling, nomadism and emigration.[66] Initially, their cluster in Levallois had only featured *Pasiegos* from the exact same mountains, called Montes de Pas. However, they were later joined by fellow highlanders from the province of Burgos (just a few miles to the south), with whom they had long-standing ties. Since the 1880s, every single one of those *padrones* from Levallois whose presence was recorded in official documents had been making a living as a strolling merchant. In summer, they would require their young charges to sell waffles, ice creams and biscuits known as *barquillos* in Spanish and *plaisirs* or *oublies* in French; in winter, they sold roasted chestnuts.

Once they started supplying glass factories in the late 1900s, the Levallois-based *padrones* scattered with their families. They flocked into a small number of tenements in the north of Paris and nearby banlieues, including the one at Nos. 96–102. Over the years, they would regularly circulate from one to the next, especially to elude police investigations.[67] Like their Italian peers, they never entirely renounced their biscuit-making business, which remained very profitable. Instead of resting on Sundays, the young glass-workers went out to sell *plaisirs* across the city. In the summer, a *padrón* from No. 96 would take his little platoon to Brittany, on a break from Legras, to sell biscuits on beaches.[68]

Around 1910, at least seven of the Spanish *padrones* based in the tenement were each providing Legras with five to ten children. They also made regular trips to their native region to recruit new ones.[69] In France, their network was not limited to the Paris area; two brothers of a *padrón* from No. 100 were supplying a coal-mine in Saint-Étienne.[70] Unfortunately for Legras and the *padrones*, scandal broke once again in late 1912, in a sort of rerun of 1898. While no children had died this time around, a few of the Spanish exploiters – some of whom were active in the tenement – were sentenced for child mistreatment.[71]

An institutionalised system

Police and prosecution documents show that the deeds of the Italian and Spanish child traffickers were part of a well-oiled machine, covering a broad spectrum of practices.[72] Most of the indentures were agreed upon orally, but some were written. One of the Italian suppliers who lived in the tenement at No. 100, for instance, would strike three-year contracts with families and sign them before witnesses. In his case, the agreements provided that parents would receive "115 lire every six months."[73] Other *padroni* offered families one lump sum up front, which allowed them to better lure families and to pay them less in the end.[74] According to several converging accounts from the early 1910s, Spanish children under 12 were leased for 100–120 francs a year; older ones went for 150–200. Yet *padrones* deducted sizeable amounts from these sums under the guise of fines or unexpected expenses.[75] Physical abuse and brutality were widespread. An Italian child worker from No. 100 would later tell his family of the terror that the *padrone*'s wife had caused him with her constant harassment. For this superstitious child, this woman came across as a "witch."[76]

Eventually, however, most traffickers escaped law enforcement; they could just move to another glasswork town and get their children employed at another factory. The Spanish *padrones* convicted in 1913 did not serve their sentences and carried on with their operations.[77] As late as 1929, one of them was still illegally procuring Spanish children for French glass tycoons.[78] He had no reason to quit the job: child-importers did well for themselves. A Spanish trafficker from No. 100 went on to buy a house in the Plaine-Saint-Denis; an Italian neighbour and colleague of his acquired a bar-hotel, secured a public contract to run the open-air market of the neighbourhood and even gave to charity like any well-to-do notable.[79]

Converging interests

By and large, the exploitation of young child workers was sanctioned by all parties to the trade – at least the adult ones. The interests of the children were a marginal concern at best, and nothing in the sources suggests that children, especially the youngest ones, were ever asked for their opinion. Not that the children were deprived of all agency, though. Flight attempts or denunciations by some of them, documented on the occasion of the aforementioned scandals, indicate that young glassworkers were not as passive as their enduring image of hopeless victims would suggest. Still, other snippets of information signal that most immigrant boys, caught in a culture of precocious masculinity and sense of family duty, would have likely chosen to participate in padronism had they been presented with the option.[80]

As for the children's families, there is little evidence to suggest that they were dissatisfied with the leasing arrangements. Most child-suppliers fulfilled their side of the bargain by regularly sending money to the boys' parents. Even Vozza sent money to the parents of his apprentices.[81] In return, caretakers expected compliance from the family. A *padrone* from No. 100 appealed before Saint-Denis local court to enforce an indenture after a father had come to fetch his children.[82] So conscious were the French judges that the child-importers had the blessings of the children's families that they felt compelled to grant extenuating circumstances to the Spanish *padrones* in 1913; they mentioned the "encouragement" they had received from the parents.[83] This also explains why people putting their own children to work illegally were almost never sued. The general acquiescence from families, predicated on their precarious economic situation, had puzzled the proponents of child labour reform throughout the 19th century.[84]

Local officials in the children's home countries also endorsed the traffic. Both leasing contracts and counterfeit birth certificates were frequently secured with their abetment. Mayors would provide inauthentic documents either out of kinship solidarity or in exchange for money or votes. "I did not cheat," Vozza claimed, "because I made the contract with the parents before the mayor of [the village]."[85] Political connections were central to both Santol's and Vozza's success; sources show that the latter personally knew the MP of Cassino.[86] Such official backing was less important in the Spaniards' case, as the *padrones* often did not bother to carry fraudulent documents. They simply flouted Spanish law by either hiding the children among sacks of goods or making them cross the border at night, far from the frontier posts.[87] As Giovanni Giolitti himself conceded, the measures imposed at the borders to prevent unlawful crossings were "ineffective."[88] This was a clear understatement.

In that indenture system, the key role was played by the factory managers themselves. They devised and fine-tuned the recruitment schemes. Despite constant and largely successful denials, the management at Legras was responsible for setting the rules of the covert operations.[89] Repeatedly pleading ignorance and good faith, the factory's director would not hesitate to lie to inspectors and change his story on workers' hiring dates from one year to the next, when he did not himself doctor his young employees' dates of birth.[90] An Italian child worker from No. 100 was first claimed to have been hired in February 1900, and the next year his starting date was altered to June 1901; that way, he was exactly 13 according to the date of birth on his work permit. All the while, this was based on a misleading birth certificate delivered in his native town in 1899.[91] These practices proved remarkably durable, and would be routinely applied to the tenement's Spanish contingent a decade later.[92] New glass-processing machines that appeared in the 1900s could have reduced this demand for child labour. However, their cost remained too high to offset the wage differential of underage employment.[93]

Contemporary observers were not fooled; bosses, *padroni* and parents had a common goal: exploit the child manpower.[94] As has been shown in other contexts, it is this convergence of interests that spurred the continuous use of underage child labour in the glass industry. Legras's lack of any real sentencing infuriated French socialists; they even brought up the matter in Parliament on the eve of the First World War.[95] Still, the alarm bells were raised after the Spanish scandal, and in the following years, the management at Legras decided to take matters into their own hands. They did so by relying less on intermediaries and expanding their own in-house boarding facility for apprentices.[96]

Women and girls

Female characters were not absent from the child import system. As early as 1890, an Italian musician was seen performing on the Avenue de Paris with the help of his seven-year-old daughter.[97] Later on, apart from the *padroni*'s wives, children could be guarded by the odd independent *padrona* – one lived at No. 100 for many years.[98] It is worth noting, however, that the young glassworkers smuggled into France were almost exclusively boys; girls, when exported, were mostly sent to work as servants or sex workers. Daughters of *padroni* and other glassworkers were made to work at Legras, too, and many served in the decoration and packaging departments. But they were rarely brought to France for that sole purpose.[99] Sources reveal that several girls from the tenement who worked at the glassworks were under the minimum age – one was as young as seven.[100] As a matter of fact, young female workers were more widely employed in the Plaine than boys, who were concentrated at Legras and a few other factories. Many features of the underage labour experience were similar across genders. A witness recalled that her mother, employed as a child at a toy factory on the Avenue de Paris in the 1920s, had been taught by managers to swiftly hide under a staircase whenever labour inspectors were paying a visit.[101]

At the glass factory, girls would not suffer from the heat and toxic fumes of the furnaces, where they were almost never employed. They were rarely assigned to night shifts either.[102] Nevertheless, they had to endure the hazards of glass etching with hydrofluoric acid, which caused severe burns and long-term respiratory illnesses.[103] As far as we can tell, a 1893 decree prohibiting the employment of women and children in workshops using toxic materials was not enforced in the Plaine. For those reasons, packaging was a safer workplace than decoration; still, when glassware broke, girls could suffer serious cuts, as the case of an 18-year-old tenant illustrates.[104]

Young girls also faced specific challenges that boys were spared. They were liable to slanderous accusations involving their so-called "morality." At Legras in 1884, a seven-year-old publicly accused an adult tenant from No. 96 of having written a malicious letter against her.[105] Such insinuations could push girls into depression and even to commit suicide.[106] Sources suggest that sexual harassment was common in mixed workshops, and girls rebutted advances at their own peril.[107] Yet young women were not bound to passively put up with difficult circumstances. In 1913, a teenage girl from a well-established family of glassworkers engineered her departure with a couple of friends. After reporting to a placement agency in Paris and perhaps working a few months as maids, the idea was to get hired as laundresses or seamstresses on transatlantic boats. To her friends, she vaunted the merits of her plan from the point of view of both "wages and freedom" (*au point de vue des appointements et de la liberté*).[108]

Men, women, boys and girls tried to exert some degree of control over their migration trajectories. But to reach the Plaine-Saint-Denis or to re-emigrate elsewhere, the inhabitants at Nos. 96–102 overwhelmingly relied on migration chains, which were sustained by ties of kinship or local solidarity. As this chapter has shown, the passage and the adjustment in the immigration context of the Plaine could at times be ensured by middle people of greater stature – often trailblazers who had succeeded financially. The Joachim de Garates and the Louis Pirollis acted as ethnic focal points and transnational chaperones. On the one hand, their connections and insider's knowledge perpetuated the ethnonational ties they were predicated upon. On the other hand, they ensured the newcomers' compliance with French administrative requirements and gave them access to local circles of sociability. As such, their role was only partly mirrored by the importers of underage manpower. Italians, Spanish and French "suppliers" took turns in carrying well-oiled indenture schemes that repurposed decade-old practices. Sanctioned by the children's families and generally tolerated by authorities at both ends of the journey, the illicit importation of minors was a distinct feature of the tenement's history until the Great War. Beyond the most egregious cases and the occasional public scandals, these shady migration chains were engineered and steered by factories like Legras. They were (sometimes begrudgingly) accepted as a legitimate, if not lawful, *modus operandi*. These schemes represented but one of many ways, based on third-party assistance, to make it to the Plaine and settle in the tenement. Once newcomers acclimatised to their new life, however, it became up to them to forge new relationships and navigate their encounters with one another. Tracking such interactions in the context of immigration will be the next step of our investigation.

Notes

1 FNA, BB/11/2235, 14792x88; SDMA, E207, SD, births, 1874, No. 765, 28.09.1874; 1F15, 1881 census, 93 av. de Paris; E213, SD, births, 1876, No. 868, 28.09.1876; E221, SD, deaths, 1878, No. 190, 20.02.1878; E231, SD, births, 1882, No. 425, 13.04.1882; APP, CB 92.2, 1905/558, 29.09.1905; AD93, 1E66/314, SD, mar., 1907, vol. 1, No. 305, 20.06.1907; *Archives commerciales de la France*, 1.11.1899, p. 1382, 4.12.1909, p. 1936; SDMA, E 294, SD, mar., 1896, No. 118, 7.04.1896; CT928, No. 485, 19.10.1888; SDMA, 1K1/37, 1893; *Le Vélo*, 15.06.1896; SDMA, E305, SD, births, 1899, No. 1285, 28.10.1899; *JORF*, 16.05.1898, 3139; *JSD*, 29.10.1903; APP, CB 92.2, 1905/558, 29.09.1905; *Bulletin des arrêts de la Cour de cassation rendus en matière criminelle*, 1909, No. 1, 84–5, 22.01.1909; *La Loi*, 28.10.1913, 6.12.1918; AD93, 1739W4, 10.11.1919; *Recueil hebdomadaire de jurisprudence*, 1926, 521–2 (57 av. Wilson).
2 Douglas Gurak and Fe Caces, "Migration networks and the shaping of migration systems," in *International Migration Systems: A Global Approach*, eds. Mary Kritz, Lin Lean Lim, and Hania Zlotnik (Oxford: Clarendon Press, 1992), 150–76; Sonja Haug, "Migration networks and migration decision-making," *Journal of Ethnic and Migration Studies* 34, No. 4 (2008): 585–605.
3 Enrico Moretti, "Social networks and migrations: Italy 1876–1913," *International Migration Review* 33, No. 3 (1999): 640–57.
4 Lillo, "Espagnols en 'banlieue rouge'," 99.
5 Claire Lemercier, "Formal network methods in history: why and how?," in *Social Networks, Political Institutions, and Rural Societies*, ed. Georg Fertig (Turnhout: Brepols, 2015), 281–310.
6 Simona Cerutti, "Micro-history: social relations versus cultural models?," in *Between Sociology and History: Essays on Microhistory, Collective Action and Nation-Building*, eds. Anna-Maija Castrén, Markku Lonkila, and Matti Peltonen (Helsinki: Finnish Literature Society, 2004), 17–40; Rebecca Scott, "Microhistory set in motion: a 19th-century Atlantic creole itinerary," in *Empirical Futures: Anthropologists and Historians Engage the Work of Sidney W. Mintz*, eds. George Baca et al. (Chapel Hill: University of North Carolina Press, 2009), 84–111.
7 Rudolph Vecoli, "Introduction," in *A Century of European Migrations, 1830–1930*, eds. Rudolph Vecoli and Suzanne Sinke (Urbana: University of Illinois Press, 1991), 1–18.
8 Clé Lesger, Leo Lucassen and Marlou Schrover, "Is there life outside the migrant network? German immigrants in 19th century Netherlands and the need for a more balanced migration typology," *Annales de démographie historique* 104, No. 2 (2002): 29–50.
9 See e.g. Miranda Sachs, "'A sad and … odious industry': the problem of child begging in late 19th-century Paris," *Journal of the History of Childhood and Youth* 10, No. 2 (2017): 188–205.
10 Pilar Arellano-Ulloa, *Le Champ de luzerne* (Paris: Le Manuscrit, 2010); int. No. 31, 18.08.2016.
11 AD93, 1E66/372, SD, deaths, 1912, No. 138, 6.02.1912; AD93, 1E66/341, SD, mar., 1921, No. 1104, 12.11.1921; FNA, 1977883/71, 14436x34, Ricci.

Chains of migration 85

12 See e.g. CVP SD-Sud, int. François Saverio Tari, 1.09.1901, in AD93, 4U7/995, *Dossier d'instruction* No. 49750, *doc. cit.*
13 FNA, BB/11/2166, 7779x88, Austett; 19770894/217, 4281x38, Caporuscio.
14 Int. No. 71, 25.07.2018; FNA, 19790858/152, 17489x51, Gonzalez.
15 SMDA, 1K1/38–47, Antoine Winckler, 1894–1903; AD93, 1E66/363, SD, deaths, 1903, No. 99, 26.01.1903; FNA, BB/11/1759, 2075x84, Legras, certificate of employment, 4.02.1885, Michel Vinckler (Antoine's son), and draft of a letter from the Minister of Justice to the Préfet de police, 8.07.1885; *JORF,* 23.02.1912, p. 1684, Feisthauer Martin (Antoine's brother-in-law).
16 FNA, BB/11/2561, 5782x91, Schiel; BB/11/4804, 5866x08, Schiel.
17 David Gerber, "Acts of deceiving and withholding in immigrant letters: personal identity and self-presentation in personal correspondence," *Journal of Social History* 39, No. 2 (2005): 315–30.
18 David Gerber, "Epistolary ethics: personal correspondence and the culture of emigration in the 19th century," *Journal of American Ethnic History* 19, No. 4 (2000): 3–23.
19 See APP, CB 92.1, 1905/41, 3.01.1905.
20 See e.g. Laurent Couder, "Les Italiens dans la région parisienne," *Publications de l'École Française de Rome,* No. 94 (1986): 501–46; or Blanc-Chaléard, *Les Italiens dans l'Est parisien.*
21 AVP, V4E3106, 5th arr., 1882, mar., No. 15, 7.01.1882; SDMA, 1F21, census, 1896, vol. II, 171.
22 *Archives commerciales de la France,* 25.06.1882, 862; AVP, D1P4 587, rue Labois-Rouillon 6 [1876]; AVP, V4E7717, 19th arr., 1883, births, No. 3110, 16.07.1882; *Le Petit Parisien,* 22.03.1884; *Le Figaro,* 23.03.1884.
23 SDMA, CT928, No. 1737; AVP, V4E3106, 5th arr., 1882, mar., No. 15, 7.01.1882; *Le Radical,* 13.07.1893; int. No. 5, 15.01.2017; AD14, 2 Mi EC 1000, Bayeux, 1895, births, No. 98, 27.08.1895, Catherine Verrecchia.
24 AD27, 4M29, Orazio Di Meo, 26.10.1884, 14.03.1885, 8.10.1885.
25 ASC Filignano, mar., 1866, 24.09.1866, Di Meo-Di Meo; 1872, births, 20.08.1872, Costanzo Di Meo; 1895, mar., 26.09.1895, Di Meo-Di Meo; AVP, V4E10510, 19th arr., births, 1893, No. 808, 15.03.1893; births, 1899, No. 127, 10.01.1899; SDMA, E309, births, 1900, vol. 2, No. 1149, 2.09.1900, Ernest Verrecchia; E313, births, 1901, vol. 1, No. 883, 10.07.1901, Vincent Di Meo.
26 Fortunata Piselli, *Parentela ed emigrazione. Mutamenti e continuità in una comunità calabrese* (Turin: Einaudi, 1981); Giovanna Campani, "Les réseaux familiaux, villageois et régionaux des immigrés italiens en France" (doctoral diss. in ethnology, University of Nice, 1988).
27 CDP SD-Sud, PV 17.08.1901, int. Angel Vettese, in AD93, 4U7/995, *Dossier d'instruction* No. 49750, *doc. cit.*
28 Int. No. 5, 15.01.2017.
29 Their names were Baltazar Gómez and Hermenegildo Saíz. See AD93, 1E66/264, SD, births, 1909, vol. 2, No. 926, 6.08.1909; 1E66/267, SD, births, 1911, vol. 1, No. 484, 19.04.1911; 1E66/275, SD, births, 1915, vol. 1, No. 555; 1E66/285, SD, births, 1922, vol. 1, No. 457, 26.03.1922. On the date of their arrival in Saint-Denis, see FNA, BB/11/12555, 32558x29; AD92, ENUMLEVN1908, Levallois, 1908, births, No. 422, 2.05.1908.
30 See e.g. AD93, 1E66/324, SD, mar., 1912, vol. 1, No. 202, 11.04.1912.
31 AHP Guipuzkoa, AHPG-GPAH 3/3504/424, Notario Berasategui, San Sebastián, 1822-3, 5.11.1884, Miguel Gárate Uranga, Consejo para contraer matrimonio a su hijo Joaquín; Archivo histórico diocesano de San Sebastián, S. Ignacio de Loyola, 1° M, 8v, No. 23, 25.11.1884, J. J. De Garate y Cipriana (Expósito); S. M. del Coro, 7°B, 187v, Np. 172, Julia Josefa Fausta Garate

Abrusa, 2.10.1885; 8°B, 86r, No. 82, 12.04.1888, José Ygnacio Garate Abrusa; 9° B, 177v, No. 228, 21.12.1890, Maria Nemesia Garate Abrusa; 10° B, p. 151, No. 157, 10.10.1892, Francisco Felisa Garate Abrusa; 11°B, 167r, No. 14, 20.01.1895, Maria Rosa Margarita Garate Abrusa; 13°B, 207r, No. 39, 1.03.1900, Tomás Garate Abrusa.
32 JSD, 24.08.1913; AVP, 14M267, 14th arr., mar., 1920, No. 2120, 19.08.1920; 3M247, 3rd arr., mar., 1922, No. 823, 29.07.1922.
33 AD93, D2M8/91, 1926, vol. 2, 57–9 av. Wilson.
34 AVP, D2U6 198, Remigio Iglesias, Gonzalez, Hocès de la Guardia, 10.01.1918; FNA, Sûreté nationale, "Fonds de Moscou", 19940453/7, No. 794, Cesar Remigo (sic) Iglesias. This man had been in France since 1902, living for years with a French-born woman with whom he had two children (see also SDMA, E358, No. 116, 31.01.1909; E369, No. 982, 6.08.1911; SDMA, 4H33, Aug. 1914, view No. 9; AD93, 1E66/334, SD, mar., 1918, No. 173, 2.04.1918).
35 Int. No. 51, 31.10.2016.
36 Humbert Nelli, "The Italian padrone system in the United States," *Labor History* 2 (1964): 153–67; John Zucchi, *The Little Slaves of the Harp: Italian Child Street Musicians in 19th-Century Paris, London and New York* (Montreal: McGill-Queen's University Press, 1992); Zeese Papanikolas, "To a Greek bootblack," *Journal of the Hellenic Diaspora* 20, No. 1 (1994): 65–85; James Flannery, *The Glass House Boys of Pittsburgh: Law, Technology, and Child Labor* (Pittsburgh: University of Pittsburgh Press, 2009).
37 Colin Heywood, "The market for child labour in 19th-century France," *History* 66, No. 216 (1981), 34–49; Marjatta Rahikainen, *Centuries of Child Labour: European Experiences from the Seventeenth to the 20th Century* (Aldershot: Ashgate, 2004).
38 FNA, F22/505, "Rapport sur le travail dans les verreries présenté par la Chambre syndicale de la Verrerie," no date.
39 Éric Vial, "Les Italiens en France," *Historiens et Géographes*, No. 383 (2003), 254.
40 See AVP, D1U6 219, 5.11.1884, No. 6088; D1U6 316, 19.11.1888, No. 5415; D1U6 373, 19.11.1890, No. 5397; FNA, F/22/505, F/22/452, BB/18/6111 (23BL164).
41 Mario Enrico Ferrari, "I mercanti di fanciulli nelle campagne e la tratta dei minori, una realtà sociale dell'Italia fra '800 e '900," *Movimento operaio e socialista* 6, No. 1 (1983), 87–108; Patrick Heiz, "Émigration et travail des enfants," in *La Traduction-migration. Déplacements et transferts culturels Italie-France*, ed. Jean-Charles Vegliante (Paris: L'Harmattan, 2000), 61–95.
42 AS Isernia, trib. Isernia II, b. 223, fasc. 19, Forte Nicandro, 6.03.1893; CDP SD-Sud, int. Nicandro Forte, 16.08.1901, in AD93, 4U7/995, *Dossier d'instruction* No. 49750, 27.08.1901.
43 AS Frosinone, b. 573, Letter from the *Delegato di Pubblicato Sicurezza* of Arce to the *Sottoprefetto* of Sora, 8.06.1895.
44 *L'Aurore*, 24.07.1898; AD93, 4U7/959; 961; 963; 966, CDP SD-Sud, PV 7.05.1897, 27.06.1897, 26.10.1897-19.11.1897 (25 times).
45 *Le Radical, Le Matin*, 25.07.1898, *Le Petit Parisien*, 28.07.1898, *La Lanterne*, 29.07.1898, 1.08.1898; *La Stampa*, 4.08.1898, 23.08.1898; *El Imparcial*, 27.07.1898; *The Portland Daily Press*, 13.09.1898, *The Washington Times*, 9.10.1898, *The Standard Union*, 19.11.1898.
46 See Raniero Paulucci di Calboli, *Parigi 1898. Con Zola, per Dreyfus. Diario di un diplomatico*, ed. Giovanni Tassani (Bologna: CLUEB, 1998 [1898]), 95–9, 105; Ugo Cafiero, "I fanciulli italiani nelle vetrerie francesi. Relazione preliminare del Comitato piemontese. Inchiesta fatta nei circondari di Sora e di

Isernia," in *Opera di assistenza degli Operai Italiani emigrati in Europa e nel Levante, Bollettino bimensile edito dal Consiglio centrale* 1, No. 2 (1901), 1–22; Ferrari, "I mercanti di fanciulli," 103; Luigi Einaudi and Giuseppe Prato, "La liberazione di ottanta piccoli martiri, una santa crociata nelle vetrerie francesi," *La Riforma Sociale* 11 (1901), 1101–13; *Le Matin,* 3.08.1898; AVP, D1U6 5661, 1898, No. 15944, 16.08.1898. The former queen of Naples was Maria Sofia von Wittelsbach, in exile in Neuilly-sur-Seine.
47 Olimpia De Gaspari, *Il racconto del piccolo vetraio* (Turin: Paravia, 1903); Giorgio Capitani, *Il piccolo vetraio* (film, 1955).
48 *Le Matin,* 2.07.1901; FNA, F/22/452, Report by M. Drancourt, 25.07.1901; AD93, 4U7/995, *Dossier d'instruction* No. 49750, *doc. cit.*
49 *JORF Lois et décrets, partie non officielle,* 30.08.1902, 5910.
50 He made the required declaration at the Préfecture on 29.01.1901 (see reference in following footnote).
51 APP, CB. 92.2, 1907/1310, 23.11.1907. Giacinto was apparently prosecuted that second time, but escaped conviction: see allusion in Ministère du Travail, *Rapports sur l'application des lois réglementant le travail en 1907* (Paris: Imprimerie nationale, 1908), 4.
52 To see through the entire imbroglio, see CDP SD-Sud, PV by M. Drancourt, 14.08.1901 about Louis and Ferdinando Pirolli in AD93, 4U7/995, No. 49750, *doc. cit.*; FNA, BB/11/13146, 16273x30; Declaration of Intention in order to request US citizenship, Ferdinando Pirolli, 16.09.1907 (accessible on www.atlanticlibrary.org). Ferdinando and Augusto were the children of Antonio Pirolli, who had migrated to the US with Giacinto in 1890. In Legras's registers, they were supposed to have left the factory on May, 26, 1901, although Ferdinando was supposed to have started on June 13 of that same year (see CDP SD-Sud, Verrerie Legras, 19.08.1901, in AD93, 4U7/995, *doc. cit.*).
53 FNA, BB/11/13146, 16273x30.
54 SDMA, 1F24, census, 1901, vol. II, 103–6.
55 Two distant clues supporting this hypothesis are to be found in FNA, BB/11/10553, 41906x27, Letter from Luigi Pirolli to the Préfet de police, 18.02.1927, in which Luigi wrote "I have lived in France since October 1901," and to a mysterious passport lost in Turin train station in early July 1901, bearing the name Pirollo (*La Stampa,* 6.07.1901, "Oggetti trovati e consegnati alle guardie municipali").
56 AD93, 4U7/952, 985, 992, 993, 1002, 1021 (1896–1905).
57 Int. No. 76, 17.03.2021.
58 "Décision du 28 mars 1901," *Bulletin de l'Inspection du travail* 9 (1901), 102.
59 AVP, D2U6168, PP, Report by M. Girardier, 27.12.1909.
60 AVP, D3U6 94, Santol, 29.03.1905.
61 AVP, D2U6 168, 26.10.1910; D3U6 94, *doc. cit.*; D3U6 175; APP, CB 92.3, 1907/689, 3.06.1907; AVP, D1U6 972, 13.08.1907, and D3U9 252, 31.01.1908.
62 See Report by M. Girardier, *doc. cit.*, and testimonies of Étienne Bertrand in AVP D2U6 168, *doc. cit.*, and of Louis Poullain in AVP, D3U6 111, *doc. cit.*
63 Sommi-Picenardi, "La tratta," 465.
64 Ministère du Travail, *Rapports sur l'application des lois réglementant le travail en 1913* (Paris: Imprimerie nationale, 1920), XXVI.
65 Patrick Gervaise, "Les Passages à Levallois-Perret. Quartier populaire, quartier de la 'Zone' (1826–1972)" (doctoral diss. in history, University of Paris VII, 1986).
66 Freeman, *Pasiegos.*
67 In addition to 96–100 av. de Paris in Saint-Denis, their successive addresses were 6 and 30 rue d'Alsace, 28 rue Deguingand, 38 rue Chaptal in Levallois, 8 rue

Chardanne and 25 rue de la Villette in Pré-Saint-Gervais, 64 and 71 rue de l'Union in Aubervilliers, 17 cité de la Moskova in Paris.
68 One biscuit (*plaisir* ou *oublie*) sold for around 0.1 franc in 1907 (*Le Journal des confiseurs et pâtissiers*, May 1907, p. 145–7). Spanish children who started in glass factories in 1908–9 were making between 2 and 2.5 francs a day (see Report by M. Girardier, *doc. cit.*).
69 See the widely circulated article by Léon and Maurice Bonneff in *L'Humanité*, 22.11.1912 (remarkably, it got translated in extenso in the *Diario de Burgos* of 29.11.1912).
70 AD42, 3E131, Saint-Étienne, 1910, mar., No. 978, 5.09.1910, Varona-Lopez; 2E152, Saint-Étienne, 1911, births, No. 2262, 3.10.1911; 1F36, Saint-Étienne, 1911 census, rue Beaubrun 39.
71 AVP D1U6 1188, TC Seine, 29.01.1913, 5.02.1913, Alonso, Ruiz, Varona, Lopez, Sainz, Lazo; D3U9 327, CA Paris, 29.05.1914; Cass., 23.10.1914 (attached to appelate ruling); *Gil Blas*, 27.09.1912; *Les Temps nouveaux*, 5.10.1912; *La Liberté*, 2.11.1912, 9.11.1912; *L'Émancipation*, 23.11.1912; *JSD*, 21.11.1912, 26.01.1913; *La Voix des verriers*, 20.01.1913.
72 Fabrice Langrognet, "Exploitation or public service? The import-export trade of underage glassmakers in Saint-Denis, France (1892–1914)," *Journal of the History of Childhood and Youth* 15, No. 1 (2022): 112–30.
73 Cafiero, "I fanciulli," 14.
74 APP, CB 82.3 (Aubervilliers), 1898/856, 19.08.1898.
75 *L'Humanité*, 23.11.1912; AGA, 54/5.933, *Contencioso* (I), 2a parte, No. 3, "*Explotación de la Infancia, asunto llamado 'Padrones'*," Letter from the General Consul of Spain to the Spanish ambassador to France, 4.05.1912.
76 Int. No. 63, 21.07.2017. The interviewee was the great-niece of Antonio Cacciarella, brought to France and the tenement at No. 100 av. de Paris in September 1900 by the *padrone* Bernardo Greco.
77 Varona went to a glasswork town in Normandy with almost three times as many children as before, while two of his fellow convicts offered their services in Corbeil, south of the capital. See AGA, 54/5.933, *Contencioso* (I), *doc. cit.*, Letter from the General Consul of Spain to the Spanish ambassador to France, 5.11.1913, and letter from Émile Tombarel to the Spanish ambassador to France, 6.05.1914; FNA, BB/11/8431, 26780x24, Ruiz.
78 *La Cruz*, 8.03.1929 (Baltasar Gómez Fernández).
79 APP, CB 92.21,1924/1282, 11.09.1924; *La Lanterne*, 11.06.1903; AD93, 4U7/1010, CDP SD-Sud, 28.03.1904, Carlesimo; JSD, 3.05.1906; FNA, BB/11/3806, 4647x00, Carlesimo; AVP D2U6 168, Report by M. Girardier, *doc. cit.*, 27.12.1909.
80 Fabrice Langrognet, "Interethnic resentment or mundane grudges? A 1900 Paris fight under the microscope," *Immigrants and Minorities. Historical Studies in Ethnicity, Migration and Diaspora* 37, Nos. 1–2 (2019): 24–43.
81 CDP SD-Sud, PV 16.08.1901, int. Jean Greco, in AD93, 4U7/995, *Dossier d'instruction* No. 49750, *doc. cit.*
82 AD93, 4U7/593, 18.10.1901, Di Benedetto c. Ranaldi.
83 AVP, D3U9 327, CA Paris, 29.05.1914.
84 Lee Shai Weissbach, *Child Labor Reform in 19th-Century France: Assuring the Future Harvest* (Baton Rouge: Louisiana State University Press, 1989).
85 Quoted by Luigi Einaudi in *La Stampa*, 26.05.1901 (my trans.).
86 Sommi-Picenardi, "La tratta," 468–9.
87 *JORF Débats parlementaires, Chambre des députés*, 10.02.1914, 653–4. In Spain, strict regulations on emigration had also been passed in the early 1870s (*Real ordenes*, 5.07.1872, 30.01.1873, 8.08.1874, 21.08.1874), and were immediately

tightened against *padrones* once the scandal of Saint-Denis broke out (*Real orden,* 18.11.1912).
88 *Le Matin,* 28.05.1901.
89 See AD93, 4U7/995, *doc. cit.,* int. Angela Reale née Quaglieri, 16.08.1901; Sommi-Picenardi, "La tratta," 475–7; *La Liberté,* 9.11.1912. Legras also offered free travel to the Plaine to any boy willing to come on his own and who committed to six months of service (APP, CB 92.12 [unbound, in CB 92.27], 746, 5.10.1915).
90 When facing a new inspector or police officer, the director would falsely claim that he had never been prosecuted nor brought to trial before (see e.g. AD93, 4U7/1002, CDP SD-Sud, 22.10.1902). For him knowingly changing a date of birth, see FNA, F/22/452, Letter from the Préfet de police to the Minister of the Industry, 13.09.1901.
91 Compare e.g. AD93, 4U7/985, CDP SD-Sud, int. Roques, head of personnel at Legras, 8.08.1900, and AD93, 4U7/995, *doc. cit.*
92 FNA, F22/452, Letter from M. Lavoisier, inspector, to the Mayor of Saint-Denis, 29.03.1915, about Mazario Peña (100 av. de Paris). See also Trib. de simple police de SD, 8.01.1913, in *Bulletin de l'Inspection du travail* 21 (1913), 51.
93 Serge Chassagne, "Le travail des enfants aux XVIIIe et XIXe siècles," in *Histoire de l'enfance en Occident,* eds. Egli Becchi and Dominique Julia (Paris: Seuil, 1998), 224–72. Also M. Martin, "Note sur les machines automatiques à cueillir et à souffler le verre à bouteilles," *Bulletin de l'Inspection du travail* 20 (1912): 507–10.
94 Beatrice Berio, "I ragazzi italiani nelle vetrerie del Lionese," *Rivista coloniale,* 1913, 16-28.02.1913: 124–7. Paulucci di Calboli was convinced that Vozza was protected by Legras (Paulucci, *Parigi 1898,* 96).
95 *JORF Débats parlementaires, Chambre des députés,* 10.02.1914, 653–4.
96 The factory extended its own boarding house to gain more independence from intermediaries (AD93, 4U7/525, 28.02.1896, Beulaigne c. Legras et Cie; APP, CB 92.12 [unbound, in CB 92.27], 746, 5.10.1915). It also placed frequent advertising in the press for potential apprentices (e.g. *JSD,* 5.06.1913; 27.12.1914; 21.03.1915).
97 *JSD,* 30.03.1890.
98 See in AD93, 4U7/995, *doc. cit.,* int. Dominique Ranaldi.
99 Heiz, "Émigration et travail des enfants," 85–93. Paulucci di Calboli reported, however, that a convoy of young girls had been brought to Lyon from Casalvieri to work in glassworks (Raniero Paulucci di Calboli, "La traite des petits Italiens en France," *La Revue des Revues,* 1897, 01.07.1897, 402).
100 Caterina Assunta Covelli, born in Songavazzo, Italy, on 10.05.1893, was employed at Legras in the spring of 1901 (SDMA, 1F24, 1901 census, vol. 2, 100 av. de Paris). For other cases, see 10-year-olds Florentine Fixari (SDMA, 1F19, 1891 census, vol. 2, 102 av. de Paris) and Marie Stéphanie Picard (SDMA, 1F21, 1896 census, vol. 2, 98–100 av. de Paris; AD93, 1E66/152, SD, births, 1885, No. 1097).
101 Int. 51, 31.10.2016.
102 François Fagnot, *Rapport sur le travail de nuit des enfants dans les usines à feu continu* (Paris: Alcan, 1908), 39.
103 Caroline Moriceau, "L'hygiène à la Cristallerie de Baccarat dans la seconde moitié du XIXe siècle. La santé ouvrière au cœur de la gouvernance industrielle," *Le Mouvement Social* 213, No. 4 (2005), 35–6. Note that in other glass factories, young girls had been observed working in the fusion halls: see Delzant, "Le travail de l'enfance," 96.

104 SDMA, CT768, "Accidents de travail, avril 1902," declaration form, 2.04.1902, Cristina Pirolli.
105 AD93, 4U7/460, 16.01.1885, Offner c. Sprisser.
106 *JSD,* 5.11.1916.
107 APP, CB 92.2, 1905/1020, 13.10.1905; CB 92.10, 1913/892, 27.09.1913; *JSD,* 12.01.1896, 4.07.1909.
108 APP, CB 92.10, 1913/1022, 22.11.1913.

Part II
Interactions and allegiances

5 Positive relationships

Saturday, May 27, 1899, in the early morning. The skies were cloudy above the smoking factories of the Plaine-Saint-Denis, the temperature unusually cold. Through the heavy wooden door of No. 96 Avenue de Paris appeared a dark-haired young man in his Sunday clothes. His name was Victor Spreisser and he was a glassworker at Legras. Born in German Lorraine, Victor had grown up in the Paris area for as long as he could remember. That morning, instead of going across to the factory for the morning shift, Victor turned right, and started walking up the Avenue towards the centre of Saint-Denis. He was accompanied by both of his parents and probably a few others. They did not want to be late; at 11:30, Victor was due to get married. The bride's name was Rosalie. She was a 19-year-old girl from the Massif Central living in Nogent-sur-Marne, an eastern suburb of Paris.[1]

Records of unions such as Victor and Rosalie's contain important information. Historians, sociologists, anthropologists and demographers have long been accustomed to studying marriages and similar social institutions. Among other benefits, these snapshots of people's lives yield precious data to assess the prevalence and enforcement of ethnonational, religious and class boundaries. In migration studies, civil and religious unions provide clues about the intensity of first- and second-generation immigrants' ethnic ties and their integration into society.[2] Among the crucial components of this type of analysis are the proportion and characteristics of so-called "mixed marriages." The problem is that identifying an intergroup marriage – or friendship – from public documents is a "messy business."[3] In the context of constructivism, scholars have indeed started to realise that the word "mixed" presupposes a clear and rigid positioning of the groups' contours.[4] A difference in nationalities, in particular, appears far from sufficient to assess the degree of actual intergroup crossing involved; although *nominally* mixed, such relationships are not necessarily *experientially* mixed.[5]

And yet to this day, there have been few practical solutions to overcome that quandary and come up with a less biased approach to mixedness. This chapter offers one such solution by looking at a non-ethnicised metric: the geodesic distance between people's towns of birth.[6] This approach relies on an exhaustive research into all Saint-Denis birth, marriage and death

DOI: 10.4324/9781003017820-5

registers from 1882 through 1931; there, I looked for all existing traces of tenants at Nos. 96–102. As will appear in this chapter, the distance-based method is meant to allow clusters of endogamy and "endophilia"[7] to stand out from the data, with a view to then assess degrees of ethnicisation by origin. This mixed-method effort differs from traditional social network analysis; its aim is not to map all social ties to understand the shape of people's networks – the tenement block was never a finite community.[8] Rather, it is focused on understanding the tenants' patterns of preference over time. This evaluation is then refined, in the chapter's second part, through a qualitative look at other grounds of solidarity and affinity between the tenements' inhabitants and their peers. The point is not so much to depict the mentality of residents as a group à la Richard Hoggart, but rather to determine what could bind tenants together.[9]

The analysis of marriage data

In the five decades of Saint-Denis civil registers, I found 282 weddings where at least one spouse was currently residing at Nos. 96–102, 615 declarations of births into families living there and 462 declarations of tenants' deaths. In marriage records, the spouses' towns of birth were always mentioned. With those in hand, I was able to obtain the geographical coordinates of their approximate centre points.[10] Then, I calculated the distance between the spouses' towns of birth, using the classic trigonometric formula for a geodesic on a sphere.[11]

From such a measurement I can at once derive, first, general statistics. The median distance over 50 years stands at 143.9 kilometres. A third of the marriages happened between spouses whose localities of birth were less than 50 kilometres apart, and a similar proportion concerns distances over 300 kilometres. Overall, the distance seems to have increased after the First World War. To explain this trend, a major role seems to be played by the marriages in which spouses had a large "origin differential" – which is the term I will be using here to refer to the geodesic distance between their towns of birth. This is shown in Figure 5.1.

This gradual increase in the interwar period does not necessarily indicate that people looked more often across their group's boundaries. It could instead be related to the presence of a second generation, born in the Paris area or another immigration destination, who would have married people from their parents' region of birth. However, this hypothesis does not withstand further scrutiny. A fine-grained analysis of the long-distance marriages in question shows that this situation is too uncommon in the data to carry any statistical weight. In fact, the major overall increase in origin differential seems to have occurred earlier in the period. In the 12-year period from 1900 to 1911, the median distance was even higher than in the 1920s. It was only at the very beginning of the period, in the late 19th century, that the distances between spouses' towns of birth were the shortest.

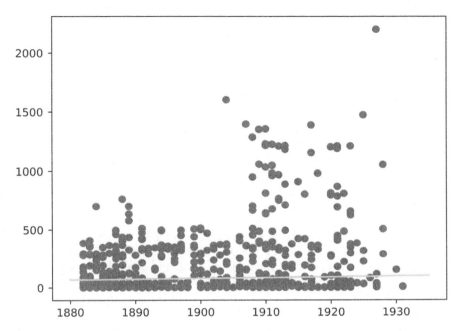

Figure 5.1 Origin differential between spouses in marriages featuring at least one tenant (in kilometres), 1882–1931.

Reasons for these evolutions must have had to do, in part, with an increasing diversity of origins in the Plaine-Saint-Denis. People tended to find their spouse in the vicinity – a mere 150 meters away, in fact. Unfortunately, there is no readily available benchmark of the Plaine's diversity in terms of origin for that period. This absence of a control baseline is a major limitation of my data. However, I can produce the next best thing: an assessment of the diversity in the tenement itself, since I have ascertained a large part of the tenants' exact place of birth across decades. Although partial, the resulting baseline of diversity is more representative of the potential pool of grooms and brides than it seems. This is because 45% of all marriages in the database happened between two occupants of the tenement.

From that evaluation of the tenant population's geographic origins, two moments of growing diversity emerge: one in the 1890s and another, at a slightly lesser pace, in the 1910s. The next step is to look at the actual distances between spouses' towns of birth when both were living in the tenement and compare them with these diversity trends. The result of that comparison is that the increase in origin differential generally matches the increase in diversity of the tenement population. There is one clear exception, however: a continuous decline of the origin differential from 1900 to the early 1910s (meaning that spouses came from origins that were closer to

96 *Interactions and allegiances*

one another) stands in contrast to the growth of the residents' diversity at that period. We will have to account for this discrepancy.

Clusters of endogamy

Now let us look at marriage patterns by origin. Instead of predetermining relevant origin groups, I ranked the origins with the highest rates of geographic endogamy (Table 5.1).

This table hints at broad geographic clusters which we can then use to analyse the data according to the tenants' origin. If we first select tenants who were born in Moselle, Meurthe, Vosges and Bas-Rhin, the median origin differential at their weddings over the half-century was 90 kilometres. Beyond the mere demographic effect of the sizeable population from these eastern regions present in the Plaine-Saint-Denis, this figure suggests a visible propensity to marry people from the same region.

Such a trend is even clearer for tenants hailing from the Sora-Cassino area, shared at the time between the provinces of Caserta and Campobasso in southern Italy. Over 80% of them married someone born in the same area; in their case, the median distance was only 21.5 kilometres. Accounting for almost a quarter of marriages in the 1901–1910 decade, these tenants' endogamy explains the overall decline in origin differential observed at that period, and therefore the aforementioned discrepancy between this diminution and a higher demographic diversity. If anything, this data suggests that people from southern Italy – present in the tenement from 1898 onwards – married among themselves for quite some time. None of their marriages in Saint-Denis took place with fellow nationals from other regions of the peninsula. Despite their smaller numbers, these compatriots were present in the neighbourhood and even in the tenement.

It should be noted, however, that despite its small radius, this regional endogamy among southern Italians had a larger perimeter in the Plaine-

Table 5.1 Districts of birth for which the median distance between spouses' towns of birth was less than 100 kilometres (marriages featuring at least one tenant)

Spouse's district of birth	Median distance between spouses' towns of birth (kilometres)
Burgos (Spain)	4.50
Campobasso (Italy)	15.27
Caserta (Italy)	20.90
Santander (Spain)	36.54
Moselle (France/Germany)	41.36
Meurthe (France/Germany)	62.17
Oise (France)	68.07
Vosges (France)	77.09
Bas-Rhin (France/Germany)	89.99

Saint-Denis than in the homeland. In other words, their "native region" only took hold as a relevant geometry of affinity in the society of immigration (this was not true to the same extent for Alsatians and Lorrainers). This becomes clear when considering a few dozen marriages of tenement residents that were celebrated back in Italy either before, during or after their sojourn in the *cités*; the overwhelming majority of those unions happened between people of the exact same village.[12] This expansion of regional solidarity among immigration populations has generally been overlooked by scholars who, because of their focus on the emergence of national identifications, have tended to take regional affinities for granted.[13]

The picture looks strikingly different for residents born in Spain. No matter their area of origin, almost all of the spouses who did not come from the same location – which was the norm back home – came from other Spanish provinces. Tenants from Extremadura did not appear in the most endogamous regions in the table above for a reason. Not only did they disproportionately marry outside of their area of origin, but when they did, close to 90% of those exogamous unions happened with people from other regions of Spain.[14] The inference here is that for Spanish residents, cross-provincial marriages were clearly preferred to unions with non-Spaniards. This indicates a greater relevance of national ties than for their southern Italian counterparts.

No other area stands out with significant geographic endogamy in our data; in some cases, the size of the sample (e.g. of Bretons) was too limited to reveal endogamy which we know as probable from other sources.[15] In others, it could be the opposite. This is the case of the Oise district, which stood out in the table as one of the areas with the lowest origin differentials. One should not read too much into that ranking, however; it derives only from five marriages, of which three feature one spouse born in Oise and the other in the Paris area – thus explaining the short distances. In any event, the Plaine's limited size of cohorts from certain origins, whose members had no real pool of "countrymen" to tap into, certainly accounts for part of the more open patterns of spouse selection.

Friendships

Aside from marriages, another set of micro-quantitative data is available to measure the importance of origin in people's affinities. At weddings, at declarations of birth and declarations of death, witnesses had to be present.[16] When returning to our corpus, the first unsurprising lesson is that the social network that mattered most to inhabitants of the tenement block was their family. Over 45% of witnesses to the tenants' weddings were family members, and there was no visible discrepancy between the spouses' genders.[17] This rate appears quite remarkable in light of the almost all-migrant demography of the Plaine. This demography, in principle, provided the tenement's occupants with fewer immediately available relatives than in their

98 *Interactions and allegiances*

localities of origin. This confirms the importance of family migration. While some scholars have argued that the bigger the distance between birthplace and place of marriage, the lower the number of family members among witnesses, my dataset does not point in that direction; coefficients of correlation between those two variables are close to zero for both brides and grooms.[18]

Even when relatives could not be present, marriages reactivated family ties through the formal consents that parents had to sign before a notary or public official in their region of origin. The mandatory character of this procedure – at least for minors, since some adults could be exempted – was a mechanism that must have at once "generated and attenuated" translocal connections.[19] The reason for this is that French and foreign residents alike had to write to their parents to ask for their blessing. They would have had to explain why they were not marrying someone from their village. They would probably also enclose money to cover the expenses of the procedure when it took place before a notary. From the parents' standpoint, this was an opportunity to take stock of their child's life in Paris; and perhaps, to also realise that their children would not come home any time soon.

Attachment to one's relatives could provide a basis, among others, for the tenants' sense of belonging to a particular group bonded by a common origin.[20] But family solidarity *per se* does not say much about these types of identification. Only the shape of networks outside the family can denote the social weight of origin, as well as its relevance within a broader ethnic or national network. Still, at more than a century's distance, it is no easy task to know who exactly the non-relatives were, and which of them would have qualified as friends or acquaintances.

In order to design a method for selecting only those "true" witnesses – at marriages as well as declarations of births and deaths – I was helped by the specific geography of the Plaine-Saint-Denis. The tenement stood miles away from the Saint-Denis city hall. For this very reason, almost all witnesses referred to as "friends" or simply left with an undefined relationship to the tenement resident and whose address was located in the vicinity of city hall can be taken out of the sample; there is very little chance that they had any actual relationship to the resident. As other historians have noticed, bar owners, craftsmen or even municipal and hospital employees were routinely asked to fill in for parties lacking witnesses.[21] The particularity here is that there is an effective way of identifying, by virtue of their address, those 11th-hour witnesses. I could thus take them out of the friends' cohort. Conversely, the distance to city hall travelled by the individuals left in the corpus attests to the existence of something more than a casual bond of solidarity between them and the tenants.

After the filtering operation, the outcome for the entire 1882–1931 period is a base of 835 pairs comprising one tenant at Nos. 96–102 on the one side (either a spouse or an individual declaring a birth or a death), and a non-family, non-last-minute witness on the other. The first striking feature echoes something we had already noted for spouses: non-family witnesses were overwhelmingly chosen among neighbours. The median distance between the addresses of residents and those of their "real witnesses" was a mere 80 meters.[22]

The next step was to determine where the witnesses were born. For 604 of the 835 pairs, I was able to retrieve the towns of origin for both individuals. From there, I could calculate the origin differential based on geodesic distances. That information retrieval proved much more challenging than in the case of marriages since the witnesses' town of birth was never mentioned in marriage, birth and death records. It is only by source-crossing that I could access that key information.

It is important to bear in mind, however, that more than a quarter of our eligible pairs of tenants and witnesses have been left out. As happens with incomplete data, results are therefore not free from distortions, which warrants caution when manipulating the statistics. In particular, it proved significantly less possible to identify the precise birthplace of witnesses who appeared to be Spanish; this is due in part to the homogeneity of Spanish surnames and to a greater scarcity of accessible individual records about Spanish immigrants at that period. As time-consuming as it was, however, retrieving all this information about the witnesses' towns of origin – which, to our knowledge, no scholar has attempted before – was a safer choice than speculating on people's origin according to the sound of their surnames.[23] This would have once again reified ethnicity or nationality on the basis of another unsatisfactory indicator.[24]

Altogether, the origin differential between tenants and their witnesses was under 50 kilometres in 46.1% of the cases and over 300 kilometres in 27.6% of the cases. Compared to the marriage data, this indicates an even stronger preference for people of the same geographic origin when it came to choosing a witness. Interestingly, one does not find a significant discrepancy between genders. While female occupants of the tenement generally had fewer acquaintances, this did not translate into tighter ethnic circles. A closer analysis of the data broadly confirms the chronological trends observed in marriages: a slow growth in diversity interspersed with more rapid increases in origin differential between tenants and their witnesses in the second half of the 1890s, in the late 1900s, and during the Great War (Figure 5.2).

As with spouses, I then identified the areas of highest tenant-witness endophilia. This time, the districts with the lowest origin differentials were Caserta, Bas-Rhin, Meurthe, Cáceres, Campobasso and Burgos. In the case of tenants from Alsace and Lorraine, 57.2% of their witnesses came from localities less than 50 kilometres away from their own. Of those tenants' witnesses who were not from their immediate area of birth, 43% came from other areas of eastern France. In total, more than 80% of those tenants' witnesses can be traced back to eastern regions.

Tenants from the Cassino-Sora area in southern Italy were even more likely to pick their witnesses among fellow regionals. 79% of their witnesses

100 *Interactions and allegiances*

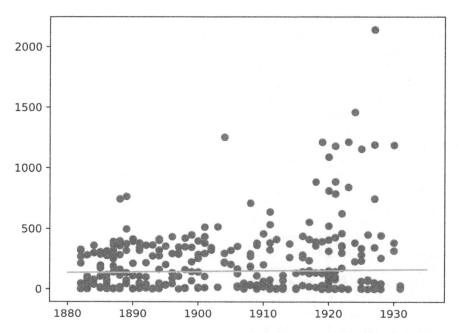

Figure 5.2 Origin differential between tenement residents and their "filtered" witnesses (kilometres) at marriages, birth declarations and death declarations.

came either from the same village or from one less than 50 kilometres away; the proportion even peaked at 96.5% in their first decade of presence in the tenement. But as was the case with marriages, there is almost a clean discontinuity in origin differentials between those inferior to 40 kilometres and those greater than 800 kilometres. In other words, statistics suggest the absence of a preference, when selecting a witness, for fellow nationals from other parts of Italy over French people. In fact, in just one instance did a Southern Italian tenant pick an Italian from another region – a man born in Tuscany. Among the French-born witnesses of Southern Italian residents, we know with certainty that 38% (8 out of 21) were born into families from the Cassino-Sora area. In the end, the overall share of witnesses either first or second generation from the exact same area stands at 85.7% for the Southern Italian cohort.

Trends observed for Spanish-born spouses are also confirmed by the resident-witness data. For natives of the province of Burgos, more than two-thirds of their resident-witness differentials were lower than 50 kilometres. Of witnesses who were not from their immediate region, 8 out of 14 came from other regions of Spain, with the remaining six coming from France and Alsace-Lorraine. As for tenants from Extremadura, the proportion of their witnesses from their area of origin was three times as great as the proportion I had found in the case of their spouses. Yet once again, the most relevant figure in their case is the number of witnesses who were not from their native area but still from Spain: ten out of 17. In short, when Spanish residents of the tenement had to select who would accompany them to city hall and did not pick someone from their micro-area of origin, they displayed a clear preference for their fellow nationals over their other neighbours.

When considered together, statistics on spouses and witnesses in that particular historical context reveal a slow increase in geographic exogamy/ exophilia over the half-century under scrutiny. It also suggests that origin-based solidarity should be considered more relevant for some cohorts of residents – Southern Italians, Alsatians and Lorrainers, Spaniards – whose regional bonds appeared disproportionately stronger than those of their neighbours from other areas. For all these subsets of residents, both geographic endogamy and endophilia seem to have declined over time, especially after the First World War. Nevertheless, they remained a defining factor in their networks' configuration throughout our 50-year period. For Spanish-born tenants, the data suggests that this origin-based dynamic took place at an ethnonational dimension. For others, like Casertans, Molisans, Alsatians and Lorrainers, the relevant geographic referential seems to have extended over a much smaller territory, albeit a larger one than the traditional matching area that prevailed back home.

Aside from these quantitative assessments, sources record a number of areas which brought people together and allowed them to forge bonds that could (but were not bound to) follow ethnic lines. This was especially the case of professional activity, religion and language.

Jobs

Class-based and professional bonds could intersect with networks based on kinship or origin. In certain crafts, like glassworks or foundry, families had alliances that went back decades. In glass factories, only recently had the tradition of reserving apprenticeships to relatives been abandoned. The name and birthplace of Alsatians and Lorrainers could themselves be a valuable currency towards securing a job: despite having no experience in the trade, some tenants probably joined Legras because they bore a well-known name in the business. Still, professional solidarity did not need to go back several generations to be relevant in people's networks. Statistics from the aforementioned tenant-witness analysis show that about a third of residents and their friends who accompanied them to city hall worked in the same profession; surely, these were not all long-time colleagues.[25]

Factory bosses, who generally did not live in the Plaine, belonged to the upper class. In principle, they had no connection to ordinary workers. That is, with the exception of the affair that M. Legras's nephew had with a 19-year-old from No. 98 in the early 1880s; when the two finally married, the Lorrainer mother of the bride remained a tenant at No. 100 but her status probably improved in the eyes of her neighbours.[26] By contrast, foremen and team leaders were far more familiar and accessible characters. In 1897, a Moselle-born tenant at No. 100 asked his Breton foreman at Legras to be the witness at his wedding. In the early 1920s, an Alsatian manager accompanied a Southern Italian glassworker all the way to city hall for the declaration of his newborn son.[27]

As for class conflicts, they were not frequent at Legras and Mouton compared to other factories.[28] For this reason, such struggles were not the same consequential experience as in other places where they would bring immigrants together.[29] Until 1905, the Plaine glassworkers did not have a union of their own.[30] Once it was founded, some women seem to have planned to join, but it is unclear how many actually did.[31] Be that as it may, labour conflicts must have concerned only a small number of tenants at Nos. 96–102.

Beliefs

More than any class consciousness, Catholicism seems to have been one of the binding forces between neighbours. This was particularly true for women, whose practice was more developed according to consistent accounts from descendants.[32] In the complete series of marriages celebrated at the Plaine's church between 1882 and 1925, I found that 49% of civil marriages of residents at 96–102 Av. de Paris were followed by a religious wedding there; and this figure probably omits multiple cases in which the religious celebration took place at another parish. Baptism rates were particularly high: 71.3% of the newborns whose births were declared at city hall by the residents between 1882 and 1902 were baptised at that same church; 76% in 1916; and 77% between 1923 and 1925.[33]

A register of communions celebrated at the parish church from 1901 to 1915 provides evidence that the residents' children attended the youth club of the local parish together, further documenting the diversity of children's networks already alluded to. In May 1904, for instance, girls taking their first communion included at least two No. 100 residents, one from Bergamo, the other born in Saint-Denis. It is true that some children did not wear the white berets of the patronage, but the red ones of a revolutionary youth group active in the early 1910s, of which an employee living for a time at No. 102 was the secretary.[34] But the latter group certainly had much fewer members. Catholicism was the norm in the *cités* – anticlericalism the exception.

Only in rare cases did Italian families try to attend services in their own language. In that respect again, they differed from their Spanish counterparts. In 1916, a Spanish mission opened in Paris, on rue de la Pompe (see Chapter 7). After the First World War, in 1923, a Spanish *patronato* (church club) comprising a chapel, a presbytery and an auditorium was founded in the Plaine, a few hundred meters north of the

Figure 5.3 Real Patronato Español de Santa Teresa de Jesús, Plaine-Saint-Denis, around 1930. Photograph A. Benoit. AD93 ref. 49Fi/6247.

cités. It provided families with services in their own language, which we know some attended (Figure 5.3).[35]

In fact, several tenants had not waited for the *Patronato*'s foundation to attend mass in Castilian. During the war, they regularly visited the Spanish Mission on rue de la Pompe – the church was a long way from the Plaine, even with the newly opened metro station at Porte de la Chapelle.[36] The mission's Spanish chaplain soon received a delegation from the Plaine's priest to administer sacraments to his parishioners. In 1916 and 1917, more than one in ten baptisms celebrated there concerned Plainards, among which a third – six out of 18 – lived either at No. 96 or at No. 100.[37] In that same biennium, Plainards also accounted for 9.5% of the Mission's marriages, including one couple of No. 96 residents.[38] In the following years, more and more people from other neighbourhoods came to the Mission, whereas Plainards turned to the *Patronato*.

Although both Mission and *Patronato* would also cater, here and there, to non-Spanish people such as Catholic Greeks and Portuguese, they reinforced people's identifications as Spanish.[39] On the other hand, this should be put into perspective by recalling the choices made by other families. The Plaine's church always remained more popular with Spanish tenants from Nos. 96–102 than the Mission, based on absolute numbers of sacraments.[40] Even after the opening of the *Patronato*'s chapel, this institution never had a monopoly on Spaniards' religious practice.

Language

The ability to communicate in a common language was critical to building and maintaining bonds of solidarity between "compatriots," as people would say at the time. Language has long been recognised as a key component of ethnic construction, and the Plaine-Saint-Denis was certainly no exception. We know that in the 1890s, some Alsatians in the area could still be heard speaking "German" to each other – in fact, a German-sounding dialect quite different from high German.[41] Most evidence suggests that they would commonly speak French, though – albeit with an accent.

Traces of the accent of tenants from Alsace and Lorraine survives in the way their names and other personal information were spelt in official documents. Censuses, despite the many misspellings due to officials' transcription, reveal alterations that are likely traceable to the direct pronunciation of the residents themselves: "Sommur" for "Sommer," "Kihl" for "Kehl," "Lintz" instead of "Lentz," "Terher" for "Derhée."[42] By contrast, later generations who attended school in Saint-Denis from the 1880s onwards would only speak French and pronounce their names with a distinctively French accent. The last name of Martin Winkler, a Lorraine-born tenant at No. 96 who had attended school in the Plaine, was recorded as "Vaincler" by the gendarmes.[43]

The situation was similar for Italians from the Sora-Cassino area. In the very first years, migrants would speak in Ciociaro dialect,[44] sometimes referred to as "Napolitan."[45] They could not necessarily make themselves understood, even in standard Italian. In 1901, a judge had trouble understanding a resident of No. 100 from the Cassino area, despite the presence of an Italian interpreter.[46] In those years, young Casertans in the *cités* were not fluent in either of the two national languages; rather, they grew up developing their own, mixed combination of French and the dialect of their region of origin. A witness in 1898 described a young Italian child worker from No. 100 as "barely able to speak his dialect."[47] Another first-hand account from 1901 mentions the "polyglot lisp" of one of them.[48] Before being caught, the *padrone** Donato Vozza offered his translation services to fellow glassworkers at the police station; unlike the children under his watch, he already had several years of practice with the French language.[49]

While the dialect remained the language of intimacy for a long time, many first-generation Casertans and Molisans in the tenement seem to have picked up French rather quickly. This does not mean that language barriers could not be feigned when necessary.[50] A perfect command of French became a precious asset for the Italian residents who climbed the ranks of their factory. An Italian-born woman from No. 102 even picked up Spanish from befriending her neighbours.[51] Having arrived at a later stage and in lesser numbers, Spaniards took more time to use French on a daily basis. This simultaneously contributed to, and resulted from, their higher tendency to mingle primarily with other Spanish speakers.[52]

But even when they kept speaking Castilian, their vocabulary denoted the influence of their French environment. One resident at No. 96 from the province of Burgos came to use the expression "*tener galeta*" for having money. This was something he had picked up – according to the story he passed on to his children – from Breton colleagues who were using the familiar form "*avoir de la galette*."[53]

Across the board, the main language disparity was the gender and generational gap, which resulted from a literacy imbalance. Migrant women of the first generation, especially older ones, had a much lower literacy rate than their husbands. Of the 145 people who were not able to sign the marriage registers on the occasion of the residents' weddings over 50 years, more than half were the mothers of one of the two spouses; and over a half of those mothers came from Alsace-Lorraine, Spain and Italy. Based on registers' mentions documenting both the presence of mothers at weddings and their inability to sign, the overall rate of literacy stood at 70.9% for Alsatian and Lorrainer mothers, 63.2% for mothers of spouses from Southern Italy and 55.2% for Spanish mothers.[54] Immigrant women in the tenement seem to have clung to their dialects for a long time, only inserting foreign-sounding words at a slow pace. Of her Casertan-born mother who lived at No. 96, an interviewee said: "My mother could speak neither French nor Italian."[55]

The second generation had an easier time communicating with each other than their parents did. Discontinuous reports in local newspapers of children obtaining their *certificat d'études* (degree) at the end of elementary school – a rather selective feat at the beginning of the 20th century[56] – hint at high rates of proficiency among the children of residents. Archives of the local *Journal de Saint-Denis* reveal that Alsatians and Lorrainers were the first to graduate; young Casertans and Molisans and Spaniards followed suit, in the 1910s and 1920s respectively. This attested to the success of the local school at fostering integration and contacts across social and ethnic lines. The significant proportion of graduates bears witness to the importance placed on schooling by their families which, interestingly, might be the same ones who had sent their children to work in factories. In 1889, Joseph Winckler, a young Lorrainer from a glassworkers' family living at No. 98, was among the first residents that we can identify as graduates. This did not prevent him from working at Legras in his early teens; but by the time he turned 20, he had secured a job as an employee.[57]

This chapter has shown, first, that the geodesic distance between birthplaces can be a useful tool to sidestep predetermined ethnic categories in the approach of mixed relationships. Thanks to the progress in digitisation and genealogical databases, I have been able to retrieve the towns of birth not only of spouses, but also of witnesses, despite the holes in civil registers. This quantitative analysis of both marriages and friendships suggests that when identifications based on origin acquired any salience in people's affinities, local solidarity was generally more operative than a broadly conceived ethnicity. Spaniards were the exception, preferring fellow nationals – after people from the same region, that is. Qualitative sources indicate that those proclivities could be alternatively reinforced or superseded by other forms of solidarity that structured the migrants' daily experiences. At the factory, bonds would be forged between colleagues, though strong ties subsisted for decades between Alsatians and Lorrainers. Going to mass or attending the church's youth club also brought people together across ethnic lines. But Spaniards were soon set apart, as they could follow services in their own religious centre. As for language, it certainly fostered affinities among tenants from the same origin, but its importance soon subsided for the second generation who bonded through schooling and a shared childhood in the Plaine.

All interactions were not so easy and gentle. For tenants at Nos. 96–102 Avenue de Paris, coexisting also meant dealing with hostility and even conflict. This darker side of people's relationships to each other also needs to be analysed to better evaluate the respective parts played, in people's negative representations and actions, by ethnicity and other dynamics of differentiation.

Notes

1 SDMA, E306, SD, mar., 1899, No. 235, 27.05.1899; *Le Journal des débats politiques et littéraires*, 28.05.1899.
2 Richard Alba and Victor Nee, *Remaking the American Mainstream: Assimilation and Contemporary Immigration* (Cambridge: Harvard University Press, 2003).
3 Miri Song, "Is intermarriage a good indicator of integration?," *Journal of Ethnic and Migration Studies* 35, No. 2 (2009), 338.
4 Augustin Barbara, "Mixed marriages: some key questions," *International Migration* 32, No. 4 (1994): 571–86; Emmanuelle Santelli and Beate Collet, "Couples endogames, couples mixtes: options conjugales et parcours de vie de descendants d'immigrés en France," *Migrations Société* 145, No. 1 (2013): 107–20.
5 Liana Grancea et al., *Nationalist Politics and Everyday Ethnicity in a Transylvanian Town* (Princeton: Princeton University Press, 2006), 209–10, 301.
6 For a more detailed presentation of the data, see Fabrice Langrognet, "Geodesic distance as metric of cross-group networks in migration history," *Journal of Migration History* 6 (2020): 405–28.
7 Jan Feld, Nicolás Salamanca, and Daniel Hamermesh, "Endophilia or exophobia: beyond discrimination," *The Economic Journal* 126, No. 594 (2016): 1503–27.
8 Robert Michael Morrissey, "Archives of connection," *Historical Methods: A Journal of Quantitative and Interdisciplinary History* 48, No. 2 (2015): 67–79.
9 Richard Hoggart, *The Uses of Literacy: Aspects of Working-Class Life, with Special References to Publications and Entertainments* (London: Chatto and Windus, 1957).
10 Both sets of coordinates were retrieved (manually) for 289 out of 292 marriages.
11 Δ = ACOS(SIN(latitude1))*SIN(latitude2))+COS(latitude1)*COS(latitude2)*COS (longitude2-longitude1)*6371. This formula is more accurate for shorter distances.

12 28 out of 34. For Alsatians and Lorrainers, the proportion is 15 out of 35.
13 Charles Tilly, "Transplanted networks," in *Immigration Reconsidered: History, Sociology, and Politics*, ed. Virginia Yans-McLaughlin (New York: Oxford University Press, 1990), 79–95; Stefano Luconi, "Becoming Italian in the US: through the lens of life narratives," *MELUS* 29, Nos. 3–4 (2004): 151–64.
14 The figures are 19 unions, of which 16 were exogamous: 14 of those happened with other Spaniards, the other two featured a spouse born in France, in both cases Paris.
15 Page Moch, *The Pariahs*.
16 Legal obligations in that respect were gradually loosened over time. Marriages only required two witnesses instead of four after September 1919, and starting in early 1924, declarations of births and deaths did not require a witness anymore.
17 So far, social historians who have limited themselves to relatives listed as such have expectedly ended up with lower percentages (e.g. a third for Maurice Garden, in "Mariages parisiens à la fin du XIXe siècle: une micro-analyse quantitative," *Annales de démographie historique*, 1998: 111–33).
18 Compare with Claire Lemercier, "Analyse de réseaux et histoire de la famille: une rencontre encore à venir?,"*Annales de démographie historique* 109, No. 1 (2005), 19.
19 Roger Waldinger, *The Cross-Border Connection* (Cambridge: Harvard University Press, 2015), 35.
20 Joseph Ruane and Jennifer Todd, "The roots of intense ethnic conflict may not in fact be ethnic: categories, communities and path dependence," *Archives européenes de sociologie* 45, No. 2 (2004): 209–32.
21 Vincent Gourdon, "Les témoins de mariage civil dans les villes européennes du XIXe siècle: quel intérêt pour l'analyse des réseaux familiaux et sociaux?" *Histoire, économie & société* 27, No. 2 (2008): 61–87.
22 This is in line with Roger Gould's insights: see *Insurgent Identities: Class, Community and Protest in Paris from 1848 to the Commune* (Chicago: University of Chicago Press, 1995), 89–90.
23 Compare with Lillo, "Espagnols en 'banlieue rouge'," 730.
24 See Guy Brunet, Pierre Darlu, and Gianna Zei, eds., *Le Patronyme. Histoire, anthropologie, société* (Paris: CNRS, 2001).
25 This is the case in our data for 32.7% of the 835 pairs. This estimate has some degree of inaccuracy because of the many declared simply as *journaliers.**
26 AD93, 1E66/146, SD, births, 1883, No. 1406, 5.12.1883; AVP, V4E 7652, 18th arr., 1891, mar., No. 1443, 26.09.1891; SDMA, E291, SD, deaths, 1895, No. 1321, 26.12.1895.
27 SDMA, E273, mar., 2.01.1892-31.12.1892, No. 162, 14.05.1892; AD93, 1E66/288, SD, births, 1923, No. 1670, 6.12.1923.
28 At Legras, brief strikes took place in 1890 (see e.g. *La Petite République*, 17.05.1890); from May 10 to 13, 1900 (see the related issues of the *JSD*) and from March 31 to April 11, 1920 (*Le Réveil des verriers*, April 1920; *L'Humanité*, 8.05.1920).
29 Dirk Hoerder, ed., *"Struggle a Hard Battle": Essays on Working-Class Immigrants* (De Kalb: Northern Illinois University Press, 1986).
30 *L'Émancipation*, 18.11.1905; *JSD*, 19.11.1905.
31 SDMA, 30Fi170, handwritten note on "Ouvrières de la verrerie Legras," photographic card, no date.
32 Int. No. 16, 17.04.2016; No. 27, 25.07.2016; No. 39, 4.09.2016.
33 APSD, Sainte-Geneviève de la Plaine.

108 *Interactions and allegiances*

34 See for an incident between the two groups, APP, CB 92.9, 1912/1036, 13.10.1912; also, SDMA, 1F27, 2I, CT533, "Répertoire des associations dionysiennes" [no date, after 1911].
35 See APSD, Spanish *Patronato*, "Registro de comuniones" : Pedro Moreno, Armancia Iglesias.
36 APSD, 25/5, Sainte-Geneviève de la Plaine, mar., 1916, No. 10. All following statistics are drawn from Archivo de la Misión católica española de París (rue de la Pompe), baptisms, No. 1 (1916–1918), 2 (1918–1921), 3 (1922–1925); mar., No. 1 (1916–1918), 2 (1918–1919), 3 (1920–1921), 4 (1922–1924).
37 This figure does not include a baptism whose witnesses were residents at No. 96: Archivo de la Misión católica española de París, baptisms, No. 1, 1916–1918 (Julio), 1916 No. 15, 30.07.1916, Fernanda Montero.
38 That couple actually went twice to rue de la Pompe in 1916, first to baptise their second child in March, and then to get religiously married in April. See Archivo de la Misión católica española de París, mar., No. 1, 1916-1918, No. 9, 24.04.1916; AD93, 1E66/329, SD, mar., 28.06.1914-31.12.1914, No. 447, 18.07.1914, Marcelo López Bola and Gabriela Varona y Varona.
39 APSD, 26/5, Spanish *Patronato*, baptisms, vol. 2, 1931, No. 7, 4.01.1931; baptisms, vol. 2, 1931, No. 8, 8.01.1931.
40 See APSD, 25/5, Sainte-Geneviève de la Plaine, mar., 1916, No. 7; 1920, No. 19, 45, 79, 139, 144; 1922, No. 4, 25, 66; baptisms, 1916, No. 24, 30, 63, 76, 140, 141, 149; 1917, No. 13, 14, 26, 27, 28, 32, 115, 154.
41 AD93, 4U7/522, 12.11.1895, Auger c. Wagner.
42 SDMA, 1F17, 1F19, 1F21, censuses, 1886, 1891, 1896, av. de Paris 96–102. Court documents confirm these variations: AD93, 4U7/457, 7.09.1883, Pfister ("Fister") c. Greiner ("Kreiner"); 4U7/460, 16.01.1885, Offner c. Spreisser ("Sprisser"). In 1893, an Alsatian tenant at No. 100 whose first name would have been spelled Joseph (in French) or Josef (in German), signed a letter to the Justice Ministry spelling his name "Josuff" (FNA, BB/11/2755, 1362x93, Bastian).
43 AD93, 4U7/921, BG Pierrefitte, PV Oswald, 26.05.1892.
44 See Francesco Avolio, *Bommèspre. Profilo linguistico dell'Italia centro-meridionale* (San Severo: Gerni Editore, 1995).
45 Sommi-Picenardi, "La tratta," 466.
46 AD93, 4U7/995, Dossier d'instruction No. 49750, *doc. cit.*, interview Tari, 18.09.1901.
47 Paulucci di Calboli, *Parigi 1898*, 98–9.
48 *Le Matin*, 2.07.1901.
49 *JSD*, 7.04.1898.
50 Compare APP, CB 92.1, 1905/41, 3.01.1905 with AD93, 4U7/1010, PV Carlesimo, 28.03.1904 and AD93, 4U7/657, 14.06.1907, Carlesimo c. Pirolli. Also, APP, CB 92.26, 1930/479, 22.03.1930.
51 Int. No. 54, 4.09.2016.
52 APP, CB 92.7, 1911/1085, 8.11.1911; CB 82.14, 1915/552, 23.08.1915.
53 Int. No. 71, 24.07.2018.
54 These figures include both the mothers of tenants and the mothers of their spouses.
55 Int. No. 18, 21.11.2016 (*"Ma mère ne parlait ni français, ni italien"*). Note that the code-switching and bilingual discourse-marking of the Plaine's Spanish women have been the object of a dissertation in linguistics: David Scott Divita, "Acquisition as becoming: an ethnographic study of multilingual style in la Petite

Espagne" (doctoral diss. in romance languages and literatures, University of California Berkeley, 2010).
56 Patrick Cabanel, *La République du certificat d'études: histoire et anthropologie d'un examen, XIXe–XXe siècles* (Paris: Belin, 2002).
57 *JSD*, 25.07.1889; SDMA, 1F19-1F21, 1891 and 1896 censuses, 98 av. de Paris; 1K1/42, 1898, Winckler Joseph Charles; AD54, 2 Mi-EC 147/R1, Croismare, 1876, births, No.11; SDMA, E326, SD, mar., 1903, No. 436).

6 Confrontations

"*You, macaroni!*" the aggressor shouted before wielding his knife in the air. That morning in 1908, tempers had flared up at Legras over a broken glass bottle. At the receiving end of both blade and racist slur was a 16-year-old Italian tenant of No. 100.[1] The expression itself was not particularly surprising; at the time, *macaroni* was one of the most common derogatory terms against Italians. In the Plaine, however, the insult had been – and would long remain – conspicuous by its absence. This is not a source-related issue; insults of all kinds were otherwise reported and recorded.[2]

This striking deficit of racist slurs is all the more troubling when considering the frequency of physical and verbal altercations. By all measures, the Plaine was a violent place. Organised delinquency was endemic in the area, which was notorious for its gangs of *apaches*.*[3] But the sheer density of the Plaine resulted in countless instances of much more ordinary disputes, brawls and skirmishes. In bars, courtyards and factory halls, people from all walks of life got involved in clashes; the tenants at Nos. 96–102 were no exception. Yet it is hard to tell what exactly fuelled those confrontations and, in particular, which sort of identifications they relied upon or enacted. Was ethnicity a factor? And if so, how did it work?

It is entirely possible that tenants' antagonisms had more to do with origin and ethnicity than their affinities. Social scientists have shown that diversity can be problematic for interpersonal trust.[4] While most conflictual interactions between people from different backgrounds are not experienced as interethnic, a disagreement can become ethnicised over the course of said interaction.[5] But that process is fundamentally contingent on specific moments in time, places and people.[6] This notion is all the more important since a conflict construed as ethnic by the people involved has the ability to produce ethnic groups, even if these groups had no tangible boundaries before. However, when a matter of origin and ethnicity is superseded by other causes in the crystallisation of violence, or it only emerges retrospectively, researchers need to proceed with caution. One should resist the common "coding bias in the ethnic direction" and not necessarily view ethnicity as a decisive factor.[7]

This chapter aims at weighing the relative incidence of various parameters in interethnic confrontations. After exposing the main features of the

DOI: 10.4324/9781003017820-6

tenants' daily antagonisms and their evolution over time, it delves into a particular incident which took place on August 19, 1900. This episode's analysis is a detailed reconstruction of the protagonists' backgrounds, networks and – ultimately – motives to act as they did.

Daily conflicts

One feature that stands out from local newspapers, as well as police and judicial archives, is the rarity of interethnic conflicts. For the most part, people of different ethnicities were not pitted against one another.

Moreover, when antagonists *did* hail from different regions, evidence of ethnically-framed identifications is very slim. Before the First World War, the quasi-absence of racial or ethnic slurs is striking. We can be confident that this silence is not due to any sugar-coating on the part of law enforcement. Throughout the period, they showed no reluctance to transcribe testimonies word for word – frequently using quotation marks and occasionally adding "*sic*" markers to underline slang or vulgar language.[8]

In fact, conflict was much more common among "compatriots." Money issues were pervasive: boarders at No. 96 could steal from their hosts, or leave without paying in full.[9] A plumber who spent three and a half years subletting a room from his cousin at No. 100 was eventually sued by his cousin's widow over an outstanding debt.[10] At other times, it was the tenants who were unable to support themselves financially who sued their children for alimony.[11] Relationships fostered by proximity could also lead to open conflicts. Whether a Spanish lodger at No. 100 actually had an affair with his host's wife or not – she denied it, but he eventually confessed – is unclear. Nevertheless, the woman's husband and son, who caught the lodger in her bed one night, certainly believed it to be the case; they ambushed and murdered the presumed lover. All four were from Extremadura.[12] The prevalence of these in-group and in-house conflicts certainly stems from the overall weight of family and micro-regional regional ties in people's social networks (as described in Chapter 5). The more interaction people have with each other, the more likely they are to engage in conflictual exchanges.

Sharing the same space must have also been at the root of occasional quarrels between neighbours, although sources yield precious little to that effect. In early 1907, a Paris-born cart-driver at No. 96 refused to let his wife spend time with one of her neighbours from Meurthe-et-Moselle. He and his family had only recently settled in the tenement, and the cause of this animus – which ended in gunshots – remains unknown. What conditioned the protagonists' reactions, in that case, was likely concerns over reputation and "morality," rather than origin.[13]

To get on each other's nerves, ethnic prejudices were far from a prerequisite; sociologists have demonstrated this for later periods.[14] After exhaustively sifting through five decades of law enforcement records, I was able to identify 48 episodes in which tenants at Nos. 96–102 were involved in a violent action – mostly physical, but at times only verbal – with someone outside their own family.[15] On the face of it, it seems possible that origin played a part in up to a third of those incidents. In these instances, the tenants and their opponents came from significantly different areas with distinct linguistic traits.

However, there is often little in the sources to support the hypothesis of ethnic attribution. Only in rare cases was an ethnic insult recorded. In 1911, an Italian-born tenant at No. 96 employed at the Mouton wire-drawing factory had an argument with a superior. Although the latter was a French citizen born in Belgium, the Italian called him a "*Prussien.*"[16] Insulting was a performative way of claiming more legitimacy than the other, branding him more or less as an outsider, if not a traitor. The actual origin was secondary, as this case illustrates. But class resentment would not automatically translate into an ethnically-charged rhetoric. In that same year, another manager from the same factory – a tenant of No. 100 from Genoa – was mobbed and beaten on the street by two of his subordinates over firing one of them.[17] "*Salaud, cochon, fumier,*" they shouted, using three common slurs. His Italian roots did not come up.[18] Even after the outbreak of the First World War triggered a flurry of derogatory terms against actual or perceived Germans, the frequency of anti-German abuse remained extremely low in the Plaine compared to other areas (the centre of Saint-Denis being one of them).

When ethnonational categories were in fact weaponised, men were more often at the receiving end than women. Abuse against the latter mostly revolved around their role as mothers and wives. Sexual depravity and dishonesty appear to have been much more prevalent in attacks against women; they were, by contrast, all but absent from tense exchanges between men, except in their attempts to slander one another's wives and daughters.

All in all, the only people that regularly faced racial slurs were North Africans – the Kabyles, in particular. Beginning in 1915, they came to the Plaine – some on a voluntary basis, others forced by military authorities – to supplement the male-depleted workforce in armament factories. Racist labels such as *bicot* and *sidi* flourished in the Plaine.[19] Even if "aggressive racism"[20] against these workers may not have been the dominant attitude in France as a whole, troubling incidents did occur in the area.[21]

It is quite likely, in that context, that the inhabitants of 96–102 Av. de Paris shared a primarily racialised vision of North-African workers. Dozens of them were actually stationed at the end of the rue Proudhon, a mere 500 metres from the *cités*. In October 1919, some of these colonial workers were spotted in the *débit** at No. 96. At that time, the bistro was run by another recently-arrived immigrant from Greece.[22] The decade-old diversity of origins in the *cités* may have made colonial workers comparatively more welcome there than elsewhere. In fact, the tenement's inhabitants must have been quite ambivalent towards the North Africans. French and Spanish men who had served in the colonies may have felt more familiarity with them, but they were also more likely to view them through a racist lens.[23]

There is no hint in the sources that residents would have made connections between physical characteristics and people's origin, despite this idea's popularity in turn-of-the-century intellectual circles. Even complexion was not a readily available criterion to distinguish individuals – at least, until the Great War. A number of tenants who were noted as *basanés* (swarthy) or *colorés* (coloured) were born to French parents in Paris, Lorraine or Nord.[24] In any case, the number of North Africans decreased in the early 1920s, and racial tensions receded.

However, the comparatively fewer number of openly interethnic confrontations does not mean that these encounters were insignificant. They may have revealed identifications and intergroup boundaries that were already there but were otherwise less visible. In order to understand how this worked, we need to reconstruct the motives of interethnic confrontations through a close critical analysis of the sources at our disposal.

A multifaceted clash

Here, one particularly resounding episode involving the tenement's occupants will be our vantage point. It belongs to the minority of instances in which Plainards from different ethnicities were pitted against each other.

Historians have only recently started to pay attention to small-scale incidents, called *faits divers* in French; those were long viewed as "uneventful events."[25] As the focus shifted onto ordinary people in the 1960s and 1970s, however, newspaper anecdotes became a precious historical source. One promising aspect was the referential level of these stories: the snippets of information they carried – albeit often with huge distortions – could help document the living conditions and social interactions of their protagonists, especially if they could be read in combination with other records. But cultural historians also developed an interest in the performative dimension of the *fait divers*; that is, the manner in which these micro-events were selected, recounted and how they came across to their readers.[26]

In the domain of interethnic violence, several major episodes have come under scrutiny, because historians felt the need to "re-write the script."[27] Lesser incidents have rarely attracted a comparable interest.[28] Yet close analysis appears valuable when assessing the ethnic component of a *fait divers*, rather than taking at face value posterior stories ascribing a major role to ethnic, national or racial differences. Competition and resentment between people from different backgrounds should not be systematically interpreted as interethnic strife.

This will become apparent in the case at hand, which dates back to the year 1900. Given the scarcity of first-hand police reports of the incident, it is essentially through newspaper sources that the facts can be known.[29] Despite mistakes and contradictions – a mainstay of the press in that period, we can hold a number of factual elements to be credible.

114 *Interactions and Allegiances*

Figure 6.1 The Avenue de Paris and rue Proudhon, no date. Neurdein postcard (detail). SDMA ref. 2 Fi 3/198 – 57.

The action started at night on Sunday, August 19, 1900. The Avenue de Paris was crowded with people enjoying the annual Fête de la Plaine, with its colourful string of food and entertainment stands. Children had been playing a variety of games in the afternoon; sack races and the greasy pole were among the most popular. At around 9 p.m., a group of young glass-workers, who had just enjoyed a few rides on the merry-go-round, went for drinks at the bar at No. 92, at the corner of rue Proudhon (Figure 6.1). The names of the glassworkers were René Abrioux, Louis Wagner, brothers Jules and Camille Derosier and the Derosiers' brother-in-law Charles Houvion. They were all in their late teens and early twenties.

As they were coming in, they bumped into Pasquale Reale of No. 100. Born in the small Italian town of Arpino in 1877, Pasquale had arrived in the Plaine in either 1897 or 1898, along with his mother and brothers.[30] That Sunday night, he asked Camille Derosier to pay for a drink. Upon his refusal, Pasquale turned to Camille's brother. The result was the same; Jules said he was broke. Pasquale then allegedly replied: "Ah! Is that so? We'll see."[31] He tried searching Jules Derosier's pockets, which led Jules to throw the first punch. Promptly retreating to No. 100, Pasquale returned minutes later with a knife, a gun and a few friends, apparently all Italian immigrants.

In the fight that ensued, Pasquale stabbed Jules Derosier and then Camille, who had tried to help his brother. Jules's friends started to run after Pasquale to avenge their wounded friends. As they did so, a friend of Pasquale's named Raffaele Tari – also from No. 100 – fired gunshots at them, injuring Abrioux in the leg. Pasquale also fired his weapon, injuring Charles Houvion; he then further wounded Charles with a few knife blows to the thigh. Pasquale is said to have gone back once more to his building, returning with even more Italians. After this, a "terrible" second fight occurred. Dozens of gunshots were supposedly heard, bystanders were hit and a newspaper set the number of injured at 22 – a gross overestimation.[32] Pasquale was eventually wounded to the neck (or shoulder) by one of Wagner's gunshots. He, along with Houvion, Abrioux and Jules Derosier, was brought to the hospital. Their injuries were not that serious. Reale, Tari and Wagner were soon released from the hospital and sent to jail. In the following days, tensions remained high at Legras. At least, that is what management thought – they asked the police to keep the factory under surveillance.[33]

Even by the Plaine's standards, this violence was quite extraordinary. What exactly had happened? According to most of the press accounts, this fight was part of a broader pattern of antagonism between French and Italian workers. The words "French" and "Italian" appeared in almost every bold-typed title recounting the event. Political leanings affected each newspaper's interpretation of the interethnic conflict. But that the conflict *was* interethnic was not in doubt. The moderate *Le Journal* connected the fight to other "atrocious scenes" of violence that had occurred in the northern suburbs, but its writers did not elaborate further.[34] Gérault-Richard, a former socialist member of parliament and editor-in-chief of *La Petite République*, took a broader view still; he linked the scuffle to a similar episode in Saint-Étienne. This sort of clash had social causes, he claimed, and the only adequate answer was to promote class solidarity. "Nothing more saddening than this fratricide war between equally destitute, equally unconscious workers." It is understandable that the arrival of more cheaply-paid workers would foster tension, he wrote. But instead of fighting one another, they should unionise and close ranks against the factory owner, who can only welcome such enmity between French and foreign workers.[35]

Others wasted no time in blaming local tensions, with little evidence to support this claim. According to the radical republican outlets *La Justice* and *Le Rappel*, the backdrop of the event was the high *"animosité"* (animosity) between French and Italian workers at the glass factory. The second even claimed that the Italian workers, "armed to the teeth,"[36] had started to wander around in the days leading up to the incident with the obvious intention to stir up conflict. Racism was reported as a potential factor by *La Justice*. It reported that French workers accused Italians of being "humble, cunning, hypocritical" and accepting lower wages from the bosses so that they could eventually replace them.

Conservative papers went further still, not distancing themselves from this racist rhetoric. For *Le Moniteur universel*, which inflated the number of combatants to over 100, Italians who had taken part in the free-for-all were "of course" (*naturellement*) armed with their knives. Motives of resentment between the two communities were many, it wrote, the main one being that "all Italians" were "more or less revolutionary," and would never hesitate to work for low wages. Never mind the absence of logic linking the two arguments; these commonplaces were two mainstays of anti-Italian rhetoric in the 1890s. The conservative local paper, the *Journal de Saint-Denis*, had by far the harshest words. It noted that the Derosiers' hatred for Italians was a very common one, since their race "is the most treacherous in the world."[37] In that particular instance, the paper went on, the French had guns and the "*Macaronis*," their "national blade" (*surin national*). Was one passerby stabbed in the back?[38] Then his assailant had to be Italian, the local paper concluded.

A conflict in which ethnicity was not paramount

From the outset, the story was riddled with issues. Some of its important aspects, likely leaked by the police, were deliberately left aside by newspapers because they did not fit their predetermined narrative. Only two outlets cared to mention, in passing, a personal grudge between the Derosiers and some of their Italian colleagues at the glass factory.

In fact, the core of the matter only emerged a few days later. It was granted limited space in the papers that bothered to follow up. Five days after the fight, the preliminary findings of the investigating judge were reported. The whole drama was not due to a mutual hatred between French and Italian workers. Rather, it could be traced back to the entrenched rancour between two families, the Derosiers and the Taris, "stemming from the rivalry of two young men in love with the same woman."[39]

In fairness, the story of Franco-Italian tensions over wages was far from implausible. Beyond the infamous Aigues-Mortes massacre of 1893, incidents of smaller magnitude between Frenchmen and Italians had been quite widespread in the 1890s.[40] But even distinguished scholars have indulged in views that overplay interethnic conflict,[41] inattentive to the variety of situations highlighted by Michelle Perrot.[42] As previously mentioned, the discontent with the arrival of Italians at Legras in 1896 had dissipated in a matter of days; no particular incident had occurred.[43] And while Italian child workers seem to have endured scoffing and occasional mistreatment at the hands of senior workers in subsequent years, this condition was not specific to Italian children – it rather affected young apprentices in general.[44] By 1900, the substantial number of Casertan and Molisan workers at the glass factory, and their non-threatening position in a context of full employment, would have helped prevent anti-Italian hostility. It was not until the first layoffs caused by the Great Depression that sources bear traces of a reactivation, at the individual level, of such tensions among the Plaine's glassworkers.

At the same time, differences in origin could reinforce other conflicts, adding fuel to the fire. A few months before the fight at the Fête de la Plaine, a similar episode – albeit of lesser proportions – had taken place at the glassworks and was settled with knives. It apparently started with an argument between two glassworkers, Dominique Pirolli (unrelated to Luigi and his family) and one of his colleagues, Pierre Feisthauer. The confrontation degenerated when Feisthauer and his friends threw bricks at Dominique and other Italians from an upper window of the factory.[45] The motive of this personal dispute is unclear, and little can be retrieved about those Pirollis, who had been in the Plaine for only a few months.

As for Feisthauer, born in German Lorraine to a family of glassmakers who had migrated to Saint-Denis shortly after his birth, he was known to be a dangerous individual.[46] A few years earlier, he and a few friends had assaulted and seriously wounded a fellow glassworker of French origin.[47] By 1900, the Feisthauers had long been associated with trouble in the Plaine-Saint-Denis. One of Pierre Feisthauer's brothers had taken part in a fight that left one worker dead in a nearby banlieue.[48] A cousin of his had stabbed a man eight times in a bar and was involved in organised crime.[49] A brother of that cousin had been taking part in night robberies as early as the mid-1880s.[50]

Proven hoodlums like the Feisthauers displayed an over-sensitivity that could rapidly trigger violence against people from very different backgrounds. Although racism may not have been entirely irrelevant, we would be at a loss to try and identify a consistent pattern of fight-picking in relation to the origin of their adversaries. In general, the family was not hostile towards Italians. At least one of Pierre's uncles, who also worked at Legras, had taken part in the Second Italian War of Independence, alongside Italian troops.[51]

As for feuds based on romantic or sexual rivalries, the motive fuelling the aforementioned antagonism between the Derosiers and the Taris was not unprecedented in the Paris area. Moreover, there could escalate into broader hostilities that had some sort of ethnic component to them.[52] Years later, the xenophobia directed at North-African and Indochinese workers who had arrived during the First World War would also have sexual underpinnings.[53] Furthermore, while Raffaele Tari and one of the Derosier brothers (probably Camille, since both were almost the same age) may initially have been motivated by their rivalry over the same girl, the Southern Italians who joined the battle may have fought the Derosiers under the impulse of a broader, ethnic solidarity.

Yet in none of the accounts, even those reconstructing the dialogue between the main antagonists, were ethnic and racialised insults to be found. Certainly, the conservative newspapers would have printed them, had there been the merest hint of one.[54] In fact, it seems that an ethnically-framed resentment, if there indeed was one, may not have been among the most relevant causes or consequences of the 1900 battle. Personal grudges seem to have been much more relevant. The young male protagonists belonged to rival street groups, and they had a history of personal violence between them.

Violent youths with scores to settle

The Derosiers were a typical, migrating glass-making family from eastern France. The two brothers had been born in Portieux, Vosges, and Bar-sur-

Seine, Aube, respectively. Their parents had married in Passavant, Haute-Saône. And after a brief first stint in Saint-Denis, the family had lived for a while in Vannes-le-Châtel, Meurthe-et-Moselle, in the mid-1890s. All of these towns had a glass factory. Both Louis Julien Derosier, who went by the first name "Jules," and his younger brother Auguste, known as "Camille," had begun engaging in violence, robberies and alcoholism at a young age.[55]

After the 1900 incident, Camille would be convicted multiple times for theft and violence and spent years going in and out of jail. He was eventually sentenced to life imprisonment in Guyana for rape in 1921.[56] Interestingly, indirect evidence indicates that Camille was friends with a boy in the 1890s whose father was an Italian shoemaker in the Plaine; a clue that would run counter to the stories of his deep-rooted racism against Italians.[57] Another Derosier brother, Léon, would join the same gang as an Italian worker.[58] He would later be on friendly terms with a soldier born to parents from central Italy.[59]

Before the 1900 fight, the Abrioux had also been involved in violence, though perhaps to a lesser extent than the Derosiers.[60] As for Louis Wagner – who, despite his impaired eyesight, was credited with neutralising Pasquale Reale – he had also been sentenced before for damaging a fence in the context of a robbery attempt.[61] The Wagners were no more allergic to contact with Italians than the Derosiers. Louis's stepmother and half-sister were well-known midwives in the Plaine who delivered babies of Italian-born mothers.[62] They also performed another sort of service to pregnant women: abortions – a serious crime.[63] Rumours of this led Mme. Wagner to be temporarily stripped of her municipal accreditation a few weeks before the Fête de la Plaine fight.[64] Overall, the Derosiers' gang was not defined by any deep-seated anti-Italian sentiment.

As for the Italian-born Raffaele Tari, he had started working in glass factories at an early age, just like the Derosiers. Beginning in the Lyon area and later working in Marseilles, Raffaele eventually settled in the Plaine in early 1900. He was joined by the rest of his family.[65] A few days before the street fight, his younger brother, aged 10, had been fired by the Legras management, after his age was uncovered by the labour inspector.[66] In the Tari family, this might have caused resentment against families whose underage children had been spared. Be that as it may, we know the Taris were friends with other southern Italian families, and it is plausible that some of their scions joined the fight.[67] Not much else is known about the Tari brothers in the early 1900s except that they rode bicycles, which assured them of a certain standing among their fellow glassworkers.[68]

While Raffaele Tari may have held a grudge against Camille Derosier over a woman, Pasquale Reale had his own motives to resent his opponents. For one thing, Pasquale and his brother Nicola were probably just as prone to violence as the Derosiers. Their involvement in another violent episode on Avenue de Paris in 1902 is one indication; this time, three workers coming back from the fête du Landy were injured.[69] Described as *"rôdeurs"* (prowlers) by one newspaper, the Reale brothers were probably after their victims' money or tobacco.[70] It is also likely that a character referred to as "Maurice Reale," who got into a bloody fight in the spring of 1899, was indeed Pasquale: they had the same age, same address, and there is no mention of any Maurizio Reale matching that profile in either Saint-Denis or Arpino archives.[71]

Also, and perhaps more significantly, a year before the 1900 fight, Pasquale's brother Nicola had witnessed an Italian friend of his get stabbed to death on the Avenue de Paris.[72] The press had already interpreted this action as the symptom of a wider conflict between French and Italians, and the highest authorities in France and Italy had been swiftly notified of the matter.[73] In this instance, a degree of ethnic hatred had indeed occupied centre stage. One of the French combatants had allegedly started the fight by defiantly asking Nicola Reale if he knew that "an Italian [had] killed a Frenchman" at another glass factory in Pantin the day before.[74] The *Journal de Saint-Denis* made matters worse by reporting that the expression used had been "*un sale Italien*" (a dirty Italian), which is not what was represented in other papers.[75] But once again, the reality was certainly more complex than it appeared.

The eventual murderers of Nicola Reale's friend were notorious *apaches*.* One of them, an alcoholic, would later beat his parents and try to assassinate his wife.[76] Another committed violent robberies on the street,[77] and his brother once threatened to kill a bar-owner.[78] A few days after the murder, the gang had tried to rob vendors on the Plaine market.[79] Another of its members had already been convicted eight times by the summer of 1900 and had spent more than five years in jail.[80] There is no proof that this band and that of the Derosiers intersected. But as the big fight broke out at the Fête de la Plaine in August 1900, Nicola and Pasquale may have been waiting for an opportunity to get their revenge against what they perceived as the same sort of thugs who had murdered their friend only a few months back.

We should not forget another important parameter in this kind of confrontation: gender. Two of the main conditions enabling violence – drinking and the possession of weapons – were disproportionately more likely to be met by males. So much so that these two things became mainstays of performative masculinity. Knives were ubiquitous among male apprentices of the glass factory.[81] And the possession of a gun became increasingly popular, if only for self-defence purposes.[82] It is unclear whether or not the coveted lover attended the fight, but Raffaele and Camille would have had the incentive to demonstrate to her and other witnesses that they were the most fearless and masculine fighters.

On the whole, the 1900 free-for-all is indicative of the variety of motives that could bring the tenement's youngsters and their peers to engage in violence branded as interethnic. When compared to other, analogous episodes, it suggests that in that particular instance, criminal history and personal rivalries were much more relevant than ethnonational identifications. If they were not entirely absent, these identifications carried much less weight than what the newspapers of the era had their readers believe. Ethnicity was very much superimposed on the *fait divers* by outsiders, whose hasty conclusions masked a more complex and contingent set of dynamics.

This chapter has shown that the residents' interpersonal hostilities were based on diverse factors. Common assumptions about the relevance of ethnic identifications are not necessarily consistent with the most frequent patterns of interaction observed in our particular case. As one set of references in a variety of motives, the salience of ethnonational categories seems to have been oscillating over the period depending both on the people's origin and its intersection with other categories of difference. While origin-based identifications remained dominant in positive interactions, out-group antagonisms were mostly driven by non-ethnic factors. These oppositions were often related to cycles of violence and retaliation among the Plaine's young males.

As important as these interactions were, the construction of difference did not happen only through interpersonal contacts. Public institutions played a major part, too, enacting differences in nationality and citizenship.

Notes

1 APP, CB 92.4, 1908/409, 29.03.1908.
2 APP, CB 92.11, 1914/550, 14.07.1914.
3 Michelle Perrot, "Dans le Paris de la Belle Époque, les 'Apaches,' premières bandes de jeunes," *La Lettre de l'enfance et de l'adolescence*, No. 67 (2007): 71–8.
4 Jon Fox and Demelza Jones, "Introduction: migration, everyday life and the ethnicity bias," *Ethnicities* 13, No. 4 (2013): 385–400.
5 Grancea et al., *Nationalist Politics*, 303–4.
6 Rogers Brubaker, *Ethnicity without Groups* (Cambridge: Harvard University Press, 2004), 110–1.
7 Rogers Brubaker and David Laitin, "Ethnic and nationalist violence," *Annual Review of Sociology* 24 (1998), 428.
8 For an example of verbatim profanities followed by "sic," see APP, CB 92.7, 1911/1085, 8.11.1911.
9 APP, CB 92.10, 1913/817, 25.08.1913; CB 92.20,1924/544, 27.04.1924.
10 APP, CB 92.5, 1909/917, 10.10.1909; AD93, 4U7/697, 26.04.1912, Carboni-Caramandré.
11 See e.g. AD93, 4U7/458, 2.05.1884, 4U7/463, 5.11.1886, 4U7/469, 18.01.1889, 4U7/642, 3.11.1905, Hepply c. Hepply.
12 APP, CB 92.21,1925/717, 16.05.1925; CB 92.21,1925/746, 2.06.1925; CB 92.22,1925/1205, 24.08.1925; AVP, D1U8 167, Cour d'assises de la Seine, 17.11.1926, Matéos Santiago.
13 APP, CB 92.3, 1907/419, 31.03.1907; AD54, 5 Mi 427/R 4, Pierrepont, mar., 19.04.1879.
14 Rabia Bekkar, Nadir Boumaza, and Daniel Pinson, *Familles maghrébines en France, l'épreuve de la ville* (Paris: PUF, 1999), 70–6.
15 Police registers for the Plaine station (APP, CB.92 series) are missing before 1905, but police and gendarmerie reports that led to prosecution survive in the local court archives: AD93, 4U7/902–1077 (with gaps for the years 1886–1890, 1911–1919 and 1923–1937). The collection of local civil rulings is complete

from 1880 to 1946 (AD93, 4U7/450–826). I have manually searched these sources for the entire 1882–1931 period. As for criminal cases brought before the Seine district court (*chambres correctionnelles du tribunal de première instance, cour d'appel, cour d'assises*) the corresponding rulings are stored without interruption (AVP, D1U6, D3U9, and D1U8 series). I have only looked at them when referenced in other sources (military registers, police registers and newspaper accounts).

16 The name of the Italian-born worker was Jean-Baptiste Tarsia. AD93, 4U7/690, 12.05.1911, Wagener ("Wagner") c. Tarsia; SDMA, 1K1/55, Electoral register, 1911, Wagener Jean Nicolas.
17 *JSD*, 28.12.1893.
18 APP, CB 92.7, 1911/1085, 8.11.1911.
19 APP, CB 92.12, 125/1916, 6.02.1916; CB 92.13, 1916/973, 20.11.1916; CB 92.15,1918/1267, 11.11.1918; CB 92.15,1919/214, 26.02.1919-2.03.1919; CB 92.15,1919/219, 2.03.1919; CB 92.18,1922/41, 22.10.1921; CB 92.18,1922/297, 7.04.1922; 92.14, 1918/208 et 209, 23.02.1918.
20 Gilbert Meynier, *L'Algérie révélée. La guerre de 1914-1918 et le premier quart du XXe siècle* (Saint-Denis: Bouchène, 2015 [1981]), 77.
21 See e.g. APP, CB 92.14, 1917/464, 13.05.1917.
22 APP, CB 92.16, 1919/707, 2.10.1919.
23 For tenants who had served in North Africa see: AVP, D4R1 697, 1892, No. 3088, Péchié; D4R1 644, 1902, No. 408, Hector; FNA, 19790858/152, 17489x51, Gonzalez.
24 AVP, D4R1 1725, 1913, No. 4265; D4R1 1613, 1911, No. 5256; D4R1 1612, 1911, No. 4957.
25 Michelle Perrot, "Fait divers et histoire au XIXe siècle," *Annales. Économies, sociétés, civilisations* 38, No. 4 (1983): 911–8.
26 Robert Darnton, *The Great Cat Massacre and Other Episodes in French Cultural History* (New York: Vintage, 1984); Dominique Kalifa, *L'Encre et le Sang. Récits de crimes et société à la Belle Époque* (Paris: Fayard, 1995).
27 Gérard Noiriel, *Le Massacre des Italiens. Aigues-Mortes, 17 août 1893* (Paris: Fayard, 2009), 11.
28 For one notable exception, see David Donham, *Violence in a Time of Liberation: Murder and Ethnicity at a South African Gold Mine, 1994* (Durham: Duke University Press, 2011).
29 See *Le Journal, Le Matin, Le Petit Parisien, Le Moniteur universel*, 21.08.1900; *Le Radical, Le Temps, Le Petit Parisien, Le Rappel, La Petite République socialiste, La Lanterne*, 22.08.1900; *La Justice, JSD*, 23.08.1900; *L'Intransigeant*, 24.08.1900; *La Lanterne*, 28.08.1900; APP, BA914, No. 116362, Telegram from the Police chief of the CDP SD-Sud, 20.08.1900; AVP, D1U6 727, 20.09.1900, T. corr. Seine, Real, Vagner, Tari (sic).
30 ASC Arpino, Stato Civile, births, 1877, No. 138, 2.04.1877, Reale Pasquale Daniele; SDMA, 1F24, 1900 census, 100 av. de Paris.
31 "*Ah! Tu n'as pas le sou. Eh bien, nous allons voir!*"
32 *Le Radical*, 22.08.1900. Among the injured was a woman selling chips, who was supposedly hit by a bullet in her right arm; another man, a concierge from a nearby building who was walking home, was allegedly hurt by Reale's knife. In reality, both sustained only superficial injuries, as did Reale, Houvion and Jules Derosier (AVP, D1U6 727, 20.09.1900, *doc. cit.*).
33 *La Justice*, 23.08.1900.
34 *Le Journal*, 21.08.1900.
35 *La Petite République socialiste*, 24.08.1900 ("*Rien de plus triste ... que cette guerre fratricide entre travailleurs également malheureux, également inconscients*").

36 *"Armés jusqu'aux dents."*
37 *"La plus fourbe qu'il soit au monde."*
38 There is no indication that he was.
39 *XIX^{e}siècle*, 25.08.1900; *JSD, La Lanterne*, 26.08.1900.
40 Noiriel, *Le Massacre des Italiens*.
41 Leo Lucassen, "A threat to the native workers: Italians in France (1870-1940)," in *The Immigrant Threat: The Integration of Old and New Migrants in Western Europe since 1850*, ed. Leo Lucassen (Urbana: University of Illinois Press, 2005), 74–99.
42 Michelle Perrot, "Les rapports des ouvriers français et des ouvriers étrangers (1871–1893)," *Bulletin de la société d'histoire moderne* 58, No. 12 (1960): 4–9.
43 *JSD*, 13.08.1896.
44 See AVP, D2U6168, PP, Report by M. Girardier, 27.12.1909.
45 *Gil Blas, Le Petit Parisien, Le Matin*, 10.01.1900; *La Croix*, 11.01.1900; *La Justice*, 12.01.1900; *L'Éclaireur*, 14.01.1900.
46 SDMA, E64, No. 94, Feisthauer, "décret de réintégration dans la nationalité française," 23.04.1881.
47 *JSD*, 3.02.1895.
48 *Journal des débats politiques et littéraires*, 3.07.1894; *XIX^{e}siècle*, 4.07.1894; AVP, D4R1 779, Military registers, 1894, No. 1490, Antoine Feisthauer; SDMA, 1F21, 1896 census, 133 av. de Paris, household No. 36.
49 AVP, D4R1 688, Military registers, 1892, No. 4036, Nicolas Feisthauer; *JSD*, 26.04.1894; AVP, D3U9 253, CA Paris, 15.02.1908, Feisthauer et autres; AD93, 1E66/338, SD, mar., 1920, No. 1308, 30.10.1920.
50 SDMA, 6I, CT234, " État nominatif des individus arrêtés par mesure de police," 1885, Feisthauer Jean Nicolas, arrested on 2.02.1885 and 6.07.1885; AVP, D4R1 689, Military registers, 1892, No. 4493, Jean Nicolas Feisthauer.
51 FNA, BB/11/1546, 2722x80, Adam Feisthauer.
52 *Le Petit Journal*, 1.10.1895.
53 Marc Michel, "Mythes et réalités du concours colonial: soldats et travailleurs d'Outre-mer dans la guerre française," in *Les Sociétés européennes et la guerre de 1914-1918*, eds. Jean-Jacques Becker and Stéphane Audoin-Rouzeau (Nanterre: Université Paris X, 1990), 393–409.
54 APP, CB 92.11, 1915/152, 8.04.1915; *Le Journal, Le Petit Parisien*, 9.04.1915; *La Lanterne, Le Figaro*, 10.04.1915; *JSD*, 11.04.1915.
55 AD70, Passavant-la-Rochère, mar., 1871, No. 4, 1.06.1871; SDMA, E321, 1902, mar., No. 374, 23.08.1902. To confirm the identity of Auguste and Camille, compare AD10, Bar-sur-Seine, 1886 census, 20 faubourg de la Gare, household No. 53; AD54, 6M33/547, Vannes-le-Châtel, 1896 census, "Le Château," household No. 110 (p. 11), and SDMA, 1F24, 1901 census, 7 imp. Chaudron (p. 114). For their acts of violence in the early 1890s, see *Le Petit Journal*, 24.07.1891 (robberies in Aubervilliers and gunshots fired at a police officer by "Louis Derosier"); *JSD* 22.03.1894 (robbery in Saint-Denis by Camille Derosier).
56 AVP, D4R1 1150, Military registers, 1902, No. 2344, Auguste Derosiers; FNA, 19940440/183, No. 15294, Auguste Derosier. See also *Le Petit Journal*, 31.10.1909; *Le Matin*, 30.04.1921. Auguste "Camille" lived at No. 96 in 1908 (AVP, D1U6 988, T. corr. Seine, 13.01.1908, Derosier Auguste). Also, APP, CB 92.10, 1913/1105, 16.12.1913; AD93, 1E66/383, SD, deaths, 1919, vol. 1, No. 1010: 14.07.1919; AD93, 1E66/368, SD, deaths, 1908, No. 179; AVP, D1U6 1013, 30.09.1908; D1U6 1240, 6.01.1914; D1U6 1500, 27.06.1919; *Le Matin*, 30.04.1921, 09.07.1924, 6.09.1925. A half-brother of the Derosiers, Émile, was himself a convicted *apache*.*

57 That boy's name was Armand Bosi. He committed thefts with Émile Winckler in 1892; the presence of Camille in Émile Winckler's group is documented in 1894 (*JSD*, 3.04.1892; *Le Figaro*, 6.04.1892; *JSD*, 22.03.1894). His brother Auguste Bosi was probably involved in the same actions; he was sentenced to one month in jail for theft in September 1894 (AD76, 1R3027, Military registers, 1897, No. 508). On the Bosis' origins (their father came from Albareto, Duchy of Parma), see SDMA, 1F17, 1886 census, 1 rue du Landy, household No. 36; SDMA, 1F19, 1891 census, 131 av. de Paris; AVP, V4E5164, Paris 19th, 1879, No. 1502, 5.06.1879, Armand Moyen (reconnu Bosi); MA Aubervilliers, 1E136, 1883, mar., No. 47, 14.04.1883.

58 *Le Radical*, 31.01.1909; APP, CB 92.9, 1912/1086, 28.10.1912; APP, CB 92.18,1922/343, 21.04.1922; AVP, D1U6 1500, 27.06.1919; APP, CB 92.11, 1915/695, 26.09.1915; APP, CB 92.12, 1916/39, 3.01.1916; 1916/274 27-28.03.1916; JSD, 9.04.1916.

59 APP, CB 92.12, 1916/39, 3.01.1916; on Mathéo and his parents, see SDMA, Fallen soldiers, 19860711/472; AD93, 1E66/379, SD, deaths, 1917, No. 926 (transcription); SDMA, E 68, vol. 1, No. 211–2.

60 *Le Petit Parisien*, 21.10.1898; *JSD*, 23.10.1898. AVP, D4R1 829, 1895, No. 2115, René Abrioux; AVP, D4R1 921, 1897, No. 2099, Adrien Abrioux; D4R1 1202, 1903, No. 4379, Lionel Abrioux.

61 SDMA, 1F21, 1896 census, 103 av. de Paris; AVP, D4R 1966, 1898, No. 1772, Louis Wagner.

62 SDMA, 1Q2, Bureau de bienfaisance, 26.07.1898; 1Q4, 27.02.1904, 29.03.1904; 1Q7, 28.11.1914; SDMA, E329, SD, births, 1904, vol. 2, No. 1413, 9.12.1904; AD 93, 1E66/270, SD, births, 1912, vol. 2, No. 1075, 20.08.1912.

63 APP, CB 92.1, 1905/315, 11.04.1905.

64 SDMA, 1Q4, 29.03.1904.

65 FNA, BB/11/8316, 21026x24, Joseph [Raphaël] Tari; BB/11/12864, 2182x30, Dominique Tari; CDP SD-Sud, PV François Saverio Tari, 1.09.1901 in AD93, 4U7/995, *Dossier d'instruction* No. 49750, *doc. cit.*

66 AD93, 4U7/985, Inspection du Travail, 12e section de la Seine, PV 16.07.1900 (Dominique Tari and Félix Tedeschi).

67 SDMA, E313, births, 1901, vol. 1, No. 79, 19.01.1901; AD93, 1E66/312, SD, mar., 1906, vol. 1, No. 440, 25.08.1906; SDMA, E351, mar., 1907, vol. 2, No. 630, 16.11.1907.

68 AD93, 4U7/1005, BG Épinay, PV Tari, 7.06.1903; APP, CB 82.4, 1904/521–23, 29.05.1904.

69 *Le Matin*, 30.06.1902; *Le Petit Parisien*, 30.06.1902; *JSD*, 3.07.1902.

70 *Le XIX^esiècle*, 1.07.1902.

71 *La Petite République socialiste*, 27.05.1899.

72 APP, BA 914, CDP SD-Sud, Report, 5.04.1898; *JSD*, 7.04.1898; *Gil Blas*, 8.04.1898; *Le XIX^esiècle*, 23.07.1898.

73 AMAE, CPCOM/90, *Correspondance politique et commerciale*, "Nouvelle série," *Italie, Italiens en France*, 1897–99, "Italiens en France. Incident Diruscio."

74 *Gil Blas*, 5.04.1898; *JSD*, 7.04.1898; *Le XIX^esiècle*, 23.07.1898. Remarkably, the Italian murderer from Pantin would end up being sentenced to 20 years of forced labour, as opposed to just one year behind bars for Nicola's friend's murderer.

75 *JSD*, 21.07.1898; *Le XIX^esiècle*, 23.07.1898.

76 *Le Journal*, 18.11.1900; *La Lanterne*, 24.06.1907.

77 *La Lanterne*, 26.09.1900.

78 *Le Journal*, 1.02.1901.

79 *Le Radical*, 24.04.1898.

80 AVP, D4R1 566, Military registers, 1889, No. 3011, Edmond Derhé. He was sentenced 48 times between 1888 and 1913. See also APP, CB 73.6 (La Villette), 1897/416, 23.03.1897.
81 On knives at the factory: APP, CB 92.1, 1905/113, 2.02.1905; CB 92.2, 1905/1199, 2.12.1905; CB 92.3, 1907/1369, 22.11.1907.
82 See e.g. APP, CB 92.1, 1905/19, 6.01.1905; CB 92.5, 1910/157, 26.02.1910; APP, CB 92.25, 1927/1622, 17.09.1927.

7 Of states and tenants

At the turn of the 20th century, tenants at Nos. 96–102 would not have much in their wallets. Along with banknotes, middle-aged men went around with their military papers and little else. Women often carried no official papers at all, except for bread cards if the family was entitled to food handouts. Men's voter cards were usually left at home, as were receipts of rent payments, membership cards and the odd bankbook. Foreigners might carry a few more sheets of paper, like a birth certificate or receipt of the mandatory residency declaration.

The period of the First World War saw a massive inflation of identity documents: residency permits; receipts of identity cards; passports with visas; proofs of military exemption; benefit cards for refugees and soldiers' spouses; not to mention coal, sugar, milk and other food stamps. And yet for all the increased state control and intervention ushered in by the conflict, the "identity revolution" had started much earlier.[1] People had long faced censuses and, as far as adult men were concerned, elections. They had appeared before law enforcement and pleaded their cases in courts. Their personal information had been written down in registers of all sorts: from city hall to local churches, police stations, factories, furnished hotels, cooperatives and corner shops. It is now acknowledged that in the 19th century, identification procedures became a crucial way of determining "who was in" and "who was out" of European nations.[2] As societies became nationalised, they found in legal citizenship the primary criterion of national membership. But this "paper nationality"[3] was neither necessary nor sufficient to enjoy citizenship in the sense of a political, social and cultural membership, which also involved imperial, class, gender and age distinctions. Following the lead of political scientists, historians have started to research those misalignments between citizenship and other modes of sociocultural belonging.[4]

At the time of our story, the new national discourse could fracture or unite parts of the local population; sometimes, it would have no significant effect. This chapter strives to explain how the tenement's inhabitants were able to either act upon, counteract or ultimately alter the outcome of official identifications that depended on their participation. The first sections

DOI: 10.4324/9781003017820-7

examine this in the context of obligations, rights and state intervention. Then the chapter focuses on naturalisation, with a view to assess the respective incentives and roles played by tenants and the state in that consequential process.

The boundaries of duty: negotiating the states' demands

One of the main, albeit infrequent, encounters with state-sanctioned categories was the census. In principle, this enumeration was conducted every five years from the early 19th century onwards.[5] Beginning in 1891, nationality became more precisely defined in censuses; the only distinctions in previous decades had been between "French" and "foreigners." This choice of words, however, depended as much on people's own declarations as it did on the interpretations of census officials. Scholars who have not attempted to cross-check multiple sources have remained on the threshold of this issue.[6] Alsatian and Lorrainer tenants at Nos. 96–102, for instance, were initially registered as French, even though many had lost their French nationality and had yet to recover it.[7] The agency of interviewees also filtered through when it came to national categories. An elderly woman identified as "Prussian," one of her neighbours said "Bavarian." These obsolete national appellations suggest that they understood the question in terms of their country of birth rather than their nationality.[8]

In other instances, traces survive of the difficulty faced by officials when dealing with naturalised citizens, and perhaps of their reluctance to take what residents said at face value. In fact, some people officially recorded as Germans, Italians or Spaniards in the registers (most likely based on their accent and place of birth) had recently acquired or recovered French citizenship; they could not have failed to mention it.[9] Sometimes uncertainty prevailed, and census officials did not press further: "Alsace-Lorraine" proved a convenient national label for people unsure about which national category they fell into.[10]

While national boundaries in the census could be somewhat fluid, registration requirements imposed on foreigners by laws adopted in 1888–1893 were supposed to draw clear demarcations between the French and the non-French.[11] International migrants who intended to work in France now had to declare their residency within a few days of their arrival. This created a specific moment in time in which names and legal citizenship were crystallised; there was little regard for self-identification. This could entail discrepancies between people's official identity and their sense of belonging – especially since a mistake in one document could be carried on to the next.[12] Born near Milan in 1859, a man living at No. 100 in the late 1880s legally became a subject of Piedmont when he was two months old, and later an Italian subject. Yet he was still listed as an Austrian national on his declaration of residency. His *livret d'ouvrier* (work permit), issued a decade earlier, was probably the original source of this error.[13]

Starting in 1893, foreigners complying with the registration obligation were issued a certificate, called the *feuille d'immatriculation* (lit. registration sheet) which conditioned their right to work. But a majority of foreigners failed to register, and the police were hardly interested in enforcing the requirement.[14] In 1907, Paris authorities estimated that about 70% of foreigners were not aware of their registration obligations.[15] The only individuals who were ever fined were those simultaneously convicted of other, more serious offences. By the time they requested their naturalisation years later, tenants from Nos. 96–102 who could prove they had initially registered were a minority: some claimed to have lost their *feuille*; others confessed to never having had one; most remained silent about it.[16] Many simply did not know (or care) about this legal obligation. Others *did* know about it, yet all were certain that it did not apply to them. This was the case of Alsatians and Lorrainers who had yet to recover their nationality, as well as French-born women who had lost their citizenship by virtue of marriage.[17]

Compliance with the 1893 registration requirement grew during the Great War; French authorities devised a system to enforce it more seriously by controlling mobility. First, a new residency permit for foreigners was created in August 1914 – with the intent to clearly identify subjects from enemy powers (see Chapter 8). Then, the decree of April 21, 1917, compelled foreigners to carry an identity card. This measure had been advocated for years as a way of fighting vagrancy and crime, routinely associated with foreigners. In the context of the war, it was also meant to restrict workers' mobility, not unlike the *livret d'ouvrier** in the 19th century. The government needed to ensure the continuous presence of foreign manpower in armament factories.

These new rules had a noticeable effect on many families of foreign origin in the Plaine-Saint-Denis. The identity card requirement, in particular, demanded a non-negligible effort. Obtaining proof of residency from one's landlord; authenticating that document at the police station; obtaining five official photographs; queuing at the Préfecture de police in central Paris, twice; and paying 5 francs of fees.[18] None of this was particularly easy for working-class families.

Once again, nationality was clearer in theory than it was in the social world. Many foreign tenants born in France thought they were exempt from the new card. Teenagers wrongly believed that only it applied only to adults; others, who had fought in the French Army, were convinced that their service had automatically made them French.[19] For many, the failure to obtain or renew their card suggests that their foreign status and the obligations it entailed were not a major concern in their daily life. At least until the mid-1920s, that is, when the right to work in factories became increasingly contingent on possession of the card.[20]

Prior to the First World War, French authorities did not require any particular document from foreigners entering French territory. Immigrants did, however, carry passports, which emigration countries had made mandatory. In Italy, two passports coexisted – one for internal movements, another for international emigration.[21] In Spain, both emigration permit and passport were necessary to travel abroad in the 1900s.[22] The effect of these paper identifications was reinforced by interactions with foreign authorities in Paris, some of which were compulsory under French law. For instance, from the late 1890s onward, Italian and Spanish fathers from the tenement who wanted their children to work at Legras needed to visit their respective consulates in Paris to have a visa stamped on their children's – sometimes counterfeit – birth certificates.[23]

The most "nationalising" of all experiences, so to speak, was military service. At any given time, several young men of the tenement were away on military duty. The days of the *tirage au sort** in February and of the *conseil de révision** in April were momentous episodes for French families, anticipated with a mix of pride and dread.[24] Foreign men would undergo their own military screenings at their country's consulate in Paris. This was yet another mandatory encounter between foreign states and their nationals. But all nationalities were not equal in that respect. Alsatian and Lorrainer tenants who had technically remained German and therefore subject to the draft in the Empire were not expected to fulfil their military duties (even though some had done so before emigrating).[25] Among Spaniards, those who had not served before their emigration were reluctant to return to do so; the notoriously hard living conditions of the troops and the high mortality rates in colonial wars acted as a powerful deterrent.[26]

In principle, Italians could not escape service either. Yet the Italian state's contradictory imperatives – encouraging the eventual, free return of emigrants once they achieved economic success and building a strong military – resulted in a policy of tolerance towards emigrant conscripts who decided to follow their own schedule and serve as they pleased.[27] Both Spain and Italy even amnestied draft-dodgers in the hope of luring them back. When his turn to leave for military service in Italy had arrived, Giustino Pirolli thought he had a solid motive of exemption: his elder brother Luigi was currently in uniform. Unbeknownst to him though, the law had changed a few months before; his request was denied. Giustino was eventually exempted at the consulate due to "mental retardation" – which we know did not afflict him. This strongly suggests that he faked his condition to dodge the draft.[28] It is unsure whether or not Italian authorities eventually saw through the deception, but they seemed to hold no grudge when they enlisted Giustino into active duty in 1915.

Military service contributed to the instrumental way in which migrants navigated their national identifications. The case of two youngsters who grew up at No. 100 and went on to decline their French nationality can illustrate this point.[29] Both were born in the Plaine in 1902 to families from southern Italy. They rejected French citizenship in 1923 – most likely to avoid military service. In order to prevent their automatic acquisition of French citizenship, the men first went to the Italian consulate. There, they obtained a certificate stating that they were regularly listed on the Italian military registers and that they intended to retain their Italian nationality. But both eventually failed to report for military duty in Italy, falling through the cracks of both systems. Once they were past the draft age, the two eventually requested French citizenship.[30]

Precisely who fell into which category was constantly in flux. Conflicting demands from emigration and immigration states as well as tenants' insufficient knowledge, lack of concern or active tactics to eschew national obligations contributed to the fluid nature of identifications.

The hazy contours of entitlements and franchises

Social policies could also divide the social fabric into different tiers of membership that were not necessarily correlated with national distinctions. According to French law, most healthcare and social benefits in the late 19th century were reserved for French nationals.[31] Although in practice, distinctions between French nationals and foreigners were unevenly enforced.[32] Local authorities displayed a tendency to apply lay understandings of social citizenship, with scant regard to the letter of the law. The need to provide relief to the poor – and the social threat posed by widespread poverty – was not only a motive for extending social protections; it long superseded, at the local level, national preferences.

In Saint-Denis and Paris hospitals, foreign tenants and their French neighbours were equally admitted to surgery hours and emergency rooms on a free basis. The law, however, did provide that most foreigners be kept out in the absence of bilateral agreements.[33] Similarly, foreigners were in principle barred from receiving handouts, orthopaedic protheses and unemployment benefits from the municipal Bureau de Bienfaisance, the local charity agency.[34] In reality, what mattered was the family's belonging to the community; each situation was assessed on a case-by-case basis. Several tenants from southern Italy received help to buy protheses for their relatives.[35] Not only had these Italian tenants been in the Plaine for several years, but they probably had some degree of familiarity with local councilmen who sat in the Bureau's committee. These elected officials were well-known shopkeepers or entrepreneurs whose networks ran deep into the neighbourhood. Over the years, two members of the city council would live in the tenement itself.[36]

Cracks in this policy of nationality-blind generosity started appearing, however, in the wake of the brief but intense wave of unemployment in 1919. First, the amount of financial support requested by families from the *Bureau de bienfaisance* became a factor. When the requested sum was too high, it might cause the Bureau to reactivate the nationality criterion and deny foreigners the help they asked for.[37] In 1921, two weeks after the communists temporarily lost their grip on Saint-Denis city hall, the Bureau went further. It decided to provide benefits only to foreigners who could justify at least six months of residency in Saint-Denis.[38] That restrictive turn soon transcended political divides. In 1926, under a communist majority, periodic handouts to destitute foreigners dwindled – officially for budgetary considerations – introducing a tangible difference in status between poor families based on their nationality. At that time, foreigners accounted for a significant portion of the needy in the Plaine; 80 Spanish and 20 Italian families, with a total of 440 children, were receiving weekly benefits.[39]

Nationality was supposed to be more sternly enforced when it came to elections. But boundaries, in this context as well, were less clear-cut than they appeared. A careful examination of electoral registers reveals that some eligible voters from Nos. 96–102 failed to register, whether they were naturalised citizens or French migrants from another region. Only Saint-Denis natives and taxpayers, which were minorities in both cases, were automatically enrolled. For migrants, active enrolment was far from effortless; they needed to obtain proof of deregistration from the previous town of residency.[40]

Even within a single family, voting rights could vary. Two brothers who had opted for French citizenship in 1872 waited eight years before filing their registration. Quite inexplicably, one was inscribed and the other was not, namely because he had failed to prove his French nationality.[41] Another factor that could blur the line between foreigners and nationals was the disenfranchisement of many male tenants due to criminal convictions. Anyone convicted of a serious crime or felonies such as indecency and vagrancy were automatically and permanently stripped of their voting rights. The same was true for those sentenced to prison for theft or fraud. Dozens of tenants at Nos. 96–102 ended up in this situation, even some of the respected shopkeepers.[42] On the other hand, some young Saint-Denis natives who in theory did not have the legal right to vote because they had been convicted of criminal offences as minors may still have cast a ballot; their name would have been automatically put on the lists.[43] When it came to voting, differences between who could and could not participate were far from black and white.

Low voter turnout in the Plaine further diminished the relevance of elections in enacting national distinctions.[44] As for the electoral participation of foreigners in their home country – a form of "external citizenship"[45] that is still largely unfamiliar to historians, it was only a remote possibility at the time. People could not vote at their country's consulate as they now can. Nevertheless, some individuals were recorded as having cast a vote in their hometowns. We know that in the case of two Italian brothers from the tenement, this was fraud – which they may or may not have been aware of. At the time of their hometown election in 1910, they were in France.[46]

Indirect state interventions

Institutional intervention in the Plaine did not require the states' direct involvement. It could go instead through secondary channels. Among these were subsidised societies pushing a national agenda. Evidence shows that Alsatian and Lorrainer tenants at Nos. 96–102 were aware of Paris-based societies that could help them recover their French nationality. These organisations would assist with the paperwork and provide the required officially stamped paper free of charge.[47] In the Plaine, tenants could also join a mutual benefit society reserved to Alsatians and Lorrainers.[48] Subsidised by both state and local authorities, this institution was regional in membership but national in purpose. Its activities encouraged members to subscribe to a full-fledged French citizenship, not only from a legal standpoint, but also from a linguistic and symbolic one. In that sense, the mission of the Alsace-Lorraine societies differed from that of other ethnonational societies. These organisations intended to foster the emigrants' sense of ethnicity in order to keep them apart from the French nation – or at least make them develop some form of allegiance to their nation of origin.

Throughout the world, the Kingdom of Italy took steps to strengthen the migrants' *italianità* (Italianness) via indirect channels.[49] Before the First World War, this was barely visible in the Plaine. It is likely, however, that some tenants already received help from some Italian organisations as they would during and after the war.[50] One of these organisations was the *Società italiana di beneficenza* (Italian benevolent society). It handed out benefits and offered train tickets to Italy to those who had been in Paris for at least six months and had become unable to work due to illnesses or old age.[51] As far as the Catholic Opera Bonomelli was concerned, it played a major role in denouncing the mistreatments of young glassmakers, including at Legras. The society claimed credit for liberating 210 children in the fall of 1901 and repatriating dozens. It then planned to open youth centres near the glass factories to undercut the *padroni*'s business but the project never materialised.[52] All in all, the *Bonomelliani's* presence in the Paris area was never permanent and their relevance in the Plaine limited at best.[53]

Little information survives about other Italian societies that might have been active in the Plaine. For instance, sources about the one founded by Louis Pirolli and his cousins are missing (see Chapter 3). We do not know if it received support from Italian authorities nor if it had a strong national overtone. In the absence of membership records, even its popularity with Casertan and Molisan families is a matter of speculation. By contrast, sources record that Southern Italian tenants at Nos. 96–102 joined non-ethnicised mutual benefit societies starting in the interwar period.[54] Established reputation may have been a reason for preferring these institutions over more recent ones like Louis's. Or these tenants were not sensitive enough to ethnicity to make it a decisive factor of their institutional affiliations.

State-sponsored efforts directed at Spaniards were more visible and more successful. The 1890s had seen a few isolated initiatives. In the 1900s, repeated calls to organise the Spanish colony in Paris remained largely unanswered.[55] The 1912 scandal caused by the *padrones* at Legras sparked a renewed interest from Spanish authorities. In 1913, a priest came to spend several months in Paris to see what could be done to "rescue" and "evangelise" the Plaine's Spaniards. The priest had the Crown's approval but no public funds; he had to raise money from the Spanish and Latin-American high society in Paris.[56] This resulted in the 1916 foundation of the Spanish mission on rue de la Pompe mentioned in Chapter 5. In addition, Spanish nuns from a Neuilly-based convent started coming to the Plaine church on Sundays, to offer catechism in Spanish.[57]

It was not until 1926, however, that a significant Spanish society was founded in the Plaine. This time, the embassy was directly involved. Called *Hogar* (lit. home), its implicit objective was to ensure that migrants would remain attached to their homeland and to the Catholic faith. Officials feared that migrants were assimilating too quickly; worse than this, Spanish workers were more and more open to radical ideas.[58] The Hogar was run by claretan priests on the premises of the Spanish *Patronato* (see Chapter 5). In addition to religious services, people would come to seek administrative help, partake in sports activities and attend theatrical shows as well as film projections. Sources also record the case of a tenant at No. 96 who came to ask for the contact of a lawyer after his son was killed in a road accident.[59] The role of the Plaine's *Patronato* and Hogar in fostering Spanishness has been rightly highlighted before.[60] Yet its impact should not be overstated. A few tenants at Nos. 96–102 did become full-fledged Hogar members. Others who did not could be seen at one-off events.[61] Still, it is likely that the majority of Spaniards from the *cités* stayed away – in early years, at least.

Naturalisation patterns

The intensity of national identifications varied over time. By contrast, from a legal perspective, nationality was supposed to be black and white. But in this case as well, tenants always retained a measure of agency in the way they negotiated nationality-related procedures. Citizenship could be declined, recovered, acquired and lost. Looking at naturalisation itself is another way to measure the extent to which nationality became relevant both for tenants and for French institutions. It also reveals the role tenants played, in practice, in co-defining the notion of citizenship itself. In the remarkably complete collection of citizenship applications stored at the French national archives, I searched for residents of the *cités*. In the process, I ended up opening about 300 files. More than half of those files concerned past, current or future inhabitants at Nos. 96–102 Av. de Paris.[62]

A serial analysis of the sample indicates that naturalisation requests were heavily concentrated in time: first around 1890, then in the late 1920s and early 1930s. The first group is almost entirely made up of Alsatians and Lorrainers who emigrated after the option period of 1871–1872 and sought to recover – or acquire, in the case of minors born after the annexation – French citizenship. Three decades later, almost all applicants were nationals of Italy or Spain.

The main stages of the naturalisation procedure remained more or less the same throughout the period. First, one had to send a request to the Minister of Justice.[63] Then, the Ministry sent along a standardised form to the Prefect of police, asking him for his opinion on the request and the level of fees that could be demanded from the applicant. Completed by local police chiefs who conducted in-person interviews with the applicants, the forms sent back to the Ministry contained a significant amount of personal information.[64] The Ministry was ultimately responsible for making decisions over whether or not the naturalisation, or the application for permanent residency ("*admission à domicile*"), should proceed and warrant a presidential decree.[65]

What emerges first from the files is the unwavering priority of the French authorities at the time: adding new soldiers to the French army, and making sure every family contributed their fair share to the military effort.[66] Having sons who were minors was, therefore, a strong asset for applicants. In my sample, applications of couples without minor sons took 55% longer, on average, to reach a positive outcome.[67] Fee exemption was also frequently granted to those who were young enough to accomplish their military duty.[68] Other criteria were clearly secondary. Absent from the form until the early 1930s, questions of language and integration were all but irrelevant; even poverty was far from detrimental.[69] Only criminal records could have adverse consequences.[70]

While the application was under review, administrative demands could be modulated and used in a castigatory way. Those regarded as having failed to request the naturalisation in time to serve in the military could see their request adjourned for a while.[71] These delays could last for years and cause trouble for those, like an Alsatian from No. 100, who needed to recover their authentic documents for private matters.[72] These so-called *droits du sceau*, which had to be paid for the decree to be issued, were entirely discretionary. They very likely contributed to delaying many applications until the late 1920s, when the fees started to be indexed to income. The overall efficiency of those bureaucratic manoeuvres is dubious at best. Applicants were not aware of the criticism expressed internally by the ministry's officials and were left to wonder why the process dragged on. As one tenant put it, "it's really unpleasant to remain without information like this."[73]

Faced with a rather complex procedure, some applicants were confused. A Lorrainer tenant from No. 100 failed to request his naturalisation before his *admission à domicile* expired, which then delayed his recovery of French citizenship by many years.[74] Another Alsatian at No. 102 thought he was "opting" for French citizenship, although a full decade had passed since that particular procedure had been closed.[75] Changing his mind in the middle of the process, an Italian tenant falsely believed that refusing to sign off on the copy of his naturalisation decree would render it ineffective.[76]

Still, most residents understood the process and developed declarative tactics to maximise their chances. First, they could lie or omit parts of their life stories. Raffaele Tari, the disgruntled lover involved in the massive 1900 fight described earlier, claimed for instance that he had a clean criminal record (which was true, strictly speaking); but he filed his application under his second name, Giuseppe, likely wary that the 1900 incident would come up in the state's records.[77] Joseph de Garate, for his part, did not mention his family in Spain. As for the Pirolli brothers, they never failed to lie about their starting dates at Legras; after a great deal of time had passed, they still did not want to attract attention to their years of illegal labour.[78] Louis Pirolli himself, while his citizenship application was under review, was arrested and briefly incarcerated for carrying an illegal firearm. He did not report anything, and the incident went unnoticed by the naturalisation office.[79] As for applicants who ran a shop, they frequently decided to remain silent about it, knowing that what mattered to the state was the contribution to the army and the workforce.[80]

Applicants were not only able to draw a veil over some elements of their lives, but they also knew what answers were expected from them. Both the request letters and the forms completed by the police bear prevailing, unoriginal expressions, which were passed among relatives, friends and acquaintances.[81] The vast majority of applications by Alsatian and Lorrainer residents, dating from the late 1870s to the early 1890s, only mentioned a single motive: "to recover French citizenship" (*pour recouvrer la qualité de Français*).[82] This reason was sufficient for the Ministry. Two young Easterners added that they wanted to register for the draft, which was sure to be even more welcome. Another Alsatian applicant intended to "settle in France for good" (*se fixer définitivement en France*), which would become a widespread leitmotiv of later applications. Mentions of "sympathy" or even "love" for France were a small minority in an ocean of standardised answers.[83] Other answers were even more systematic; a whopping 99% of the applicants in the sample stated – unrealistically – that they were unconcerned by politics, and that they had lost all intention of returning to their home country.

What were people's real incentives? Based on the most candid answers, it appears that considerations related to military service could be genuinely important to applicants. Aside from avoiding the draft in one's own country – and if possible, in France as well, by deferring one's application until a later age[84] – some files denote a real desire to serve in France. There is little doubt, for instance, over the sincerity of Louis Chevrier, from No. 100, and Chrétien Lentz, from No. 96. Both enlisted for the draft before officially becoming French.[85]

Economic reasons were not far behind. Fear of losing one's job in case of an economic downturn was explicitly mentioned in some requests. And though I have not come across, in this particular context, concrete instances of residents being turned away from jobs on account of their foreign nationality, it is possible that this practice did take place at some factories in the Plaine.[86] M. Legras may have occasionally pressured his employees to apply for French citizenship, especially at a time when employing German personnel was not particularly auspicious. In 1893, he apparently threatened to fire an Alsatian glassworker living at No. 100 if he failed to recover his French nationality.[87] On the other hand, an opposing signal can be found in the management of the workers' housing units owned by the factory at No. 133 Av. de Paris. There, various nationalities coexisted from the 1890s onwards, reflecting – albeit with some delay – the diverse make-up of the factory's personnel.[88]

Other naturalisation hopefuls from 96–102 Av. de Paris confessed to being enticed by welfare benefits. In addition to the ones already mentioned, the pension for parents of a soldier killed in the war was another benefit reserved to French nationals; it was explicitly referred to by one applicant.[89] Apprehension and uncertainty over one's foreign status should not be discounted, either. Alsatians-Lorrainers seem to have been unsettled by the new declaration requirement imposed by the decree of 1888. Perhaps because they feared that this requirement could eventually lead to deportation, or bring some form of differential treatment, many decided to recover their French nationality at that moment precisely.[90] Other scholars have pointed out that the mere hope of not being singled out by the police and staying out of trouble was a powerful, though unexpressed, impetus behind citizenship applications.[91] One former resident at No. 100 saw his acquisition of French citizenship as a way to "comply with the law" (*en règle avec la loi*). As the process dragged on, he complained that he was "very worried" *(très tourmenté)* as this might "get him into trouble" *(avoir des ennuis)*.[92]

In 1927, the new law on nationality made it easier and cheaper to apply. It also convinced many that it was the right time to obtain citizenship. At the same time, they did not necessarily have strong feelings about it; up to that point, some may have felt that the application was not worth the effort. Soon enough, nativist considerations caused more detailed questions to be included in the administrative forms. The new elements included information on people's health and their degree of integration.[93] The law was also amended to impose restrictions on recently naturalised citizens. These new Frenchmen, whose degree of Frenchness might have already been questioned by their peers, would now be legally denied some rights associated with full-fledged citizenship.[94]

Some researchers have described naturalisation as an "official certificate of integration" that did not alter the immigrants' deep feelings.[95] That assertion rings mostly true for the specific cohort of people under scrutiny in this book. For a former tenant, born in France to Italian parents and whose own children were automatically French, it had always been clear that "France is my Fatherland" (*ma Patrie, c'est la France*); her naturalisation only confirmed an existing state of mind.[96] Other individual evidence points to more complex identifications, in which the act of naturalisation took centre stage. After his naturalisation, a former tenant at No. 96 was heard saying he was more French than French-born citizens. As opposed to them, he had chosen to be French.[97]

136 *Interactions and allegiances*

Most of the time, nationality changes did not mean severing transnational ties. In Louis and Maria Pirolli's case, they had been exposed to the French state, and to French national culture, for a long time. After going back and forth across national borders, they had decided, however, to cross the major legal boundary of citizenship. This decision is likely to have validated a sense of belonging that had been underway for some years. The love for France that Louis would profess a few years later as he was stripped of his nationality by the Vichy regime suggests as much.[98] After becoming a French citizen though, Louis would periodically return to Italy. Paradoxically, this may have reinforced his sense of Frenchness, as he travelled back and forth with a French passport.

On the other hand, Louis and Maria's identification as "Italian" in 1931 and 1936 censuses may suggest either that they did not answer to the census officials in person, misunderstood the question as relating to their country of birth or (more likely) were still being identified by concierges and census officials as foreigners regardless of their "paper nationality." After the Second World War, however, when multiple traumatic experiences would have reinforced the importance of their French citizenship – the *Exode* in May 1940, their son's captivity in Germany and their denaturalisation, which was nullified at the *Libération* – their French nationality would show for the first and last time on census registers, shortly before they passed away.[99]

As we have seen, interactions between the tenement's occupants and public authorities could result in contingent and hybrid forms of participation. The content of such citizenship could vary not only between individuals but also over time. It depended on shifting lines of belonging at various levels: in the neighbourhood, at the city level and according to national regulations, whether issued by France or by people's countries of origin.

Although compulsory procedures like mandatory registration and military conscription certainly participated in nationalising people's identifications, they never followed, nor entailed, unambiguous boundaries in the tenement's population. Ignorance, negligence and active avoidance strategies, combined with variable zeal from law enforcement, often blunted the effectiveness of nationality-based rules. The exercise of social rights also enacted idiosyncratic and mutable systems of difference. To secure welfare benefits, people's reputation and insertion in social networks often mattered more than their paper nationality, until the interwar period. Even the right to vote, the paradigmatic marker of male political citizenship, could see its nationalising effect limited by widespread disenfranchisement as well as a persistently low turnout of eligible voters. By contrast, political participation also took local forms; this was due to the propensity of foreigners to navigate between national and transnational allegiances.

As for naturalisation, it often marked a moment of major reckoning in the evolving relationship between the applicants and two nation-states, to which

Of states and tenants 137

people held varying degrees of allegiance. For many tenants, the procedure sanctioned a physical migration and a sociocultural integration. Still, it was almost always the result of complex individual identifications, not to mention pragmatic choices. People rarely cut ties with their country of birth, nor did they regard themselves – or be perceived by others – as unconditionally and exclusively French.

There was another, crucial moment when nation-states attempted to drive a national wedge in the tenants' complex transnational identifications. That moment was the First World War, which will be the object of the final chapter.

Notes

 1 Gérard Noiriel, *La Tyrannie du national. Le droit d'asile en Europe (1793–1993)* (Paris: Calmann-Lévy, 1991), 156.
 2 John Torpey, *The Invention of the Passport Surveillance, Citizenship, and the State* (Cambridge: Cambridge University Press, 2000), 121.
 3 Marco Meriggi, "La cittadinanza di carta," *Storica*, No. 16 (2000): 107–20.
 4 Stephen Castles and Alastair Davidson, *Citizenship and Migration: Globalisation and the Politics of Belonging* (Basingstoke: Macmillan, 2000); Hakan Sıcakkan, Yngve Lithman, eds., *Envisioning Togetherness: Politics of Identity and Forms of Belonging* (New York: Edwin Mellen, 2004); Alexis Spire, *Étrangers à la carte. L'administration de l'immigration en France (1945–1975)* (Paris: Grasset, 2005); Lewis, *The Boundaries of the Republic*.
 5 In Saint-Denis, census operations did not take place 1906 and 1916. On censuses and nationality construction, see Éric Guichard and Gérard Noiriel, eds., *Construction des nationalités et immigration dans la France contemporaine* (Paris: Presses de l'École normale supérieure, 1997).
 6 See e.g. Lillo, "Espagnols en 'banlieue rouge'," 187–8.
 7 See the example of M. Cantin, who was listed as French, but technically German: SDMA, 1F17, 1886 census, 100–102 av. de Paris, and FNA, BB/11/1976, 1919x87.
 8 SDMA, 1F19 (1891), 1F24 (1901), 100 av. de Paris.
 9 Raphaël and Catherine Spreisser (FNA, BB/11/1728, 6337x83; SDMA, 1F17, 1886, av. de Paris 87); Domenica Carbone née Cocorocchia and her son Roger (FNA, BB/11/10398, 34199x27, Carbone and SDMA, 1F33, 1931 census, 100 av. de Paris); Feliciano and Encarnación Sedano (FNA, BB/11/12897, 3823x30; SDMA, 1F33, 1931 census, 100 av. de Paris).
10 SDMA, 1F21, 1896 census, 102 av. de Paris, Landry family; AD93, D2M8 205, 1921 census, 96 av. Wilson; AD93, D2M8 91, 1926 census, 96 av. Wilson.
11 The most important pieces of legislation were the decree of 2.10.1888 on the regulation of foreigners, the law of 26.06.1889 on nationality, and the law of 8.08.1893 on the sojourn of foreigners in France and the protection of national labour (see Noiriel, *La Tyrannie du national*, 170–4).
12 Pierre Piazza, *Histoire de la carte nationale d'identité* (Paris: Odile Jacob, 2004), 125–6.
13 SDMA, CT928, No. 156.
14 From 1894 to 1900, no more than 20 foreigners were sentenced every year in the Paris area for violating the 1893 law (FNA, F7/12601, "Seine").
15 Clifford Rosenberg, *Policing Paris: The Origins of Modern Immigration Control Between the Wars* (Ithaca: Cornell University Press, 2006), 47.

138 Interactions and allegiances

16 For those 45 inhabitants, we can know both the date of entry in France and that of their declaration of residency (mostly from the naturalisation file). Extremely rare (just one case in the sample) were those who had filed the declaration more than once, even though in principle a new declaration was mandatory for each town where foreigners settled for work.
17 FNA, BB/11/3735, 6006x99, Schwartz née Mohr; BB/11/8198, 15099x23, Pirolli née Billères.
18 *Guide to the Formalities for Foreigners in France (Orléans: Pigelet et fils, 1920)*.
19 APP, CB 92.23,1926/1702, 3.11.1926; FNA, BB/11/6155, 17652x14, Gómez.
20 From 1924, the right to work was conditional upon having a visa on the card from the French Ministry of Labour, after a recommendation from the Office régional de la main-d'œuvre étrangère.
21 Italian law on emigration of 31.01.1901, Art. 5.
22 Germán Rueda Hernanz, "Emigración," in *Diccionario político y social del siglo XX español*, eds. Javier Fernández Sebastián and Juan Francisco Fuentes (Madrid: Alianza editorial, 2008), 460–9.
23 FNA, BB/18/6107, F/22/452, 23BL164. Foreign consulates proved largely unable – or unwilling – to detect fraud in that context, despite repeated diplomatic efforts from the French government (see e.g. the Franco-Italian agreement signed on 15.06.1910 in *Bulletin de l'Inspection du travail* 20 (1912), 2).
24 Eugen Weber, *Peasants into Frenchmen: The Modernization of Rural France, 1870–1914* (Palo Alto: Stanford University Press, 1976); Odile Roynette, *Bon pour le service, l'expérience de la caserne en France à la fin du XIXe siècle* (Paris: Belin, 1999).
25 There was some ambivalence from the French authorities though, with an expeditious naturalisation procedure granted to those who had indeed served in the German Army.
26 See cases of Spanish tenants at Nos. 96–102 who requested French citizenship just before they could be called to serve in Spain: FNA, BB/11/12221, 15851x29, Luengo; BB/11/12649, 37296x29, Esteban. For context, see Fernando Puell de la Villa, *El soldado desconocido: de la leva a la 'mili' (1700–1912)* (Madrid: Biblioteca Nueva, 1996), 255–72.
27 Caroline Douki, "The 'return politics' of a sending country: the Italian case, 1880s–1914," in *A Century of Transnationalism: Immigrants and Their Homeland Connections*, eds. Nancy Green and Roger Waldinger (Urbana: University of Illinois Press), 36–50.
28 ASC Pozzilli, lista di leva, classe 1888, No. 23, Giustino Pirolli; Royal decree No. 553 of 10.12.1896, Art. 14; Italian law No. 763 of 15.12.1907, Art. 6; FNA, BB/11/13146, 16273x30, Giustino Pirolli.
29 French-born sons of immigrants who declined French citizenship were rare. In total, only 21 people born in Saint-Denis did so between 1893 and 1945, against several hundreds who remained French. See Ministère de la santé publique et de la population, Direction du peuplement et des naturalisations, 7e bureau, *Liste alphabétique des enfants d'étrangers ayant décliné ou répudié la nationalité française (déclarations enregistrées entre le 22 juillet 1893 et le 31 décembre 1945*, ed. Maurice Loisel (Paris: Imprimerie nationale, 1946).
30 FNA, BB/11/8198, 15099x23, Pirolli née Billères; BB/11/7971, 3729x23, De Bellis.
31 Foreigners were excluded from labour conciliation boards (law of 1.06.1853) and from the leadership and management of unions (law of 21.03.1884). Only societies made of French people could tender for public contracts (4.06.1888, 29.07.1893). Foreigners were also barred from boards of mutual benefit societies, unless the members were all foreign (law of 1.04.1898). The assistance to the elderly and incurables was reserved to French citizens (law of 14.07.1905), while

the law on free medical assistance (15.07.1893) conditioned the foreigners' eligibility upon diplomatic reciprocity.
32 Caroline Douki, David Feldman, and Paul-André Rosental, "Pour une histoire relationnelle du ministère du Travail en France, en Italie et au Royaume-Uni dans l'entre-deux-guerres: le transnational, le bilatéral et l'interministériel en matière de politique migratoire," in *Les Politiques du travail (1906–2006). Acteurs, institutions, réseaux*, eds. Alain Chatriot, Odile Join-Lambert, and Vincent Viet (Rennes: Presses universitaires de Rennes, 2006), 143–59.
33 SDMA, CT812, "Registre des entrées d'urgence dans les hôpitaux de Paris," 1892–3; SDMA, 1I227, PP, bureau d'hygiène, "État des entrées dans les hôpitaux," 25.10.1915; SDMA, 1Q14, 20.03.1930
34 Nissim Samama, *Questioni riguardanti la condizione giuridica degli Italiani all'estero (Francia)* (Florence: Ariani, 1911), 117. The decree requiring French nationality for annual and temporary benefits in Paris was issued on 15.11.1895.
35 SDMA, 1Q7, 26.11.1913; 1Q8, 27.02.1915, 24.04.1915; 28.08.1915.
36 And a third one was the landlord at No. 100–102 after 1907. On Louis Gustave Gambon, see Brunet, "Une banlieue ouvrière," 922; *Bulletin des convocations et ordres du jour des LL*** de la région parisienne de la Fédération du Grand-Orient de France*, 15.03.1908, 10; on Eugène Péchié, SDMA, CT833, "Demandes d'inscription au bénéfice du legs Fontaine, 1912–1918," Letter from André Bayer to the Mayor of SD, 12.06.1912; on Joachim Louis Lutel, SDMA, CT94, Petition from the Plaine residents to the Préfet de Police, 13.02.1894; *Le Rappel*, 25.10.1910; Int. No. 24, 15.02.2017). There would be yet another councillor at No. 98 after the Second World War (see SDMA, 2ACW9, 96 av. Wilson, Letter from M. Fauvel to the Mayor of SD, 17.03.1952).
37 See e.g. SDMA, 1Q10, 27.09.1919, 29.01.1920.
38 SDMA, 1Q11, 21.07.1921.
39 SDMA, 1Q13, 25.11.1926.
40 Law of 7.07.1874.
41 SDMA, E42, No. 36, 17.03.1872, Nicolas Blimer; E44, No. 589, 30.06.1872, Jean Blimer; SDMA, 1K1/25, 1881; AD93, 4U7/452, 18.02.1881, Nicolas Blimer; 1E66/146, SD, births, 1883, No. 732, 24.06.1883.
42 AVP, D4R1 557, Military registers, 1888, No. 3653, Voyenne.
43 For an example of a tenant who was improperly registered for four years before being struck out: AVP, D4R1 1398, 1907, No. 2948; SDMA, 1K1/53-6, 1909–1912, Jules Guyonvernier.
44 See SDMA, CT513, 514, 519.
45 Rainer Bauböck, "The rights and duties of external citizenship," *Citizenship Studies* 13, No. 5 (2009): 475–99.
46 AS Caserta, b. 23, f. 229, "Elezioni politiche del 17 aprile 1910," 16.05.1910 (Gabriele).
47 On these societies, see Wahl, *L'Option*, 195–9. See also the birth certificate in FNA, BB/11/2561, 5782x91, Schiel; the letter from M. and Mme. Lauber, 22.08.1888 in FNA, BB/11/1838, 2415x85, Lauber; the translated documents in FNA, BB/11/4843, 8848x08, Müller.
48 See FNA, BB/11/3608, 4656x02, and BB/11/4600, 2010x07, Pierre Studer.
49 Matteo Sanfilippo, "Nationalisme, 'italianité' et émigration aux Amériques (1830–1990)," *European Review of History–Revue européenne d'histoire* 2, No. 2 (1995), 177–91; Mark Choate, *Emigrant Nation: The Making of Italy Abroad* (Cambridge: Harvard University Press, 2008).
50 SDMA, CT103, Letter from the *Società italiana di Beneficenza* to the Mayor of SD, 20.11.1919, CT45, idem, 20.02.1922 (Puzzuoli family); SDMA, 4H3/131, 172, Letter from the *Società italiana di Beneficenza* to the Mayor of SD, 20.10.1917

(Palma family); SDMA, 4H3/137, Letter from the director of the *Società Italiana di Beneficenza* to the Mayor of SD, 3.11.1917, and reply from the Mayor, 13.11.1917 (Carbone family).
51 Samama, *Questioni*, 130-2. The poor state of the Society's archive makes it impossible to check in detail if Italians in the Plaine knew about it and requested its services at an early stage (FNA, F7/15908–9, Société italienne de Bienfaisance).
52 Sommi-Picenardi, "La tratta," 481–2.
53 Luigi Taravella, "La pratique religieuse comme facteur d'intégration," in *L'Intégration italienne en France: un siècle de présence italienne dans trois régions françaises: 1880–1980*, eds. Pierre Milza, Antonio Bechelloni, and Michel Dreyfus (Brussels: Complexe, 1995), 71–83.
54 Int. No. 39: J. Verrecchia's membership card of the Fédération mutualiste de la Seine (member since 1.07.1930). See the Pirollis and Zonfrillis in SDMA, 5Q61, Société de secours "la Mutualité" de la Plaine-Saint-Denis.
55 *La Correspondencia de España*, 9.06.1901, and the reference to the letter by Luis Bonafoux to the Count of Romanones in 1906 in *El Mótin*, "¿Se puede?," 12.12.1912. As early as 1890, a Spanish priest had travelled to Levallois to establish a camp for Spanish peddlers and beggars: see Eusebio Blasco, "Españoles sueltos," *Alrededor del Mundo*, 29.09.1899.
56 CDEE, "El Hogar de los Españoles," 001/009, Letter from Gabriel Palmer to Manuel Hernández, chairman of the Hogar, Madrid, 17.03.1930; Ana Fernández Asperilla, "Los emigrantes españoles en París a finales del siglo XIX y en el primer tercio del siglo XX. La sociedad de socorros mutuos El Hogar de los Españoles," *Hispania: revista española de historia* 62, No. 211 (2002), 505–19.
57 APP, BA2154, PP, RG, 11.04.1914, Report about Spanish Catholic charities in the Plaine-Saint-Denis.
58 Antonio Niño Rodríguez, "Políticas de asimilación y de preservación de la nacionalidad de los emigrantes españoles en Francia, 1900–1936," *Hispania: revista española de historia* 62, No. 211 (2002): 433–82.
59 AGA, 54/11001, leg. 25, "Patronato Saint-Denis, Plaine-Saint-Denis."
60 See e.g. Laura Oso Casas, "La comunidad: relaciones sociales en la diáspora," in *Trans-ciudadanos: hijos de la emigración española en Francia*, ed. Laura Oso Casas (Madrid: Fundación Francisco Largo Caballero, 2008), 191–2.
61 CDEE, "El Hogar de los Españoles," 001/006, List of donors to the project of monument of the queen Maria Cristina, 18.06.1929 (Francisco Mateos, Emilio Fernández, Basilio Curiel).
62 Only six out of the 288 requests I examined had been filed by single women.
63 In 1927, the Préfet de Police replaced the Minister as the authority to which applications had to be addressed.
64 The main questions remained stable over the years: the applicants' identities and profession; their parents' and siblings' names, nationalities and places of residency; the date of arrival in France; the various places of residency in the country; the general behaviour and morality; the reputation; the military situation; the earnings of the family; the rent and taxes paid; the motivation of the application; the applicants' political behaviour; their intent of returning to their home country; their mastery of French and their degree of assimilation. After each World War, questions about the applicants' and their siblings' occupations during the conflicts were inserted. After the Second World War was added the obligation to state the places of residency before coming to France, and also a list of all the employers since the arrival in France. Annexed to the form was an excerpt of the applicants' criminal record, retrieved by the Ministry itself, and supporting documents produced by the applicants, such as original birth

Of states and tenants 141

certificates, medical certificates, military documents, certificates of residency and employment.
65 Until 1927, the *admission à domicile* was a mandatory first phase of three years – unless applicants could already demonstrate their residence in France for ten years. At the end of the three years, the persons could apply for citizenship.
66 Paul Lawrence, "Naturalisation, ethnicity and national identity in France between the wars," *Immigrants & Minorities* 20, No. 3 (2001): 1–24.
67 The statistic is based on 19 couples of past, current or future tenants without a minor son at the time of their request, and 62 with at least one minor son.
68 FNA, BB/11/3743, 6860x97, Messmer; 19770879/4, 7312x33, Cassanego.
69 I found no correlation in the sample either between the time to process applications and the families' income.
70 See e.g. FNA, BB/11/3806, 4647x00, Carlesimo.
71 "Avis du Préfet de police," in FNA, BB/11/7112, 274x20, Rosso.
72 Letter from Chrétien Lienhardt, 100 av. de Paris, SD, to the Minister of Justice, 18.05.1893, in FNA, BB/11/2609, 10501x91, Chrétien Lienhardt.
73 "*C'est vraiment désagréable de rester ainsi sans renseignement.*" Letter from Filippo Quaglieri to the Préfet de police, 16.01.1931, in FNA, BB/11/12172, 13433x29, Quaglieri.
74 FNA, BB/11/2609, 10501x91, Lienhardt.
75 FNA, BB/11/1650, 3545x82, Herholt.
76 FNA, 19770898/107, 48623x38, Ricci.
77 FNA, BB/11/8316, 21026x24, Tari.
78 FNA, BB/11/13146, 16273x30, Giustino Pirolli.
79 APP, CB 92.25, 1927/1622, 17.09.1927; AVP, D1U6 2144, 20.09.1927; FNA, BB/11/10553, 41906x27, Louis Pirolli. Note that it was not unheard of for applicants to volunteer criminal information that the government was not aware of (see e.g. FNA, BB/11/11124, 70451x28, Girardi).
80 Zalc, *Melting shops,* 138–40.
81 Unsigned police report [no date, probably 1941], in FNA, BB/11/10553, 41906x27, Louis Pirolli. Compare with application letters in FNA, BB/11/6172, 18503x14, Fraioli; BB/11/12583, 33988x29, Gabriele; BB/11/12595, 34552x29, Carlesimo.
82 13 out of 17 files that bear mention of the motives of the request, a category that was not filled systematically on the forms in those years.
83 See Jean-Charles Bonnet, "Naturalisations et révisions de naturalisations de 1927 à 1944: l'exemple du Rhône," *Le Mouvement social,* No. 98 (1977): 43–75.
84 Individuals in our tenants' sample applied on average at 37.5 years of age. A contemporary observer suspected that very reason when noting that most applications were made after 27 years of age: Gaston Dallier, *La Police des étrangers à Paris et dans le département de la Seine* (Paris: Rousseau, 1914), 117.
85 FNA, BB/11/2155, 6602x88, Chevrier; BB/11/2475, 9087x90, Lentz.
86 For job-related motives to the residents' applications, see FNA, BB/11/2609, 10501x91, Lienhardt; BB/11/7112, 274x20, Rosso. On the relation between naturalisation and foreigners being denied job opportunities, see Jean-Charles Bonnet, "Les Italiens dans l'agglomération lyonnaise à l'aube de la Belle Époque," in *L'emigrazione italiana in Francia prima del 1914,* eds. Jean-Baptiste Duroselle and Emilio Serra, 87–106 (Milan: Franco Angeli, 1978).
87 FNA, BB/11/2609, 10501x91, Letters from Chrétien Lienhardt to the Justice Minister, 21.09.1893, 25.12.1893.
88 FNA, F/12/5190, Légion d'honneur de François-Théodore Legras, 1906; AD93, 1E66/368, SD, deaths, 1908, No. 137; AD93, D2M8 205, SD, 1921 census, 133 av. Wilson; SDMA, 1F33, 1931 census, 133 av. Wilson.

89 FNA, BB/11/7928, 1592x23, Messmer. Art. 28 of the law of 31.03.1919 conditioned the pension on the French nationality, in addition to the age (over 60 for fathers and 55 for mothers) and income criteria (the beneficiaries must be too poor to pay the income tax).
90 See Société de réintégration des Alsaciens-Lorrains, *Rapport sur l'exercice 1888* (Paris: Pariset, 1889).
91 Alfred Sauvy, *Théorie générale de la population*, vol. 2, *Biologie sociale* (Paris: PUF, 1954), 331.
92 FNA, BB/11/11367, 82663x28, Gélorme ("Jérôme") Pirolli.
93 See Laurent Gauci, "Les critères de naturalisation: étude des conséquences de la loi du 10 aout 1927 à travers des formulaires de demande de naturalisation (1926–1932)," *Cahiers de la Méditerranée* 58 No. 1 (1999): 179–99.
94 See e.g. the law of 19.07.1934 denying the access to elected offices, civil service, bar and notary-type functions to naturalised citizens for ten years.
95 Couder, "Les Immigrés italiens," 230.
96 FNA, 19770875/184, 18950x32, Louise Zangrilli née Jacovissi.
97 Int. No. 31, 18.08.2016. For an example of the questions immigrant children could experience in the interwar period when they learned that they had changed nationality, see Monique Rouch, Catherine Brisou, and Carmela Maltone, eds., *"Comprar un prà." Des paysans italiens disent l'émigration (1920–1960)* (Bordeaux: Maison des sciences de l'homme d'Aquitaine, 1989), 337.
98 See FNA, BB/11/10553, 41906x27 and Langrognet, "The crossings of Luigi Pirolli."
99 SDMA, 1F33, 1F35, 1931 and 1936 censuses, 4 imp. Trézel.

8 A war-torn tenement

Thursday, February 14, 1918, 9:30 pm. Sergeant major Isaac-Friang, 27, records the death of one of the colonial workers of his Plaine-Saint-Denis detachment. His name is Mabrouk ben Mohamed Boubila. Born in Tripoli, Ottoman Libya, around 1877, he was a resident of Tunis before the war. Mabrouk was fatally stabbed around the corner from the tenement. His last words were "Englishmen beat me" and "Spaniards struck me with knives."[1]

Mabrouk's tragic fate illustrates, first and foremost, how the Great War marked both an acceleration in the Plaine-Saint-Denis migration flows, as well as an increase in their diversity. This was bound to impact the experience of the tenants at Nos. 96–102. The increase in incoming and outgoing migrations echoed the situation of a great number of French cities on the home front. The First World War has now been recognised as a period of intense mobility – forced or otherwise.[2] Movements of soldiers, factory workers, refugees, detainees, sex workers and deserters happened on unprecedented scales throughout Europe, ushering in a new era of migration management and control. More and more attentive to that particular feature of the war period, researchers have tried to investigate issues of race and nationhood by studying the legal and political treatment of foreigners and colonial subjects during the war. This line of research, which started in the 1980s and 1990s,[3] has resulted in studies that include analyses of the war experience from the standpoint of national, ethnic or racial minorities.[4] A strong interest in migrant people's own understanding and agency has informed discussions on the complex issues of their "loyalty." That is, loyalty to their state of residence on the one hand, and loyalty to the state of their birth on the other;[5] and these issues were relevant even in regions of the world remote from the conflict's main stage.[6]

Yet to this day, few studies have attempted to look at migrants in order to understand the reconfigurations brought about by the war in terms of integration.[7] The tenement at the centre of this volume provides an interesting opportunity to understand, at close range, the impact of war on social boundaries. The nexus of nationality, race and gender visibly evolved under the new circumstances, particularly through the deeper involvement of public authorities in people's lives. And yet this increased state-meddling

DOI: 10.4324/9781003017820-8

was not merely a top-down process; people were not passive recipients of new rules and legal categories. The extent to which these parameters of difference were enacted in people's daily lives was a consequence of more mundane issues: employment, money, sex, health, death, mourning – in other words, the petty catalysts of human passions. The stakes here are then to try and see how these dynamics altered the tenants' identifications, sense of belonging and sense of place during the conflict, and how much they depended on the war's specific social conditions. Let us first assess the importance of nationality in the displacements triggered by the war's outbreak. Then, we will turn to the symbolic reconfigurations that this period entailed for the tenement occupants.

Nationality and migration

From the outset, the tenants experienced the war through the prism of nationality. In early August 1914, the departure of French and Belgian men to their regiments had an unmistakable national component. For the other residents who did not have to go – say those of Italian or Spanish origin – it was one of the first times that their identity as foreigners translated into such a consequential difference.

Still, few could escape the havoc wrought by war, as well as the civilian migrations it entailed; they were not exclusive to any particular group. The subjects of enemy powers were targeted by particularly restrictive measures. In the Plaine, however, "Austro-Germans" quickly became hard to find. Few would be arrested as suspects and deported to internment camps out west, as most of them swiftly departed on their own.[8] On August 28, 1914, nationals of the Central Empires made up only two out of about 5,000 Plaine families. And there is no evidence that any neighbours would have known that these two Italian-speaking families were "enemy aliens." For once, it seems that the police had not tipped the local press about its investigations.[9]

Dozens of tenants at Nos. 96–102 were among the area's 1,500 adult foreigners who obtained residency permits at the police station; these were a new requirement put into place in early August.[10] They certified individuals as foreigners, reinforcing the effect of pre-existing documents like the *feuille d'immatriculation* which many had lost or never bothered to get (see Chapter 7). For young men who otherwise looked and sounded as French as anyone, the permits acted as precious proofs of military exemption. Aside from these identity papers, French authorities soon offered logistical help to foreigners – in coordination with emigration countries. Newspapers and posters informed Italians, Belgians, Spaniards and the Swiss that they could be repatriated by their Consulate with no cost.[11] Many were quick to seize this opportunity, including a hefty number of tenants at Nos. 96–102.[12] This was no ground for envy on the part of the French, since Saint-Denis inhabitants hailing from French provinces could receive similar assistance. By mid-September 1914, more than 2,000 free or half-priced train tickets had been issued by the municipal authorities to locals who could not afford them.[13] If so many flocked to their home regions, it was because they had few alternatives in view of the rapidly worsening military situation and the brutal economic standstill. An inhabitant of No. 100 would later testify that she had returned to Italy because she "feared the German invasion."[14] Financial constraints were no less pressing; factories all but halted their production for want of both customers and manpower. Legras was left with only 250 employees in November 1914 – an 80% drop. Louis Pirolli and his entire family were among those who departed in September.[15] At Mouton, the steel-casting department closed altogether, and jobless Spanish tenants at No. 96 had no choice but to go back to Spain, if only temporarily.[16] In some ways, the war was just another economic crisis, and returning home, a classic solution. In times of hardship, people had been used to coming back to their region of origin. In that regard, the economic effect of the war could be felt in a variety of ways. Some French tenants of rural extraction, for instance, had to promptly return to their village of origin in order to help with the harvest. Now that so many men had left for the army, crops were in jeopardy. This further contributed to the rare reversal of the push and pull factors in favour of emigration regions.[17]

Although homecomings were not structurally different from one country to the next, they were more national than ever before. Until then, occasional "repatriations" had been private and individual affairs, whether national institutions had provided financial help or not.[18] Now multiple trains were entirely paid for by the embassies.[19] Aboard, there were no French travellers to be found – only fellow nationals. And in Italy as in Spain, state-backed committees raised funds to help returning migrants reach their hometowns. State representatives at the local level were also involved in assisting – and registering – emigrants on their way back.[20]

French authorities, who needed to devote nearly all the railway system to military purposes, soon stopped subsidising tickets to the needy. Southern European states dit the same.[21] French and foreign tenants who remained at Nos. 96–102 were either too poor, deterred by the impossibility of taking their furniture with them or had ties in the Plaine-Saint-Denis too strong to sever.[22] By early October, as the last families decided to leave, some returnees were already thinking of coming back. An Italian who had left in August was already back by December.[23] As for Louis Pirolli, he returned quickly to the Plaine. He was already back at his Legras post by March 1915, with neither his wife nor children.[24]

Louis's parents also had every intention to come back to the Plaine but they ended up staying in the village a bit longer. As a consequence, they had to go through a more demanding procedure than their son to be allowed back into France. In Italy, a passport for foreign travel had now become compulsory. The pre-approval from the *Commissariato generale dell'Emigrazione*, the institution controlling emigration, was also required, as was a visa of a French consulate which was conditioned on a labour contract (see Figure 8.1).[25] As

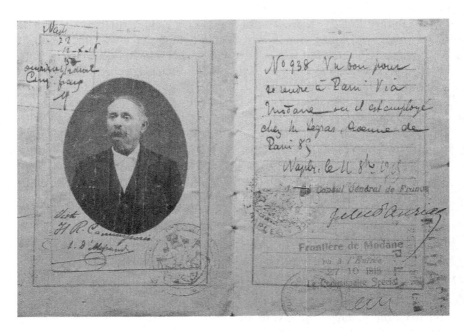

Figure 8.1 Giacinto Pirolli's passport, issued in Isernia, 1915. Private collection of Mr. and Ms. Parravano. Photograph by the author.

the war dragged on, the intervention of national institutions became more and more tangible in people's cross-border mobilities and life choices.

Archival traces suggest that returning families of residents faced similar experiences across France and Europe. They went to work in agriculture, as they had before their migration, only to wait for an opportunity to go back to Saint-Denis. There were certainly local differences, especially with regard to the urgency people felt to try and travel back to the Plaine. Factors could diverge in that respect. In southern Italy, for instance, the heavy damage to the region caused by an earthquake in January 1915 may have made the re-emigration even more necessary.[26]

Crossing national boundaries

During the war, national boundaries could be experienced in ways other than border crossing. First, a number of Italian and Spanish residents decided to join the Foreign Legion.[27] Besides a genuine sympathy and enthusiasm for the French cause, their decision to enlist was based on various motives.[28] The automatic protection against any potential deportation of the *légionnaire*'s family must have crossed people's minds. This was all the more likely because they might have heard stories of Italian-speaking families being forcibly removed from the Plaine. Deportation and denaturalisation eventually spared the *cités* during the First World War. But some inhabitants may have dreaded these measures, upon which war governments increasingly relied.[29]

Also, it would soon be known that families of foreign volunteers would be entitled to the same benefits as families of French soldiers.[30] At a time of sudden and widespread unemployment in the summer of 1914, this was a major aspect to consider.

Once Italy entered the war, the French government agreed to return the Italian soldiers living within its borders to its ally. In the Spring of 1915, the so-called Garibaldi regiment of the Foreign Legion was disbanded. Some tenants followed orders from the Italian army and went on to fight on a second front, under a second uniform. Others were less inclined to do so. A former resident who had been serving in that regiment had initially placed his hopes in a naturalisation request, filed a few months earlier. But he ultimately decided to withdraw it. He had seen enough in the first months of the war – he himself was injured, and the Garibaldians suffered over 25% of casualties – and had no intention of serving further for France. As for Italy, he figured he would simply dodge the draft, which he did. But after the war ended, he changed his mind again and confirmed his intention of becoming French.[31]

On the face of it, some Italian, French, Spanish and Belgian families in the *cités* might have felt on an equal footing; no matter the army, their husbands and sons were fighting for the Allies. International agreements provided that the children of Belgian immigrants, like two brothers in the *cités*, would be enrolled in the French Army.[32] In people's minds, the enrollment of sons from the same family (or even of the same individual) in two different armies of the Allies' camp could lead to a secondary form of patriotism. This patriotism was inclusive and somehow denationalised. Certain well-known families, while foreign from a legal standpoint, symbolically joined the "us" group: a plural pronoun which could be used by the non-nationals themselves, like the Spaniard who would say "we" when referring to the French government.[33] At No. 100, an Italian-born tenant initially enrolled in the French Foreign Legion before joining the Italian Army in 1915. He would disappear on the Isonzo front before one of his brothers, a French citizen, was killed at Verdun.[34] Yet casualty rates on the Italian and French fronts soon proved very dissimilar. When for the first time (apparently) an Italian tenant lost his son in 1917, his French neighbours had already borne the brunt of the war toll. There had been at least five deaths of French tenants during the first six months of the war.[35] At No. 96, the concierge Barbe Sommer ended up losing three of her four sons. Upon her request, the municipal authorities helped ensure that the last one was sent to a safe assignment (Figure 8.2).[36]

As the conflict settled in and became a fact of life, the importance of military episodes – which were all over national newspapers – waned in

Figure 8.2 No. 96's porter Barbe Sommer in her apartment, late 1914. Private collection of Ms. Besson. Photograph by the author.

people's daily interactions. As early as the first weeks of the war, tensions against putative "Prussians" observed in the centre of Saint-Denis barely had any echo in the Plaine. Based on false rumours of German ownership, three Maggi dairy shops were vandalised in the area, including that of No. 96. Though this was bound to have frightened tenants of Alsatian and Lorrainer origin, the act was committed by a looting mob that came from afar and attracted general scorn in the neighbourhood.[37] In subsequent years, Plainards generally remained unconcerned with the ins and outs of military operations.[38]

Asymmetrical decisions made by national governments could also fragment the social fabric of the *cités* and further embed national differences in people's minds. Born in 1899, Louis Carbone was among the "*ragazzi del '99,*" i.e. the 18-year-olds that Italy decided to enlist in early 1917.[39] "Loulou," as he was called, attended his medical examination at the Italian consulate in June 1917, was soon declared fit and promptly headed to the front. At the same time, Jules Brulé was a French national and former schoolmate of Loulou's who also lived at No. 100. Born only two months after Louis, he stayed with his parents and would not serve until April 1918.[40] So whether people participated in the nationalist rhetoric or not, national decisions and ascribed allegiances splintered a context in which nationalism previously had little salience. In that regard, the Plaine was not unlike other cosmopolitan contexts.[41]

Other differences

A family's national origin proved more important in wartime, but it was not necessarily a game-changer. Other distinctions could run athwart differences based on nationality. Undesirability became as much a criterion of foreignness as legal nationality. From 1915 to 1916, those who were being sought and denounced as unwelcome were the so-called *embusqués* (cowards), detached in factories by industrial necessity, but also by favour or outright fraud. In the Plaine-Saint-Denis, most (but not all) of these privileged workers were French. We know of several Frenchmen living in the *cités* who were mobilised in factories and bore the distinctive armband of the *détachés en usine* (detached in factories).[42] The management at Legras filed the necessary papers to spare several of their long-time employees from active duty and had to defend themselves against rumours of helping draft dodgers by sheer favouritism.[43]

The most significant number of tenants in this enviable situation came from the *Compagnie du Nord*, a railway company. They were either long-standing Plainards or recently arrived refugees.[44] From 1915 onwards, some Italian workers positioned in factories supplying the French Army also became exempt from service in Italy by virtue of provisional agreements between the French and Italian governments. As a consequence, their fate was closer to that of French residents placed in the same situation than to their countrymen in uniform. These lucky Frenchmen and Italians kept working together, and they became the targets of the same sort of smears for not being either French or Italian enough. This contributed to redrawing the boundaries of belonging and citizenship.[45]

Resentment against real or perceived cowards redefined everyone's right to residency. For newcomers, such as a soldier on leave or Belgian refugees, it could paradoxically be the local police officer whom they – as many French people from the home front – viewed as idle and anti-patriotic; in other words, a stranger to the social fabric. "Go to the front, your place isn't here," policemen would be told, when not beaten up or escorted by angry civilians to the nearest military base for an identity check.[46] Naturally, this construction of cowardice, like that of prostitution, was an easy way to express or settle pre-existing antagonisms. But one of the originalities of the Plaine's demographic context is that such rhetorical devices could be wielded by non-nationals against French people.[47]

Gender issues also became intertwined with norms of patriotic correctness. The masculinity of those who were not fighting on the front became increasingly questioned starting in 1916. Boys under 17, the minimum age for a voluntary enlistment, were in principle protected against such insinuations. Masculinity being primarily attached to military service, boys who were not old enough to serve had to find other ways to subscribe to this model. For a Paris-born tenant, Raymond Hatterer, the beginning of the war was a period when he tried to show off his fitness for service. The teenage son of a local baker, Raymond used the courtyard to practice rifle shooting after work.

This may have been a way to prevent negative feelings among his neighbours because Raymond's family enjoyed an enviable position. His father's departure for the front had been deferred because of his status as a baker. And as a probable result of his father's connections with local politicians, Raymond had secured a white-collar job at the local bank. Lastly, the youth bore an Alsatian last name and had tangible family connections with enemy powers – one of his aunts was married to a German, and one of his uncles had long been an employee at the Austro-Hungarian embassy – hence the need to act like a man and a patriot. Raymond's eventual departure for the front and his subsequent war injury may have been, in a strange way, a reward for his efforts: it served as his passport to a masculine, militarised and anti-German version of French citizenship.[48]

Discrepancies between tenants of the same nationality, and even between members of the same family, were not only apparent through uneven exposure to the perils of war. They could also consist in differences in microeconomic conditions. In the fall of 1917, when Paul Carbone – Loulou's brother – came back from the Italian front for a month of leave, he may have paid a visit to the family of yet another brother of his, Dominique, at No. 100. Whereas Paul's wife received a daily 1.15-franc allowance as the wife of an Italian soldier, Dominique earned a daily salary of 7 francs at a local metal factory supplying the French military.[49] Benefits for Italian wives were only slightly inferior to their French equivalents.[50] But they were notoriously insufficient when it came to making ends meet, and some foreign families were authorised to receive the refugee allocation instead.[51]

Other foreigners of the *cités* did rather well during the conflict and were not singled out by the authorities. Born in Italy, Maria Giacinta Reale – who now went by the French name of Georgette – took control of the *débit** at No. 96.[52] Her sister-in-law Angèle, at No. 100, worked at the toy factory across the Avenue[53] and amassed a significant amount of money from suspicious ventures with local *apaches*.*[54] This sort of accomplishment by residents was not framed in national terms, either by the protagonists or by those who wished them ill.[55] The national divide between long-time neighbours was counterbalanced by years of familiarity. Lastly, there was another series of issues in which the state would try to impose a national framework over a more complex reality, which contributed to redefining the residents' cognitive boundaries surrounding citizenship. These issues had to do with race, gender and empire.

Intersectional fault lines

During the war, the arrival of colonial and Chinese subjects to the Plaine-Saint-Denis was viewed as a potential social peril by state institutions. The presence of these populations, imported nationwide by the Ministry of War from late 1915 began to be documented in the area in 1917.[56] As opposed to the "white" foreign workers that the Ministry of Armament was in charge of recruiting – Italians, Greeks, Swedes, Portuguese and Spaniards – the assimilation of this exotic manpower was regarded as neither feasible nor desirable.[57]

Officially, authorities encouraged a paternalistic approach as well as humane treatment of colonial workers. Yet one of the main concerns of public officials and employers on the ground was to prevent colonial subjects from interacting with the French metropolitan population.[58] Part of the explanation for this lay in the fear that enjoying too much freedom in France could lead indigenous people to demand the same rights in the colonies. This restrictive policy was also grounded in sexual considerations.[59] However, actual cases of racialised antagonisms based on sexual competition remained rare in the Plaine. In any case, it is hard to tell whether this factor may have been at play in certain incidents. The Plaine's lack of race-based sexual conflict is all the more comprehensible when considering that the offer of paid sex was abundant and affordable – at least for the men who worked in armament factories.[60]

There were probably never as many sex workers as in those years. The *fleurs des fortifs* (lit. flowers from the walls of Paris) who picked up clients "near the gas factory," as the popular Georgius would sing after the war, were everywhere.[61] Prostitution fostered positive interactions between clients of different origin; in the café at the corner of rue Proudhon, sex workers would solicit both British noncommissioned officers and local heads of households, who befriended one another.[62] And when in order to rein in this immoral pastime, the British command denied its soldiers any local shop or bar altogether, every bar-owner from around the tenement protested in outrage.[63]

As for colonial subjects, they were not treated equally by French authorities and the local population. The state's racial prejudices, which would hold true for years, contrasted the "brutal mores" of the North Africans with the docile tranquillity of sub-Saharan and Indochinese subjects.[64] None of them, in any case, were supposed to gain a pathway to full French citizenship. From the locals' point of view, by contrast, it seems that whatever tensions existed, they remained muffled until the last months of the war. More and more soldiers came back around this time and had a hard time finding work.[65] However, violent arguments among the North-African workers, which were sometimes related to imported rancours, could feed into the racialisation of public discourse and cast them on the side of the *indésirables*.[66] This was all the more true when some of them, possibly out of revenge, began engaging in nightly robberies on passers-by, an activity of which they had long been at the receiving end.[67] It is also possible that such tension would have triggered yet another evolution of the racialised image of Spaniards and Italians in the area. They could have experienced a "whitening" in contrast with the North Africans, although they were no less likely to be involved in violent scuffles.[68]

Yet once again, fault lines would not fall neatly along ethnonational separations. The newcomers who managed to settle in (like those who took over bars) did not seem to face particular opposition, whether they came from Greece or Algeria. And in factories, during the great strikes of May 1918, people's resentment was mostly directed at the upcoming arrival of American and Japanese workers.[69] Just as welcoming attitudes often depended on language, resources and conditions of the newcomers' arrival (alone/in barracks/with pre-existing networks in the neighbourhood), hostilities seem to have been driven by factors other than origin; it rarely came up in people's expressions of despise or insult, even when tempers flared up. On the other hand, state intervention could act as a decisive factor in driving wedges between people along racial lines. At the local level, an imperial and racialised understanding of the nation could spark social questions that had rarely been raised before in the metropolis, let alone in the Plaine-Saint-Denis. A story involving a young female tenant is indicative of this.

Born in 1897 in a small village in Tonkin, Indochina, the young Trân Đinh Long – who went by the nickname of Năm – enlisted voluntarily as a military worker when recruitment took place in Hanoi. He arrived in mainland France in September 1915. After probably changing places several times, Năm was assigned to the Plaine-Saint-Denis group of Indochinese workers in early 1918. Accommodated in barracks about 600 metres to the east of the *cités*, his mission consisted in repairing the damaged railway tracks of the area.

The extent to which these colonial workers mingled with outsiders is not easy to determine. On the one hand, racism and harassment were not absent. One of Năm's fellow workers was hurt by a stone thrown by an 18-year-old who later confessed that the worker had done nothing to provoke him. Yet we know that Indochinese men, like their North African counterparts, certainly engaged with women.[70]

In late 1918, Năm had an affair with 15-year-old Yvonne. Born in Oise, to the northwest of Paris, she had grown up at No. 98 Av. de Paris. As her pregnancy became more obvious, Yvonne's mother wrote to the *Président du Conseil* (Prime Minister) to ask permission for Năm to marry her daughter. In the following months, the French authorities tried their best to discourage the marriage. That stance was inspired by a general segregationist policy, clearly exposed in confidential exchanges among high-level government officials as early as February 1917. Allowing such unions and the subsequent return of these married couples to Indochina, the reasoning went, could harm the prestige of France within the indigenous society.[71]

As one inspector put it, the *indigènes*' ambitions of marrying French women were spurred by "false ideas on naturalisation," and the hope of increasing their social status in the colony. "They believe that the presence in their family of a French woman would result in a greater consideration from the part of colonial Frenchmen or of their fellow indigenous subjects."[72] From the government's standpoint, such aspirations were fanciful; the imperial conception of the nation implied that colonial subjects remained second-class citizens. In principle, they may have enjoyed a legal equality to French nationals when it came to marrying whomever they wished. Yet in practice, they were not permitted to exercise this right. The emergence of a class of mixed-race French citizens – Năm and Yvonne's children would be French by birth – was something the French authorities were determined to prevent.[73]

It is in this spirit that the Governor-General in Hanoi ordered an inquiry into the material situation of Năm's family. The report, for which the authorities even commissioned photographs of the family, was supposed to paint a dire picture to Yvonne's family. Năm's 60-year-old father owned a small, straw-covered cob and thatch cottage, while his mother earned a meager income by selling *nước chè* (tea). But what with the life conditions that Yvonne's family was used to in the Plaine-Saint-Denis, as well as the real bond between Năm and Yvonne, her mother persisted in August 1919. Now, the baby girl was born, Yvonne was an unmarried mother and Năm had already left the Plaine for a new assignment farther north. Yvonne's mother maintained her request but yielded to the government's persuasion on one crucial point: she conditioned the marriage upon the right for Năm to remain in metropolitan France at the end of his service. This effectively amounted to an opportunity for the ministry to torpedo the marriage altogether. Just like most of the foreign and colonial manpower that had been exploited by the Allies during the war, Năm was barred from staying.[74] Two years later, Yvonne married another man who recognised the baby child as his.[75]

This case illustrates how the offspring of white women were deemed too important to be left under the authority of their colonial fathers, although they legally should have been. It also highlights how racially-tinged considerations could be intertwined with a gender and age component. Năm was not the only one who was prevented from exercising his civil franchises; Yvonne was also frustrated in her plans to choose a spouse, because of her double status as a female and a minor. Had she been a male adult, her lover would have been able to remain in France and become a French citizen. For the first time, colonial definitions of citizenship, with their different tiers of membership according to racial categories, could gain currency in metropolitan locations and disrupt the social life of ordinary people.[76]

154 *Interactions and allegiances*

All in all, as national governments and local authorities tried to regulate social participation and allegiances, the inhabitants of the *cités* and the nation-states maintained a constant dialogue. Constantly reconfigured by formal and informal decisions on both ends, this relationship was far from balanced. It was always the states who had the final say over letting people vote; granting them a new nationality, visa or free loaf of bread; and sending them to fight in the trenches. Nevertheless, individual cases show how the rules were constantly resisted and negotiated. The official versions of citizenship had loopholes, and tenants at Nos. 96–102 had a more fluid understanding of what it meant to belong in the *cités*, neighbourhood and society as a whole.

Networks remained paramount in people's interactions with public authorities, and often superseded the effect of national differences in social life. Political connections to accelerate one's naturalisation, obtain a municipal benefit or procure official documents for unlawful purposes; contacts at companies that could help avoid being sent to the front or cross international borders in wartime; know-how exchanged with friends, concierges and friendly police officers, in order to give the authorities the information they expected …. All of these levers probably constructed as much difference in the tenement as the legal notion of nationality, between those who could pull them and those who could not.

At the same time, the outcomes of these interactions between tenants and the state were sanctioned by a variety of material and biological markers such as passports, forced departures, injuries or even deaths. This created sociocultural differences which intersected with daily distinctions emerging from both the residents' spatial movements and their affinity-hostility dynamics. In other words, the institutional discourse of belonging and citizenship was a powerful force, but not an irresistible one. When it did permeate the micro-context of the *cités* – always after some degree of diffraction – this rhetoric contributed to reconfiguring the boundaries of difference in tenants' lives.

Notes

1 APP, CB 92.14, 1917/2009, 17.12.1917; CB 92.14, 1918/172, 14.02.1918; *JORF*, 13.10.1945, 6497.
2 Matthew Stibbe (ed.), *Captivity, Forced Labor and Forced Migration in Europe during the First World War* (Abingdon: Routledge, 2009); Santanu Das, ed., *Race, Empire and First World War Writing* (Cambridge: Cambridge University Press, 2011); Peter Gatrell and Liubov Zhvanko, eds., *Europe on the Move: Refugees in the Era of the Great War, 1912–1923* (Manchester: Manchester University Press, 2017).
3 Horne, "Immigrant workers"; Stovall, "Colour-blind France?"

4 Andrew Horrall, "The 'foreigners' from Broad Street: the Ukrainian sojourners from Ottawa who fought for Canada in the First World War," *Histoire sociale/Social history* 49, No. 98 (2016): 73–103; Laurent Dornel and Céline Regnard, *Les Chinois dans la Grande Guerre. Des bras au service de la France* (Paris: Les Indes savantes, 2018); Jacqueline Jenkinson, ed., *Belgian Refugees in First World War Britain* (Abingdon: Routledge, 2018); Janiv Stamberger, "The 'Belgian' Jewish experience of World War One," *Les Cahiers de la mémoire contemporaine* 13 (2018): 95–124.
5 Ben Braber, "Living with the enemy – German immigrants in Nottingham during the First World War," *Midland History* 42, No. 1 (2017): 72–91.
6 Galante, John, 2016, "Distant loyalties: World War I and the Italian South Atlantic" (doctoral diss. in history, University of Pittsburgh, 2016).
7 Stacy D. Fahrenthold, *Between the Ottomans and the Entente: The First World War in the Syrian and Lebanese Diaspora, 1908–1925* (Oxford: Oxford University Press, 2019).
8 APP, CB 92.11, 1914/589–590, 3.08.1914.
9 They were Austrian subjects from Trentino: APP, CB 92.11, 1914/634, 27-28.08.1914; CB 92.12, 1916/274 *bis,* 20-29.03.1916.
10 *JSD,* 9.08.1914.
11 Becker and Audouin-Rouzeau, *Les Sociétés européennes et la guerre.*
12 APP, CB 92.11, 1914/835, 17.12.1914.
13 See *L'Émancipation,* 12.09.1914; SDMA, 4H3/4, Letter from the Head of the Chemins de fer de l'État to the Mayor of SD, 12.08.1914.
14 AD93, 4U7/723, 27.10.1916, Veuve Gréco c. Lutel.
15 Compare FNA, F/12/8649, Légion d'honneur, Charles Legras (stating that the factory had 1,250 employees in 1909); SDMA, 4H3/13, Letter from the Legras factory's director to the Mayor of SD, 17.11.1914.
16 See e.g. letter from J. Mouton to Manuel Arellano, Bohonal de Ibor, 28.11.1914, private collection (int. No. 31, 18.08.2016).
17 See e.g. SDMA, 4H3/8, Letter from Reine Gauthier [no date, Sept. 1914].
18 See e.g. SDMA, 1I12, Letter from the Mayor of SD to the Head of the 4th bureau of the PP, 7.08.1895, about Mme Brulez, 100 av. de Paris. On the repatriation of Spanish emigrants before the Great War, see Noguer, 1912.
19 On the general situation for Spaniards and Italians, see Gaziel, *Diario de un estudiante: París 1914,* trans. José Ángel Martos Martín (Barcelona: Diërensis, 2013 [1914]), 289–90; Giovanni Gesare Majoni, "Relazione sull'opera svolta dal Commissariato a tutela delle nostra emigrazione in conseguenza dello scoppio della guerra europea," 36, in ACS, *Min. interno, Dir. gen. p. s., Div. polizia, Div. polizia giudizaria,* fasc. 11900.a, 1913–1915.
20 See Archivo histórico de las Merindades, Villarcayo, Spain, sig. 1597, "Antecedentes de la suscripción de caracter nacional para soccorrer a los repatriados con motivo de la actual guerra europea. Agosto de 1914"; *El Castellano,* 10.08.1914, 13.08.1914, 19.08.1914, 28.08.1914, 22.09.1914; ACS, *Min. interno, Dir. gen. p. s., Div. polizia, Div. polizia giudizaria* fasc. 14800.A, "Vitto e alloggio a indigenti, rimpatrio dalla Turchia, rimpatrio dall'estero a causa della guerra (per provincia)," 1913–5.
21 SDMA, CT225, Letters from the Consul general of Italy to the Mayor of SD, 18.08.1914, 27.08.1914, 6.09.1914, 10.09.1914; and AGA, sig. 54/5.932, 1914, No. 5, Letter from P. Balaguar to the Spanish ambassador in Paris, 4.09.1914.
22 The Italian ambassador in Paris affirmed in June 1915 that the Italians who had stayed in Paris in the Fall of 1914 were about 15,000 and were the "most needy" (ACS, *Min. interno, Dir. gen. p. s., Div. polizia, Div. polizia giudizaria,* 1913–5,

fasc. 14800.a, "Reale Ambasciata di Parigi," Letter from the Italian ambassador in Paris to the Presidente del Consiglio, 2.06.1915).
23 FNA, BB/11/9615, 23796x26, Greco.
24 FNA, BB/11/10553, 41906x27, Pirolli.
25 Int. No. 52, 28.10.2016; APP, CB 92.15, 1918/395, 11.04.1918. On Article 2 of the decree of 2.05.1915 modifying the decree of 21.01.1901, see Ernest Lémonon, *L'Après-guerre et la main-d'œuvre italienne en France* (Paris: Félix Alcan, 1918), 54–5.
26 AS Frosinone, b. 565, "Edifici danneggiati dal terremoto nel circondario di Sora," 24.11.1917.
27 This was the case of least four tenants from Nos. 96–102: Costantino Gio Batta Orsi (FNA, BB/11/11264, 77542x28), Feliciano Sedano (FNA, BB/11/12897, 3823x30), Giolormo Pirolli (FNA, BB/11/11367, 82663x28), Rodríguez Mateos (SDMA, 4H1/2587, Fallen soldiers, 1914-1918, "Mathéo"); SDMA, CT209, "Disparus. Guerre 1914-1918," 24.06.1916; AD93, 1E66/388, SD, deaths, 1921, vol. 2, No. 1298, transcription of a ruling from 9.05.1915).
28 Stéfanie Prezioso, "Les Italiens en France au prisme de l'engagement volontaire: les raisons de l'enrôlement dans la Grande Guerre (1914–1915)," *Cahiers de la Méditerranée*, No. 81 (2010): 147–63.
29 I found only one denaturalisation procedure targetting a former inhabitant of the *cités*, who had been born in German Saarland. The procedure was dropped after no incriminating element could be found (FNA, BB/11/4456, 1564x06, Steinmann). By contrast, revisions of naturalisation undertaken during the Second World War would result in the denaturalisation of one current resident (FNA, 19770904/174, 103514x41, Barquin) and of several former inhabitants of the *cités*, like Louis Pirolli (see Chapter 7). On this subject, see Daniela Caglioti, "Subjects, citizens, and aliens in a time of upheaval: naturalizing and denaturalizing in Europe during the First World War," *The Journal of Modern History* 89, No. 3 (2017): 495–530; Stefan Manz, Panikos Panayi, and Matthew Stibbe, eds., *Internment During the First World War: A Mass Global Phenomenon* (Abingdon: Routledge, 2018).
30 *L'Émancipation*, 29.08.1914.
31 FNA, BB/11/4698, 9356x07, Carlesimo.
32 Art. 2 of the Franco-Belgian convention of 30.07.1891. See AVP, D4R1 1202, 1901, No. 4133; D4R1 1726, 1913, No. 4505, Vandepontseele brothers.
33 *JSD*, 28.03.1915; APP, CB 91.23, 1917/1039, 27.11.1917.
34 SDMA, 4H1/2587; FNA, BB/11/7235, 6407x20, Mattéo.
35 On the Italian tenant who was killed, the name is Jean Baptiste Pirolli: see Emilio Pistilli, *Acquafondata e Casalcassinese* (Acquafondata: Comune di Acquafondata, 2004), 121. The Spaniard is Rodríguez Mateos (see above, note 27). For the French residents, see AVP, D4R1 1101, 1901, No. 1932, Granger; SDMA, 4H1/3420, Sommer; SDMA, CT209, "Disparus. Guerre 1914-1918," Dubuffet; AVP, D4R1 1612, 1911, No. 4957, Dubrulle; *JSD*, 8.3.1915; AVP, D4R1 1669, 1912, No. 5056, Rocher. Casualties are much higher when taking into account former residents, and also gas victims who died after 1918.
36 SDMA, CT177, Letter from Mme Sommer, 96 av. de Paris, to the Mayor of SD, 16.05.1916.
37 CB 92.11, 1914/594, 4.08.1914; 1914/685, 2.09.1914; SDMA, 4H3/223, "Laiteries de la Plaine-Saint-Denis," 26.11.1918.
38 Fabrice Langrognet, "Contingent minorities: what the Great War meant for the migrant youth of the Plaine-Saint-Denis," *The Journal of the History of Childhood and Youth* 11, No. 2 (2018): 208–26.

39 Enzo Raffaelli and Lorenzo Cadeddu, eds., *I ragazzi del '99: Il racconto dei diciottenni al fronte* (Udine: Gaspari, 2016).
40 ASC Pontecorvo, *leva* 1899-1900, *classe* 1899, No. 20; births, 1899, No. 214; FNA, BB/11/10398, 34199x27, Carbone; *La Lanterne, Le Gaulois, Le Petit Parisien,* 27.01.1924; AVP, Military registers, D4R1 2101, No. 5250.
41 Tobit Vandamme, "The rise of nationalism in a cosmopolitan port city: the foreign communities of Shanghai during the First World War," *Journal of World History* 29, No. 1 (2018): 37–64.
42 AVP, D4R1 1558, 1910, No. 3822, Victor Muller, mobilised at Legras (his brother Joseph was in the same situation, which suggests a particular protection of the family by the factory's management –see AVP, D4R1 1509, 1909, No. 5477, Muller); D4R1 1966, 1917, No. 5904, Piers. Some tenants were placed in factories because of their age or a medical condition, and were not technically on draft-deferral (see e.g. AVP, D4R1 644, 1891, No. 410, Joseph David Sommer).
43 SDMA, CT208, Certificate issued by Legras for Dimnet Antoine, 16.10.1917; Brunet, "Une banieue ouvrière," 191–2; *JSD*, 10.11.1915, 5.12.1915, 12.12.1915.
44 See e.g. AVP, D4R1 780, 1894, 1530, Barbier; D4R1 879, 1896, 4079, Isz; D4R1 780, 1894, 1737, Jean-Baptiste dit Langlois; D4R1 1202, 1903, No. 4379, Abrioux; D4R1 1398, 1907, No. 2657, Piers; D4R1 1613, 1911, No. 5161, Monnet. Refugee tenants could also mobilised at the *Compagnie du Nord*: see AD93, D7 42–9, Malderez, Duclermortier, Sauvage.
45 APP, CB 89.48, 1914/1332, 23.10.1914; CB 92.11, 1915/520, 3.04.1915; CB 92.12, 1915/917, 24.11.1915-7.12.1915; 1916/576, 3.07.1916.
46 APP, CB 92.11, 1915/520, 3.04.1915; 1915/551, 5.08.1915; 1915/561, 18.08.1915; *JSD*, 10.09.1916; APP, CB 92.15, 1918/598, 27.05.1918.
47 APP, CB 92.12, 1915/917, 24.11.1915-7.12.1915; 1916/576, 3.07.1916.
48 FNA, BB/11/2910, 13770x93, Hatterer; APP, CB 92.11, 1915/98, 27.01.1915; SDMA, 4H3/16; SDMA, H40, 1917, and H42, 1919; SDMA, 20C 001-001, 39–41; ASSD, 1E66/377, SD, deaths, 1916, vol. 1, No. 283, 19.02.1916; AVP, D4R1 2101, 1919, No. 5479, Hatterer; D4R1 1966, 1917, No. 5692, Hatterer.
49 SDMA, 4H3/137, Letter from the Director of the Italian Benevolent Society to the Mayor of SD, 3.11.1917, and reply from the Mayor, 13.11.1917; FNA, BB/11/10387, 33613x27, Paul Carbone; BB/11/10398, 34199x27, Dominique Carbone.
50 Auguste Saillard and Henri Fougerol, *Les Allocations aux familles des mobilisés, réfugiés et victimes civiles de la guerre* (Paris: Berger-Levrault, 1917).
51 Jérôme Hervé, "Réfugiés italiens dans le Maine-et-Loire pendant la Grande Guerre," *La Trace. Cahiers du Centre d'études et de documentation sur l'émigration italienne*, No. 14 (2001), 32.
52 APP, CB 92.14, 1918/207, 24.02.1918.
53 SDMA, CT158, N. Clerc factory, list of workers back at work, 17.10.1914.
54 APP, CB 92.15, 1918/607, 4-6.06.1918; CB 92.25, 1927/1596, 15.09.1927.
55 *Ibid.*
56 APP, CB 92.14, 1917/708, 24.07.1917; CB 92.14, 1917/906, 29.09.1917; AD93, 1E66/379, SD, deaths, 1917, No. 1807, 28.12.1917.
57 FNA, 94AP/120, Ministry of the Armament, "L'introduction de la main-d'œuvre étrangère pendant la guerre, et la politique d'immigration," 12.07.1917, 2. For a general outline of wartime policies regarding foreign and colonial manpower, see Bertrand Nogaro and Lucien Weil, *La Main-d'œuvre étrangère et coloniale pendant la guerre* (Paris, New Haven: PUF/Yale University Press, 1926).
58 See e.g. FNA, 94 AP 130, Report by M. Berrue, 13.06.1916.
59 Mireille Favre-Le Van Ho, "Un milieu porteur de modernisation: travailleurs et tirailleurs vietnamiens en France pendant la Première Guerre mondiale" (doctoral diss. in history, École nationale des Chartes, 1986); Marc Michel,

"'Immigrés malgré eux': soldats et travailleurs coloniaux en France pendant la Première Guerre mondiale," *Historiens & Géographes*, No. 384 (2003): 333–44; Kimloan Vu-Hill, *Coolies into Rebels: Impact of World War I on French Indochina* (Paris: Les Indes savantes, 2011).

60 APP, CB 92.11, 1915/489, 23.07.1915; APP, CB 92.15, 1918/732, 23.06.1918; CB, 1919/563, 30.07.1919.
61 *On l'appelait "Fleur-des-fortifs,"* lyrics by Georgius, music by Jean Lenoir, 1930.
62 APP, JC58, 181.746. M.R; CB 92.12, 1916/421, 22.05.1916; 1916/518; 26.06.1916. See also Fabrice Langrognet, "Accueil et représentations des migrants en temps de guerre: les étrangers à la Plaine-Saint-Denis, 1914–1919," *Migrance*, Nos. 45–6 (2016): 161–72.
63 SDMA, 4H3/58, Lettre-pétition en date du 1.05.1916 des commerçants de la Plaine-Saint-Denis.
64 See e.g. ANOM, 1slotfom/4, Ministry of the Colonies, SCAFICF, "Note pour M. le Général, directeur des services militaires," 13.09.1924.
65 APP, CB 92.14, 1917/464, 13.05.1917; 1918/289 and 310, 20.03.1918; CB 92.16, 1919/310, 3.03.1919; 1919/595, 25.08.1919.
66 APP, CB 92.13, 1916/824, 1.10.1916; *JSD*, 8.10.1916, 24.02.1918.
67 APP, CB 92.16, 1919/707, 2.10.1919.
68 APP, CB 92.14, 1918/172, 14.02.1918.
69 APP, CB 92.15, 1918/208 et 209, 23.02.1918; CB 92.16, 1919/707, 2.10.1919; FNA, F/7/13367, "Compte rendu," 14.05.1918.
70 We can deduct as much from the sexually transmitted diseases reported among Indochinese workers of the Plaine-Saint-Denis in ANOM, 1slotfom/9, "Rapport de Tri-Phu Le Quang Liem Dit Bay au sujet de sa visite dans les hôpitaux de Saint-Denis ...," 07.04.1919. See also APP, CB 92.11, 1915/564, 18.08.1915; CB 92.15, 1918/208–9, 23.02.1918; CB 92.16, 1919/447, 26–7.06.1919.
71 On the importance and effects of the "politics of prestige" in colonial Indochina, see Emmanuelle Saada, *Les Enfants de la colonie: les métis de l'Émpire français entre sujétion et citoyenneté* (Paris: La Découverte, 2007), 71–8.
72 ANOM, 1slotfom/9, Note rédigée par M. Nguyen-Van-Vinh, Tri-Phu de Cochinchine, Délégué au Service du Contrôle des Tirailleurs et Travailleurs indochinois en France, 27.05.1918, 18 (*"Ils pensent que la présence dans leur famille d'une femme française attirerait une plus grande considération des Français coloniaux ou de leurs compatriotes."*)
73 Saada, *Les Enfants de la colonie*, 131–6. For a recent discussion of the interplay of anti-miscegenation policies and racial boundaries of citizenship in another colonial context, see Pamela Ballinger, *The World Refugees Made: Decolonization and the Foundations of Postwar Italy* (Ithaca: Cornell University Press, 2020), 134–74.
74 Jacqueline Jenkinson, *Colonial, Refugee and Allied Civilians After the First World War: Immigration Restriction and Mass Repatriation* (Abingdon: Routledge, 2020).
75 See ANOM, 6slotfom/7; 1slotfom/1, Confidential letter from René Viviani, Minister of Justice, to the Procureur général, 2.02.1917; APP, CB 92.14, 1918/281, 13-14.03.1918; APP, CB 92.15,1918/1369, 30.12.1918; AD93, 1E66/280, births, 1919, No. 555; 1E66/281, births, 1920, No. 253; 1E66/341, mar., 1921, No. 709.
76 Ann Laura Stoler and Frederick Cooper, eds., *Tensions of Empire: Colonial Cultures in a Bourgeois World,* (Berkeley: University of California Press, 1997); Laura Levine Frader, "From muscles to nerves: gender, 'race' and the body at work in France 1919-1939," *International Review of Social History* 44, No. 7 (1999): 123–47.

Conclusion

The end date of this book's story, 1932, was neither an ending for the tenement, nor for its inhabitants. Both still had a future ahead of them. For the buildings, what lay ahead turned out to be much of the same – perhaps even worse. They continued to deteriorate but remained too expensive to repair and too crowded to demolish. By the start of the Second World War, the sight of No. 100 was more appalling than ever. "The walls have cracks, the coats are crumbling, the woodwork's fastenings do not hold anymore, the floors could collapse at any moment…." The list of defects compiled by health inspectors went on and on.[1]

The bombings of the Plaine-Saint-Denis by the Royal Air Force in 1944 did not help.[2] On the night of April 21, hundreds of bombs were dropped on the area. One exploded about 40 metres from the tenement, blowing out the windows and riddling the front buildings with shrapnel. That night, most residents took shelter in the cellar at No. 98. Cautiously emerging the next morning, they were startled by the sight of corpses and dead horses spread across the Avenue.[3] Louis and Maria Pirolli's shop at No. 119 had been entirely destroyed; what remained of the glass factory was looted (Figure 9.1).[4]

Three months later, on August 25, 1944, the old tenement was hit once again; street combats sprayed the façade at Nos. 100–102 with bullets. The next day, an incendiary bomb fell on No. 104 and caused part of No. 102's roof to collapse.[5]

Blaming the bombings, Mme. Carbone later complained that the ceiling of her apartment at No. 100 was sagging.[6] Not long afterwards, the "balcony" (see Chapter 1) would collapse under the feet of her daughter.[7] Finally, in the late 1960s and early 1970s, the remainder of the old constructions at Nos. 96 and 100–102 were torn down.[8]

Over the years, the population of the *cités* slowly dwindled as more of their buildings were sealed up or levelled. But its diversity did not wane.[9] After the Second World War had brought another round of newcomers – including Italian-born GIs who were relatives of former residents[10] – new origins complemented the rich demographic history of the tenement at Nos. 96–102. For the first (documented) time, the hotel at No. 102 checked in Algerians, Yugoslavians and Englishmen.[11]

DOI: 10.4324/9781003017820-102

Figure 9.1 The glass factory after the bombing of April 1944. AD93, ref. war damages WWII, 99/18E11.

The glass factory, which had managed to withstand the impact of the Great Depression, saw its profitability plummet after the war; production stopped in 1958.[12] As for the wire-drawing factory Mouton, it changed hands several times and struggled in the 1960s. Eventually, its doors closed in 1971. In the Plaine, the economic downturn started well before the crisis of the 1970s, due in large part to government initiatives in favour of industrial decentralisation.[13]

After the tenement was razed, some former inhabitants stayed in the area. One of the last to leave, Mme. Carbone's life ended in nearby rue Trézel.[14] A woman born at No. 96 in 1925 was still living on rue Proudhon in the 2000s.[15] Others never returned to the neighbourhood, even when they settled only a few kilometres away.[16] Most families lost contact with their former neighbours. But others kept ties for decades – especially children who had grown up together at Nos. 96 and 100.[17]

From a socio-economic standpoint, the passing of time brought about change, but not as much as people had hoped. While most of the families I was able to track down saw their material situation improve after the Second World War, the majority of them remained – by their own account – far from well-off. Long-term wealth mobility in 20th-century France is a puzzling issue on which more research is needed.[18]

Today, former inhabitants and their descendants live far from the brick-and-mortar stage at the centre of this book. That distance is one of time and space, but also one made of multiple layers and lapses of memory. Some of the issues I came across in that regard are well-known to ethnographers and oral historians, others less familiar.

First, I observed that the Second World War largely obliterated the previous stories passed down by families. François Mauriac had noted the substitution of World War II memories for those of World War I: "what we keep calling the 'Great War' is disappearing under the muddy tide of 1940."[19] To this day, the residents who resisted, collaborated or were sent to concentration camps are well-remembered by their kin.[20] Moreover, old-enough tenants vividly recalled its most traumatic episodes: the flight in 1940, the 1944 bombings. Also, the hunger and cold suffered under the Occupation are still a painful memory for many. In instances where crucial details of the 1940s were not known to descendants, this was in all likelihood because they had been deliberately concealed by the protagonists. To cite only one example, Louis Pirolli probably never told his children that he had been stripped of his French citizenship in 1941.[21] Details could also be lost or distorted by the mere passage of time.[22]

Second, some of the interviewees were prone to idealise their family's own migration and life choices, compared to later migrants of other origins. Sometimes these claims had a distinct economic aspect. This was the case, for instance, when more recent ethnic groups were blamed for the declining value of a family property.[23] Likewise, the fondness that many descendants expressed for the Plaine's "village life" in the 1940s and 1950s also partly romanticised a peaceful, and forever lost, diversity. "Everybody got along well," several interviewees said in identical terms.[24] "There was no hostility," others concurred.[25] "The Algerians were good Algerians."[26]

This study has shed light on a third, less familiar, aspect: these memory gaps and alterations started at an early date. In 1925, there had been so much turnover in the *cités* that no one remembered a man who had spent several years at No. 100 two decades earlier.[27] Ten years later, the police had no way to check the accuracy of another former resident's account, when he claimed – accurately – that he had worked at Legras as a child before the First World War. The factory had ensured that its rolls bore no memory of illegal child work.[28]

For others who had resided in the tenement as children, this part of their life receded from memory, when it was not deliberately kept secret.[29] The accuracy of recollections could also vary between members of the same family. Thirty years after the fact, one of three brothers failed to remember his stay on rue Curial, in Paris, where the family had resided before moving to the tenement. Another, despite being the eldest, had forgotten the family's passage in yet another street of Paris. The third brother, for his part, could recall both.[30] When the son of Spanish immigrants showed his daughter around in the 1960s, he was not quite sure whether he had been born at No. 96 or at No. 100.[31]

As intricate as it is, the tenants' memory was not the only source of interference in this investigation. All the public information recorded on paper was the result of a production – hence, of a distortion. Offering at best versions of what happened, archives never grant access to the elusive – some might say illusory – reality of the past, which can be tentatively reconstructed but never recovered. By contrast, what does not need reconstruction (at least in the material sense) is the small bit of *cités* that is still standing today. The building at No. 98, owned by a public housing company, underwent repair works in 2017–2018, extending its life into the future. But more repairs also mean more erasures of the material record. One would now look in vain for the old wooden floors; the courtyard faucet has long been replaced; bullet impacts on the façade are nowhere to be found.

While the vestiges of the old Plaine are vanishing fast, the majority of its inhabitants are still working-class and from a migrant background. They often reside in overcrowded quarters and work long hours to make ends meet. Unbeknown to them, they perpetuate a long tradition of struggle and perseverance that neither wars nor economic and demographic transformations brought to a halt. Insights from the social sciences would suggest that these new Plainards share many characteristics with the protagonists of this microhistory. As much as I would love to share more information about present-day inhabitants, I could hardly go beyond informed guesses. Rather, let us briefly return to their predecessors. A few additional points can be made about them.

The first is that none of the inhabitants of the tenement was a famous figure and they rarely met any. They were not the "forgotten" or "silent" heroes of anything. The point of this study was never to emphasise, or somehow rehabilitate, its protagonists' historical importance. Research of great quality has emerged from this sort of ambition – and it still does. Yet this was not the perspective of this particular investigation.

On their own, the residents at Nos. 96–102 av. de Paris did not play any major social, political, economic or cultural role. Save for a few child-importers and a handful of local elected officials, they did not wield cultural, social or political influence outside of their own networks. Besides, we should not automatically regard their trajectories as exemplary of lower-class migrants in Paris at the turn of the 20th century. Rather, they made up one diverse sample of people – and a rapidly changing one, at that – whose particular experiences can inform and expand our understanding of what was possible at that time, in that place, under those circumstances. Whether or not others were in similar situations and made similar choices was outside of the purview of this research.

On the other hand, the lesson of microhistory is that residents were not mere pawns buffeted by the great currents of history. They played their full part in the collective configurations that mattered to them. In the apartments and in the courtyards, at the factory, the wash house and the *débit*,* they constantly acted and interacted with others. Thereby, they contributed to shaping and defining the parameters of their individual experiences.

These experiences were inseparable from the place in which they took place. Both the evolution of the tenants' life settings and changes in their physical location were not exogenous, passively-received phenomena. On the contrary, the first part of this study has highlighted the contingency of these processes, as well as the role residents played in moulding their life conditions and constructing their own representation of space and mobility. Always cultural, their sense of place depended on a variety of intertwined criteria: what the buildings looked like, sounded like, smelled like; how they were connected to their surroundings; who else lived there; what sort of joys or grief oneself and one's neighbours were experiencing. As for the tenants' migration decisions, those were influenced by resources, networks, and circumstances; and in turn, they altered and reconfigured those very parameters. Episodic and contingent enactments of either ethnicity, gender, class or age differences were often among the causes, and consequences, of the residents' many migrations. Even when they were not on the move themselves, the spatial movements of others could significantly affect their identifications. The level of granularity of this study's migration stories has allowed me to substantiate these points with a degree of precision and complexity generally unseen at the macro level. From a methodological perspective, I have offered a way of intertwining small-scale human geography and socio-demographic analysis with an in-depth inquiry into individual migrations, based on the critical examination of multiple sources.

Changes of, and between, places combined with the constant interactions with others. As the second part of this book has shown, others could be people or institutions. With respect to the former, the tenants' relationships were always diverse and not over-determined by one single category of difference. When they were based on common geographic and cultural origin, affinities tended to bring people together from micro-regions, and not broader territories. Spaniards, whose relationships to their fellow nationals often extended beyond their strict area of origin, were a possible exception to this pattern. As for hostilities, they could sometimes feed off of perceived differences in ethnicity or race, but they were rarely triggered by them. More mundane considerations, and more idiosyncratic characteristics, could put people in opposition to each other. The overarching narratives of migration history often leave the impression that the migrants' ethnicisation took place along national lines, and that interethnic violence was primarily fuelled by racism. This book's qualitative and quantitative evaluations offer one counterpoint to these ideas. They also form an innovative combination of methods, which will hopefully inspire others who try to find common ground between microhistory and statistical analysis.

In addition, this study has demonstrated that with both hard and soft power, states competed for the residents' allegiances, and citizenship was never a foregone conclusion. Rules could be flouted, policies resisted, procedures circumvented. Divided loyalties and changes in nationality show that residents could carve their own paths in between and across national boundaries. All the same, identification papers, administrative decisions and military orders could deprive people of the freedom they had hoped for. They also might leave visible, sometimes indelible, national divides running through the courtyards of a single housing complex. These delineations provided an important, though not exclusive, symbolic repertoire for dynamics of solidarity and hostility by which the tenants constantly rearranged their social life.

Migration history is now part of a global field of study. With the institutional recognition of this cross-cutting topic, the appetite has grown for a canon, a grand narrative with its share of migration laws, turning points and authoritative statistics. This book's story, narrated from the peephole of one tiny fraction of territory and population, should give pause to those hoping for such definitive accounts of migration, integration or racism. By making room for counter-intuitive stories and non-linear evolutions, the only gospel this work attempts to preach is one of critical circumspection. Today, migration and cultural diversity often elicit ready-made, dogmatic and knee-jerk responses. Academic research cannot afford to shy away from the values of nuance and caution.

Notes

1. SDMA, 16AC5, Av. Wilson 100, Letter from M. Lutel and M. Coulon to the Mayor of SD.
2. "Le bombardement de la Plaine du 21 avril 1944," in *La Plaine. Il était une fois*, No. 8 (2001).
3. Int. No. 42, 23.04.2016. 641 people were killed in the bombings, among whom 218 in the Plaine, where another 150 were injured.
4. AD93, War damages, WWII, box No. 75, RB4097, Les Fils de Nicolas Clerc; No. 99, 18E11, Verreries de Saint-Denis; int. No. 52, 28.10.2016; int. No. 51, 31.10.2016. At least one former tenant was killed in the bombings (int. No. 18, 21.11.2016).
5. AD93, War damages, WWII, box No. 90, RB43221, Lutel et Coulon.
6. SDMA, 16AC5, Av. Wilson 100, Letter from Mme Dominique Carbone to the Mayor of SD, no date [received 20.07.1948].
7. *L'Humanité*, 10.08.1950.
8. SDMA, 16AC5, Av. Wilson 100–102.
9. In 1962, there were only 64 people left at No. 96, and 24 at No. 100 (SDMA 1F39, 1962 Census, 96–102 Av. Wilson).
10. Int. No. 22, 24.09.2016.
11. SDMA, 16AC5, Av. Wilson 102, Petition from the tenants at No. 102 Av. Wilson to the Mayor of SD, 06.12.1949; 1F38, SD, 1954 census, 102 Av. Wilson; 1F39, SD, 1962 census, 96–102 av. Wilson.
12. The former Legras factory still had 284 workers in 1939. See S.A. Verreries de Saint-Denis et de Pantin réunies, 6.06.1944, "État numérique du personnel de l'usine," in AD93, War damages, WWII, box No. 99, *doc. cit.*; *Base inventaire historique de sites industriels et activités de service* (BASIAS), file No. IDF9300040, last accessed July 27, 2021, https://www.georisques.gouv.fr/donnees/bases-de-donnees/inventaire-historique-de-sites-industriels-et-activites-de-service.

13 Serge Adda and Maurice Ducreux, "L'usine disparaît. L'industrialisation remise en question. Saint-Denis, Aubervilliers," *Les Annales de la recherche urbaine* 5, No. 1 (1979): 27–66; Raymond Guglielmo, "Désindustrialisation et évolution de l'emploi à Saint-Denis," *Villes en parallèle* 11, No. 1 (1986): 116–33; Alain Bertho, "La Plaine-Saint-Denis dans l'entre-deux," *Projet*, No. 2 (2008): 23–30; Sébastien Radouan, "La rénovation du centre-ville de Saint-Denis aux abords de la basilique, de la Libération au Mondial 98: une modernité à la française" (doctoral diss. in art history, University of Paris IV, 2008).
14 Int. No. 43, 23.04.2016.
15 Antonia Gonzalez, a daughter of Estanislas González (int. No. 71, 25.07.2018).
16 Int. No. 49, 6.07.2016.
17 Int. No. 71, 25.07.2018; int. No. 42, 23.04.2016.
18 Economists started in the 1990s to study intergenerational mobility of wealth. A fairly recent paper on France from 1848 and 1960 highlighted an upward trend in wealth mobility after the First World War, but suggested a negative impact of rural-to-urban migrations (Bourdieu et al., "Intergenerational wealth mobility in France, 19th and 20th Century," *Review of Income and Wealth* 65, No. 1 (2019): 21–47). For what it is worth, the few descendants of residents who live in the United States seem to have enjoyed a much higher degree of economic success.
19 *Le Figaro littéraire*, 14.12.1957.
20 Int. No. 51, 31.10.2016; int. No. 31, 18.08.2016; int. No. 71, 25.07.2018. At least one former tenant, Thomas Sánchez, was deported to Auschwitz. Other deportees included Alphonse and Michel Pelayo, the sons of a couple of residents at No. 100 in the late 1900s, and possibly the shoemaker at No. 100, as well (int. No. 32, 19.04.2016).
21 FNA, BB/11/10553, 41906x27, Louis Pirolli.
22 Louis Pirolli's nephew had always heard that his family came from Venafro, not Pozzilli. According to his cousin's photo album, the place of origin of the family was Apulia, not Molise. Int. No. 52, 28.10.2016; int. Thomas, 31.10.2016.
23 Int. No. 40, 21.08.2016.
24 Int. No. 42, 23.04.2016; int. No. 43, 23.04.2016; int. No. 22, 24.09.2016 *("Tous le monde s'entendait bien")*.
25 Int. No. 19, 14.09.2016; int. No. 14, 30.09.2016 *("Il n'y avait pas d'animosité")*.
26 Int. No. 42, 23.04.2016 ("*Les Algériens, c'était des bons Algériens*").
27 FNA, BB/11/6172, 18503x14, Fraioli.
28 See AVP, D2U8 390, Dossier d'assises, Lopez Rufo; for another example, see FNA, BB/11/8141, 12218x23, Ranaldi.
29 FNA, 19770876/18, 25377x32, Salvatore.
30 FNA, BB/11/10387 33613x27, Paul Carbone; BB/11/13261, 22005x30, Antonio Carbone; BB/11/10398, 34199x27, Dominique Carbone.
31 Int. No. 31, 18.08.2016.

Sources

1 Primary manuscript sources

France

Municipal archives

- Saint-Denis municipal archives (by series):
  - D, "Administration générale de la commune": 2D2 31–3, 37, 43–45, 48; CT7, 37, 43, 45–6, 58, 64, 67, 69, 70, 72, 74–75, 77, 83, 84, 87, 90, 92, 94, 96–97, 100, 103, 111, 114, 118–21, 124, 12–7, 131, 136, 139–40, 144–5, 147, 151, 154, 278.
  - F, "Population, économie, statistique, travail": 1F41, 44, 50–3; CT208, 807, 1353.
  - H, "Affaires militaires": CT177, 223–5, 929–30; H26–43; 4H3.
  - I, "Police. Justice. Hygiène publique": 1I12, 19, 34, 44, 207, 227, 249; CT234, 238, 241–2, 250, 253, 255, 314, 392, 398, 40–1, 405, 414, 424, 433, 539, 546, 556, 559, 560, 569, 573, 575, 904, 925, 928, 935, 940, 1005, 1199, 1200, 1332, 1333.
  - K, "Élections, personnel municipal": 1K56, 513–4, 519, 1192.
  - O, "Travaux publics. Voirie. Transport. Eau": 2O238–41.
  - Q, "Assistance et prévoyance, hôpital": 1L272; 1Q2–17; 2Q1; 3Q4; 5Q29, 48, 61; CT206, 209, 261, 343, 384, 720, 768, 806, 811–2, 833, 1162, 1328, 1358, 1454.
  - R, "Instruction publique, culture, sports": 1R27.
  - Deposited between 1940 and 1983: "Hygiène," 16AC5, 10, 2ACW 9–10; "Logement et immobilier," 40AC74–5; 30ACW64.
  - "Permis de construire": 358W51, 404W15, 42ACW58, 574W21.1; 717W44.
  - Private archives: Legs Tissot, 21S055.
  - Digitised archives: births, marriages, deaths (E246–336, 351); censuses (1F14–29); military censuses (CT199, H9–12, 15, 24–39); electoral lists (1K22–59); schools (1R20); nationality (E42–67); tax rolls (1G87–110); cadastre (10Fi2/1–4).

- Other municipal depositories:
  - Aubervilliers: "État-civil" (individual records in 1E48–258), naturalisations (3E2–6).
  - Saint-Ouen: "État-civil" (individual records in 1E112–180).
  - Other towns: digital depositories.

Departmental archives

- Seine-Saint-Denis (AD93):
  - Censuses: D2M8 205, 91 Saint-Denis, 1921, 1926; D2M830, Aubervilliers, 1911, D2M840, Pré-Saint-Gervais, 1911.
  - "État-civil": Saint-Denis, 1881–1932: births (1E66/142, 146, 149, 152, 257–305); marriages (1E66/126, 131, 134, 140, 312–61); deaths (1E66/176, 183, 189, 195, 363–409); Aubervilliers, births (1E01/144, 151); Pré-Saint-Gervais, births (1E61/48, 49), deaths (1E61/100, 102).
  - P, "Finances. Cadastre. Postes": "bulletins préparatoires à l'établissement du cadastre" (D4P4 57); "croquis d'arpentage et de délimitation de Saint-Denis," Sept. 1929 (2048W83–4); "matrices des propriétés bâties" 1900, 1910 (Nos. 695, 697, 704–5).
  - Q, "Domaines. Enregistrement. Hypothèques": 4Q5 191, 229, 435, 469, 451 2460, 5686, 6170, 7397, 7704 7840, 8428, 8450, 8644, 8948.
  - R, "Affaires militaires": "secours aux réfugiés" (WWI) (DR741–50); war damages (WWI) (10 R 1 47, DR7 76).
  - 4U: Justice de paix du canton de Saint-Denis: civil rulings 1880–1931 (4U7/450–789); seizures, rulings 1896–8 (4U7/350–4); expert reports (4U7/416–7); work accidents (4U7/429–30); gendarmerie's *procès-verbaux*," subpoenas 1885–23 [missing: 1886–90, 191–19 and 1923–37] (4U7/902–1042).
  - W, "Enregistrement": "Fichier du répertoire général" (1744W1–85), "Répertoire général" (1742W); successions (1748W6; 1729W48, 72, 73, 75, 78–9, 89, 102, 107, 110, 113, 114, 122, 143, 208, 1730W8, 1730W1, 8, 12); "renvois" (1738W6, 8, 13–7, 20, 24, 25–6, 29, 32, 34, 38, 39, 65); "actes civils publics" (1740W201, 273, 284, 310, 343, 470); "actes sous seings privés" (1739W3–4, 9–11, 13–4, 20, 22, 25–6, 30, 35, 41, 43–4, 49; 1742 W 1, 4, 5, 7, 9–16, 18).
  - War damages (WWII): 5, 10, 45, 90, 99, 152, 219, 243.
  - Notary records, Me Maillard: 2E8/1317, 1692.
  - Parish Sainte-Geneviève de la Plaine-Saint-Denis: baptisms, marriages, 1882–5 (4L2).

- Paris (AVP):
  - P: "Calepins du cadastre" D1P4/320 (rue Curial), 313 (rue de Crimée), 346 (passage Desgrais), 587 (rue Labois-Rouillon).

- Q: successions (DQ7/30677, 32914, 34888).
- R: military registers (D4R1–D3R1, 1880–1933), WWI refugees (D1R7/147–8).
- S: transports, "Gare de la Plaine-Saint-Denis," 1871–1914 (6S9 5).
- U: Cour d'appel de la Seine, chambres correctionnelles (D3U9/136, 240, 252–5, 304, 327); Tribunal de première instance de la Seine, chambres correctionnelles, rulings (D1U6/166–8, 219, 225, 226, 305, 316, 362, 373, 478, 508, 512, 513, 533, 539, 544, 575, 680, 709, 716, 726–7, 729, 732–3, 735, 742, 775, 778, 797, 880, 913, 963, 972–3, 977, 985, 988, 993, 1008–9, 1013, 1040, 1061, 1078, 1091, 1128, 1135, 1166, 1172–3, 1184, 1188, 1200, 1217, 1240, 1269, 1370, 1394, 1438, 1450, 1500, 1554, 1585, 1591, 1636, 1660, 1807, 1865, 1998, 2144, 2165, 2186, 2278, 2298, 2357, 2796, 5747), files (D2U6/166, 194, 198; D3U6/94, 111, 175, 196); Cour d'assises de la Seine, rulings (D1U8/93, 97, 108, 127, 129–30, 142, 145, 160, 163, 167, 176, 182), files (D2U8/293, 300, 390); Conseil de prud'hommes de la Seine (D1U10/3, 719, 729, 770–1).
- W: Hygiene (17W73–4).
- DV: Religion (DV14).
- DW: Unions (1070W1/40, 55).
- Digitised archives: births, marriages, deaths 1880–1950 (V4E).

- Calvados (AD14):
  - M, "Police": "nomades et ambulants," 1862–1910 (M3163); "condamnations des étrangers," 1890–3 (M3318); "étrangers, expulsions," 1870–81, 1877–85 (M3073–4, 3077).
  - U, "Justice": Tribunal de première instance de Lisieux (3U4/905, 956, 966); Tribunal de première instance de Bayeux (3U1/135); Cour d'appel de Caen (2U4/535, 1599).

- Moselle (AD57):
  - 7E: Births, marriages, death registers (by town).
  - 3AL: Emigration permits.

- Seine-et-Marne (AD77):
  - Notary records: Me Dangoise (214E460), Me Fauvel (214E461, 477, 482, 484), Me Greppe (224E897).

- Eure (AD27):
  - M, "Police": "Carnets de saltimbanques" (4M29).

- Seine-Maritime (AD76):
  - M, "Police": Le Havre, "État nominatif des étrangers italiens" (4M739).

- Rhône (AD69):
  - M, "Police": foreigners (4M415, 650–1; 4313W1–4).
- Other departments: digital archives only (censuses, births, marriages and deaths records, military registers).

Archives of the Préfecture de police

- CB, "Commissariats: répertoires analytiques": Saint-Denis Sud, 1905–40 (CB 92.1–35); Saint-Denis Nord, 1917–8 (CB 91.23); Aubervilliers, 1898–9 (CB 82.3), 1904 (CB 82.4), 1914–7 (CB 82.13–5); Pantin 1914–5 (CB 89.48), 1917–8 (CB 89.49–50); La Villette, 1895–1900 (CB 73.5–7).
- BA, "Cabinet. Affaires générales": strikes (BA/170); Saint-Denis (BA/914); "Physionomie de Paris," 1917–9 (BA/1587–8); "État d'esprit de la population de Paris," 1918–9 (BA/1614), "Étrangers" (BA/2247); "Guerre de 1914–1918, Commission des étrangers" (BA/896), "Situation industrielle" (BA/20); Spain (BA/2154–7), Italy (BA/2162, 2165, 2169).
- DA-DB, "Police administrative": children (DB/70, 76, 92–3), foreigners (DB/301), First World War (DA/199; DB/336, 341, 343, 364).
- IA, "Naturalisations": 9 individual files (IA/71, 99, 152, 157, 164, 169, 171, 216–7).
- JC, "Répression du proxénétisme": First World War (JC58).

National archives

- Pierrefitte-sur-Seine:
  - BB11, naturalisations and related procedures: 181 individual *"extraits"* (from BB11/1464 to BB11/13877); naturalisation files brought back from Fontainebleau: 106 individual *"extraits"* (from 19770862/110 to 20010479/1).
  - F7: "Société de bienfaisance italienne de Paris" (F7/15908–9); "Région parisienne, agitation dans les usines de guerre, 1918" (F7/13366–7); "Renseignements généraux," "Associations et groupements espagnols en France" (F7/14721).
  - F12: "Légion d'honneur" (F/12/5190, 8649); "Verrerie" (F/12/7824).
  - F14: "Main d'œuvre étrangère et coloniale" (WWI) (F14/11332).
  - F22: "Travail des enfants" (F22/452, 505–6), "Usines, Première Guerre mondiale" (F22/530).
  - Direction générale de la sûreté nationale, fichier central ("fonds de Moscou"), 57 individual files.
  - LH: "Légion d'honneur" (LH/1562/64).

- BB18, "Correspondance de la division criminelle du ministère de la Justice" (BB/18/6107, 6109–11, 6116, 6129, 6534, 6538).
- Private archives: Albert Thomas (94AP/120, 129–32).

- Paris (CARAN):
  - Notary records: Barillot (AN, MC/ET/LVII/1637, 1669), Faÿ (MC/RE/CXIX/27), Gamard (MC/ET/XXXVIII/1224).

Archives nationales de l'Outre-mer
- Control of the colonial manpower, 1915–22 (1slotfom/1, 4, 9; 3slotfom/139; 6slotfom/7; 7slotfom/1).

Archives of the Ministry of Foreign Affairs
- "Correspondance politique et commerciale. Nouvelle Série": Spain (Vol. 80), Italy (CPCOM/90–3, 97).
- Control of foreigners: passports for Italian nationals, 1916–29 (418QO/28).

Archives of the French Army (SHAT)
- "Conseils de Guerre": individual records (GR11J/3047, 3212, 3515, 2703; GR5J/650, GR10J/78, GR10J/883.
- Industry (GR6N/149), foreign and colonial manpower, 1914–19 (GR7N/144, 435, 496, 114, GR10N/63).
- Weekly reports for the military district of Paris, 1914–19 (GR23N/77).

Notary offices
- Me Genin and Me Brunet, Bourg d'Oisans (Isère): transcripts from Me Pellissier, succession Lutel ("notoriété," 14.05.1927; "inventaire" 8.07.1927).

Religious archives
- Archives from the parishes of Saint-Denis:
  - Sainte-Geneviève de la Plaine-Saint-Denis (25/5): "livres des annonces," 1908–11; 1925–30; "livre de réunion des dames de Charité au presbytère," 1927–38; "listes annuelles des enfants qui ont fait leur Première Communion dans la paroisse," 1903–15; baptisms, 1886–1902, 1916–7, 1923–6; marriages, 1886–1925.
  - Real Patronato español Santa Teresa de Jesús (26/5): baptisms (1923–35), marriages (1925–32).

- Archive of the Misión catolica española de París (51 bis, rue de la Pompe, Paris):
  - Baptisms, Nos. 1 (1916–8), 2 (1918–21), 3 (1922–5); marriages, Nos. 1 (1916–8), 2 (1918–9), 3 (1920–1), 4 (1922–4).
- Diocesan archives, Seine-Saint-Denis:
  - "Paroisse Sainte-Geneviève de la Plaine-Saint-Denis" (25.1.8, 3F, 21010).

School archives

- Elementary school Saint-Just, Saint-Denis (formerly 120 Av. Wilson):
  - Boys' school, "Registre matricule des élèves" (after 1945).
  - Girls' school, "Registre matricule des élèves admis à l'école à partir du 4.11.1924."

Archives of diplomatic missions

- Spanish General Consulate in Paris: births (1909) and marriage transcriptions (Vol. IV–V).

Private archives

- Fédération d'associations et citoyens espagnols en France, FACEEF (10, rue Cristino-Garcia, Saint-Denis): "Archivos – El Hogar de los Españoles," 1925–59.

Italy

Municipal archives

- Acquafondata
  - "Registri della popolazione," 1911, 1945; "Schede individuali."
  - RGN, "Regno d'Italia": "elenchi dei poveri" (RGN9–11); "emigrazione, immigrazione" (RGN41); "liste di leva" (RGN 19–25).

- Pozzilli
  - "Stato civile," 1850–1930.
  - "Liste di leva," 1885–92.
  - B. 13, "Catasto fabbricati."
  - "Fogli di famiglia," 1890–1960.

172 *Sources*

- Casalvieri
  - "Stato civile."

- Rocca d'Arce
  - "Stato civile."
  - "Registro di popolazione."
  - "Schede individuali."

- Arpino
  - "Stato civile."
  - B. 180, cat. XV, fasc. 12, "Mentecatti"; fasc. 14, "Oziosi, vagabondi, rimpatriati."
  - "Registro della popolazione," 1800–1900.

- Pontecorvo
  - "Stato civile."
  - "Leva. Ruoli," 1881–1910.

Provincial archives

- Archivio di Stato, Roma
  - "Tribunale penale civile di Roma": b. 4100, fasc. 28765.

- Archivio di Stato, Isernia
  - "Sottoprefettura di Isernia," "Atti di Polizia" (11-39-1868, 11-19-1868, 11-13-1868, 10-42-1868, 12-6-1880, 12-7-1880).
  - "Tribunale di Isernia" II (b. 223, fasc. 19).

- Archivio di Stato, Frosinone
  - "Sottoprefettura di Frosinone": Roccasecca, 1894 (b. 265).
  - "Prefettura di Frosinone": emigrants (b. 533, 554 bis, 571, 612), 1915 earthquake (b. 501, 565), child labour in glass factories in France (b. 565 bis), criminal groups (b. 573), municipal affairs (b. 3, 71, 123, 429, 443, 495).

- Archivio di Stato, Caserta
  - "Corte d'assise di Cassino": individual cases (b. 119, No. 510; b. 128, No. 552; b. 164, No. 740; b. 52, No. 230; b. 101, No. 427; b. 160, No. 716).
  - "Prefettura, Gabinetto": emigration (b. 22, No. 213); municipal affairs, Casalvieri (b. 138, No. 1477; b. 149, No. 1562);

Acquafondata (b. 148, No. 1546; 156, No. 1618; 249, No. 2550); Reports on the circondario of Sora, 1899–1902 (b. 303, No. 3442, 3450; b. 304, No. 3455; b. 304, No. 3458).

National archives

- Archivio centrale dello Stato

  - Ministry of the Interior, "Direzione generale della Pubblica sicurezza, Divisione Polizia": "associazioni in Italia e all'estero," 1912–45 (b. 1); "affari generali di polizia giudiziaria" (b. 39); emigrants (b. 85–86, 91, 113, 166, 190, 820; old Nos. 96, 291); "Reati. Avvenimenti" (b. 177, 224).
  - Ministry of the Interior, "Direzione generale della Pubblica sicurezza, Divisione Affari generali riservati": Ordine pubblico, Caserta, 1914 (b. 15).
  - Ministry of the Interior, "Direzione generale della Pubblica sicurezza, Divisione Polizia giudizaria," 1919–21 (b. 1400, 1363).

- Archivio storico diplomatico

  - Italian embassy in Paris, 1896–1919 (b. 16–26).
  - "Commissariato generale all'Emigrazione" (b. 30, 46–7).
  - Affari Politici, P, 1891–1916: Italians in France (b. 572, 619).
  - Archives of the Ministry's personnel: Armao Ermanno, Vice-Consul in Marseilles, 1915–7 (b. 385/884).

Spain

Municipal archives

- Archivo histórico de las Merindades, Villarcayo (Burgos)

  - Repatriations, 1914 (sig. No. 1597).

- Merindad de Sotoscueva (Burgos)

  - Births, marriages, deaths, 1880–1910.

- Merindad de Valdeporres (Burgos)

  - Births, marriages, deaths, 1893–1935.

- Valle de Valdebezana (Burgos)

  - Births, marriages, deaths, 1873–1911.

174 *Sources*

- Mesas de Ibor (Cáceres)
  - Births, marriages, deaths, 1883–1928.

- Navalmoral de la Mata (Cáceres)
  - Leg. 63, "1898–1916: Junta auxiliar de suscripción nacional" (1898).
  - Leg. 100, "Copia del padrón," 1898–9.

- Peraleda de la Mata (Cáceres):
  - Births, marriages, deaths, 1883–1910.

Provincial archives

- Burgos
  - Audiencia territorial: "sentencias," 1883–97 (No. 269), 1900–9 (No. 270–2); "juicios orales" 1910–5 (1381/2).

- Cáceres
  - "Interior, Gobierno civil": Passports, 1924–43 (GC/1536, 2458:1).
  - "Correspondencia ordenada por pueblos": Belvís de Monroy, 1924–35 (GC/2685).
  - "Expediente de responsabilidades políticas contra Ambrosio Luengo Marcos" (JIRP/19:33).
  - "Real Audiencia, Cáceres, Sentencias," 1934 (RA-LIB, 328:L768).
  - Tribunal Superior de Justicia de Extremadura, "Desobediencia imputado a Luengo Marcos A," 21.11.1950 (RA 1540:26).

National archives

- Archivo histórico nacional (AHN)
  - Juzgado de Instrucción del Distrito del Congreso de Madrid: "Infracción de la Ley de Emigración" (FC-AUDIENCIA_T_MADRID_CRIMINAL, 4, Exp. 33).

- Archivo general de la Administración (AGA)
  - Spanish embassy in Paris: children in glass factories, 1905 (54/5.861); "contencioso" (54/5.926, 932, 933); Spanish workers in Saint-Denis (54/5954), "Patronato Saint-Denis, Plaine-Saint-Denis" (54/11001); emigration, 1909–31 (54/6.072).
  - "Comercio": emigration (54/1695–6).
  - "Repatriaciones y otros": 1914–5 (51/00047, 51/00051).

- Centro documental de la memoria histórica (Salamanca)
  - "Delegación Nacional de Servicios Documentales de la Presidencia del Gobierno, Secretaría General, Fichero de la Secretaría General y de la Sección Político Social, fichero N° 37": Ambrosio Luengo Marcos.

Private archives

- Archives de la Fundación 1° de Mayo/Centro de Documentación de la Emigración española
  - "El Hogar de los Españoles" (001/001–25).

Other countries (United States, Great Britain):
- Digital depositories (censuses, immigration records).

2 Primary printed sources

Official publications

- *Bulletin municipal officiel de Saint-Denis*, 1878–1912 (digitised).
- *Bulletin municipal officiel de la ville de Paris*, 1880–1938 (digitised).
- *Journal officiel de la République française, Lois et décrets*, 1880–1978 (digitised).
- *Bulletin de l'Inspection du travail*, 1893–1936.
- *Bulletin des usines de guerre*, 1916–8.
- *Gazzetta ufficiale del Regno d'Italia*, 1895–1931 (digitised).
- *Gaceta de Madrid*, 1886–1922 (digitised).

Press and periodicals

- Local publications
  - *Journal de Saint-Denis*, 1889–1932 (digitised).
  - *L'Émancipation*, 1902–32 (digitised).
  - *L'Éclaireur*, 1896–1900.
  - *Le Réveil de Saint-Denis*, 1901–8.
  - *Le Petit démocrate de Saint-Denis et de la Région*, 1912–4.
  - *L'Écho des Chaumettes*, 1908–9.
  - *Le Bonhomme normand*, 1882–1910 (digitised).
  - *El Castellano. Diario* católico (Burgos), August–December 1914.
  - *El Diario de Burgos* (Burgos), August–December 1914.

Sources

- National publications

  - *Le Matin, La Presse, Le Petit Journal, Le Petit Parisien, Le Radical, Le Journal, Le XIXe siècle, La Lanterne, Gil Blas, L'Aurore, Le Figaro, Le Journal des Débats politiques et littéraires, La Petite République socialiste, L'Humanité, Le Soleil,* 1881–1932 (digitised and searchable).
  - *Le Réveil des verriers (La Voix des verriers),* 1892–1924.
  - *La Stampa,* 1898–1904 (digitized and searchable).
  - *La Correspondencia de España,* 1912–4 (digitised).

- Other

  - *Bollettino dell'Emigrazione,* 1907–20.

3 Primary oral sources

For privacy purposes, I have decided not to publicise in this volume the identity of the former tenants and descendants interviewed for this research. The interviews have been referenced by numbers 1–76. More information can be obtained by contacting the author.

Bibliography

Adda, Serge, and Maurice Ducreux. "L'usine disparaît. L'industrialisation remise en question. Saint-Denis, Aubervilliers." *Les Annales de la recherche urbaine* 5, No. 1 (1979): 27–66.
Ageron, Charles-Robert. *Les Algériens musulmans et la France (1871–1919)*. Paris: PUF 1968.
Alba, Richard, and Victor Nee. *Remaking the American Mainstream: Assimilation and Contemporary Immigration*. Cambridge: Harvard University Press, 2003.
Albera, Dionigi, Patrizia Audenino, and Paola Corti. "I percorsi dell'identità maschile nell'emigrazione. Dinamiche colettive e ciclo di vita individuale." *Rivista di storia contemporanea* 20, No. 1 (1991): 69–87.
Alietti, Alfredo, *La Convivenza difficile. Coabitazione interetnica in un quartiere di Milano*. Turin: L'Harmattan Italia, 1998.
Alter, George. *Family and the Female Life Course: The Women of Verviers, Belgium, 1849–1880*. Madison: University of Wisconsin Press, 1988.
Amar, Marianne, and Pierre Milza, eds. *L'Immigration en France au XXe siècle*. Paris: A. Colin, 1990.
Andall, Jacqueline. *Gender and Ethnicity in Contemporary Europe*. Oxford, New York: Berg, 2003.
Anderson, Benedict. *Imagined Communities: Reflections on the Origin and Spread of Nationalism*. London: Verso, 1991 (2nd ed.).
Anderson, Bridget. *Doing the Dirty Work? The Global Politics of Domestic Labour*. London: Zed, 2000.
Appadurai, Arjun. *Modernity at Large: Cultural Dimensions of Globalization*. Minneapolis: University of Minnesota Press, 1996.
Arellano-Ulloa, Pilar. *Le Champ de luzerne*. Paris: Le Manuscrit, 2010.
Artières, Philippe, and Dominique Kalifa. "L'historien et les archives personnelles: pas à pas?" *Sociétés et Représentations*, No. 13 (2002): 7–15.
Artières, Philippe. *Rêves d'histoire. Pour une histoire de l'ordinaire*. Paris: Gallimard, 2014.
Assouline, David, and Mehdi Lallaoui. *Un siècle d'immigrations en France. Première période 1851–1918: De la mine au champ de bataille*. Paris: Au nom de la mémoire/Syros, 1996.
Atouf, Elkbir. *Aux origines historiques de l'immigration marocaine en France, 1910–1963*. Paris: Connaissances et savoirs, 2009.

178 Bibliography

Avolio, Francesco. *Bommèspre. Profilo linguistico dell'Italia centro-meridionale*. San Severo: Gerni Editore, 1995.

Bacqué, Marie-Hélène, Emmanuel Bellanger, and Henri Rey, eds. *Banlieues populaires. Territoires, sociétés, politiques*. La Tour d'Aigues: l'Aube, 2018.

Bade, Klaus, ed. *Migration – Ethnizität – Konflikt: Systemfragen und Fallstudien*. Osnabrück: Universitätsverlag Rasch, 1996.

Baldassar, Loretta, and Donna R. Gabaccia. eds. *Intimacy and Italian Migration: Gender and Domestic Lives in a Mobile World*. New York: Fordham University Press, 2011.

Ballinger, Pamela. *The World Refugees Made: Decolonization and the Foundations of Postwar Italy*. Ithaca: Cornell University Press, 2020.

Barbara, Augustin. "Mixed marriages: Some key questions." *International Migration* 32, No. 4 (1994): 571–86.

Barroux, Marius, André Barroux, and André Marie. *Saint-Denis*. Paris: Grasset, 1938.

Barth, Frederik, ed. *Ethnic Groups and Boundaries: The Social Organization of Cultural Difference*. London: George Allen & Unwin, 1969.

Barton, Nimisha. *Reproductive Citizens: Gender, Immigration, and the State in Modern France, 1880–1945*. Ithaca: Cornell University Press, 2020.

Barzman, John, and Éric Saunier, eds. *Migrants dans une ville portuaire (XVIe–XXIe)*. Rouen, Le Havre: Publications des universités de Rouen et du Havre, 2005.

Bastié, Jean. *La Croissance de la banlieue parisienne*. Paris: PUF, 1964.

Baumann, Gerd. *Contesting Culture: Discourses of Identity in Multi-Ethnic London*. Cambridge: Cambridge University Press, 1996.

Bayor, Ronald. *Neighbors in Conflict: The Irish, Germans, Jews and Italians of New York City, 1929–1941*. Baltimore, London: Johns Hopkins University Press, 1978.

Becker, Jean-Jacques, and Stéphane Audoin-Rouzeau, eds. *Les Sociétés européennes et la Guerre de 1914–1918*. Nanterre: Université Paris-X-Nanterre, 1990.

Bekkar, Rabia, Nadir Boumaza, and Daniel Pinson. *Familles maghrébines en France, l'épreuve de la ville*. Paris: PUF, 1999.

Benoist, Charles. "Le travail dans la grande industrie." *Revue des deux mondes* LXXIII (1903), 1.11.1903: 169–94.

Benveniste, Annie. *Le Bosphore à la Roquette. La communauté judéo-espagnole à Paris (1914–1990)*. Paris: L'Harmattan, 1989.

Berio, Beatrice. "I ragazzi italiani nelle vetrerie del Lionese." *Rivista coloniale* (1913), 16–28.02.1913: 124–27.

Berlanstein, Lenard R. *The Working People of Paris, 1871–1914*. Baltimore, London: Johns Hopkins University Press, 1984.

Bertho, Alain. "La Plaine-Saint-Denis dans l'entre-deux." *Projet*, No. 2 (2008): 23–30.

Bevilacqua, Piero, Andreina De Clementi, and Emilio Franzina, eds. *Storia dell'emigrazione italiana*. Rome: Donzelli, 2001.

Bevilacqua, Piero, ed. *Storia dell'agricoltura italiana in età contemporanea*. Venice: Marsilio, 1989.

Bhabha, Homi K. *Location of Culture*. London and New York: Routledge, 1994.

Blanc-Chaléard, Marie-Claude, Antonio Bechelloni, and Bénédicte Deschamps, eds. *Les Petites Italies dans le monde*. Rennes: Presses universitaires de Rennes, 2007.

Blanc-Chaléard, Marie-Claude, Caroline Douki, Nicole Dyonet, and Vincent Milliot, eds. *Police et migrants. France 1667–1939*. Rennes: Presses universitaires de Rennes, 2001.
Blanc-Chaléard, Marie-Claude. "Les Italiens à Paris au XIXe siècle." *Studi Emigrazione* 35, No. 130 (1998): 229–49.
Blanc-Chaléard, Marie-Claude. *Les Italiens dans l'Est parisien. Une histoire d'intégration (années 1880–1960)*. Rome: École française de Rome, 2000.
Blanc-Chaléard, Marie-Claude. "Les immigrés et la banlieue parisienne. Histoire d'une aventure urbaine et sociale (XIXe–XXe siècles)." In *Banlieues populaires: Territoires, sociétés, politiques*, edited by Marie-Hélène Bacqué, Emmanuel Bellanger, and Henri Rey (La Tour d'Aigues: L'Aube, 2018), 95–109.
Blanchard, Pascal, and Éric Deroo. *Le Paris Asie: 150 ans de présence de la Chine, de l'Indochine, du Japon, dans la capitale*. Paris: La Découverte, 2004.
Blanco Rodríguez, and Juan Andrés. *La migración castellana y leonesa en el marco de las migraciones españolas*. Zamora: UNED, 2011.
Bodnar, John, Roger Simon, and Michael P. Weber. *Lives of Their Own: Blacks, Italians, and Poles in Pittsburgh, 1900–1960*. Urbana: University of Illinois Press, 1982.
Bonnet, Jean-Charles. *Les Pouvoirs publics français et l'immigration dans l'entre-deux-guerres*. Lyon: Presses de l'Université de Lyon, 1976.
Bonneval, Loïc, and François Robert. *L'Immeuble de rapport. L'immobilier entre gestion et spéculation, Lyon 1860–1990*. Rennes: Presses universitaires de Rennes, 2013.
Bonneval, Loïc, François Robert, Florence Goffette-Nagot, Roelof Verhage, and Olivier Lemire-Osborne. *Les Politiques publiques de contrôle des loyers, comparaisons internationales et enseignements historiques (1914–2014)*. Lyon: Ministère de l'égalité des territoires et du logement, 2015.
Boucau, Henri. *L'Île-de-France et Saint-Denis*. Paris: Grasset, 1938.
Bourderon, Roger, and Pierre De Perreti, eds. *Histoire de Saint-Denis*. Toulouse: Privat, 1988.
Bourdieu, Jérôme, Lionel Kesztenbaum, Gilles Postel-Vinay, and Akiko Suwa-Eisenmann. "Intergenerational wealth mobility in France, 19th and 20th century." *Review of Income and Wealth* 65, No. 1 (2019): 21–47.
Bourdieu, Pierre. *Esquisse d'une théorie de la pratique*. Paris: Droz, 1972. Translated by Richard Nice. *Outline of a Theory of Practice*. Cambridge: Cambridge University Press, 1977.
Bourdieu, Pierre. "et la représentation: éléments pour une réflexion critique sur l'idée de région." *Actes de la recherche en sciences sociales* 35, No. 35 (1980): 63–72.
Bourdieu, Pierre. "The forms of capital." In *Handbook of Theory and Research for the Sociology of Educa*tion, edited by John Richardson, 241–58. New York: Greenwood Press, 1986.
Bourillon, Florence. "Un immeuble dans Paris." *Cahiers d'histoire* 44, No. 4 (1999): 701–15.
Braber, Ben. "Living with the enemy – German immigrants in Nottingham during the First World War." *Midland History* 42, No. 1 (2017): 72–91.
Brown, David. *Contemporary Nationalism. Civic, Ethnocultural and Multicultural Politics*. Abingdon: Routledge, 2000.

180   Bibliography

Brubaker, Rogers, and David Laitin. "Ethnic and nationalist violence." *Annual Review of Sociology* 24 (1998): 423–52.
Brubaker, Rogers, and Frederick Cooper. "Beyond 'identity'." *Theory and Society* 29, No. 1 (2000): 1–47.
Brubaker, Rogers, Mara Loveman, and Peter Stamatov. "Ethnicity as cognition." *Theory and Society* 33 (2004): 31–64.
Brubaker, Rogers. *Citizenship and Nationhood in France and Germany*. Cambridge, London: Harvard University Press, 1992.
Brubaker, Rogers. *Nationalism Reframed: Nationhood and the National Question in the New Europe*. New York: Cambridge University Press, 1996.
Brubaker, Rogers. *Ethnicity without Groups*. Cambridge: Harvard University Press, 2004.
Brunet, Guy, Pierre Darlu, and Gianna Zei, eds. *Le Patronyme. Histoire, anthropologie, société*. Paris: CNRS, 2001.
Brunet, Jean-Paul, ed. *Immigration, vie politique et populisme en banlieue parisienne*. Paris: L'Harmattan, 1995.
Brunet, Jean-Paul. "Aux origines de l'industrialisation de Saint-Denis." *Études de la région parisienne*, No. 22 (1969): 16–22.
Brunet, Jean-Paul. "Une banlieue ouvrière: Saint-Denis (1890–1939). Problèmes d'implantation du socialisme et du communisme." State dissertation in history, University of Lille III, 1978.
Brunet, Jean-Paul. *Saint-Denis, la ville rouge: socialisme et communisme en banlieue ouvrière, 1890–1939*. Paris: Hachette, 1980.
Bueno Rocha, José. *Navalmoral, 600 años de vida*. Navalmoral de la Mata: Ayuntamiento de Navalmoral de la Mata, 1985.
Burke, Peter. *History and Social Theory*. Ithaca: Cornell University Press, 2005.
Burke, Peter. *New Perspectives on Historical Writing*. Cambridge: Polity Press, 2001.
Cabanel, Patrick. *La République du certificat d'études: histoire et anthropologie d'un examen, XIXe–XXe*. Paris: Belin, 2002.
Cafiero, Ugo. "I fanciulli italiani nelle vetrerie francesi. Relazione preliminare del Comitato piemontese. Inchiesta fatta nei circondari di Sora e di Isernia." In Opera di assistenza degli Operai Italiani emigrati in Europa e nel Levante, *Bollettino bimensile edito dal Consiglio centrale* 1, No. 2 (1901): 1–22.
Caglioti, Daniela. "Subjects, citizens, and aliens in a time of upheaval: Naturalizing and denaturalizing in Europe during the First World War." *The Journal of Modern History* 89, No. 3 (2017): 495–530.
Calhoun, Craig. *Nationalism*. Buckingham: Open University Press, 1997.
Campani, Giovanna. "Les réseaux familiaux, villageois et régionaux des immigrés italiens en France." Doctoral diss. in ethnology, University of Nice, 1988.
Carbone, Annalisa. *Le cento patrie dei Molisani nel mondo*. Isernia: Cosmo Iannone, 1998.
Cassarino, Jean-Pierre. "Theorising return migration: The conceptual approach to return migrants revisited." *International Journal on Multicultural Societies* 6, No. 2 (2004): 253–79.
Cefaloglì, Fernando. *Il Molise nell'Unità d'Italia*. Isernia: Cosmo Iannone, 2011.
Centre de documentation et d'histoire des techniques. *Évolution de la géographie industrielle de Paris et sa proche banlieue au XIXe siècle*, vol. II: *Vers la maturité de l'industrie parisienne, 1872–1914*. Paris: CDHT, 1976.

Certeau, Michel de. *The Practice of Everyday Life*. Berkeley: University of California Press, 1984.
Cerutti, Simona. "Micro-history: Social relations versus cultural models?" In *Between Sociology and History: Essays on Microhistory, Collective Action and Nation-Building*, edited byAnna-Maija Castrén, Markku Lonkila, and Matti Peltonen. (Helsinki: Finnish Literature Society, 2004), 17–40.
Chanut, Jean-Marie, Jean Heffer, Jacques Mairesse, and Gilles Postel-Vinay. "Les disparités de salaires en France au XIXe siècle." *Histoire & Mesure* 10, Nos. 3–4 (1995): 381–409.
Charle, Christophe. *Histoire sociale de la France au XIXe siècle*. Paris: Seuil, 1991.
Chassagne, Serge. "Le travail des enfants aux XVIIIe et XIXe siècles." In *Histoire de l'enfance en Occident*, edited by Egli Becchi and Dominique Julia, 224–72. Paris: Seuil, 1998.
Châtelain, Abel. "Les migrations temporaires françaises au XIXe siècle. Problèmes. Méthodes. Documentation." *Annales de démographie historique* 1967: 9–28.
Châtelain, Abel. "L'attraction des trois plus grandes agglomérations françaises: Paris-Lyon-Marseille en 1891. Migrations parties des départements français selon le lieu de naissance." *Annales de démographie historique* 1971: 27–41.
Cho, Sumi, Kimberlé Williams Crenshaw, and Leslie McCall. "Toward a field of intersectionality studies: Theory, applications, and praxis." *Signs* 38, No. 4 (2013): 785–810.
Choate, Mark. *Emigrant Nation. The Making of Italy Abroad*. Cambridge: Harvard University Press, 2008.
Choudhry, Sultana. *Multifaceted Identity of Interethnic Young People. Chameleon Identities*. Farnham: Ashgate, 2012.
Cohen, Jean-Louis, and André Lortie, eds. *Des fortifs au périph*. Paris: Picard, 1992.
Colin, Marielle, and François Neveux, eds. *Les Italiens en Normandie: de l'étranger à l'immigré*. Caen: Musée de Normandie, 2000.
Colin, Marielle, ed. *L'Immigration italienne en Normandie de la Troisième République à nos jours: de la différence à la transparence*. Caen: Musée de Normandie, 1998.
Colombijn, Freek, and Aygen Erdentug. *Urban Ethnic Encounters: The Spatial Consequences*. New York: Routledge, 2003.
Consejo provincial de fomento de Burgos. *Estadística emigratoria de la provincia: causas principales de la emigración y medios para que disminuya*. Burgos: Díez y Compañía, 1914.
Conzen, Kathleen Neils *et al.* "The invention of ethnicity: A perspective from the USA." *Journal of American Ethnic History* 12, No. 1 (1992): 3–41.
Corbin, Alain. *Le Monde retrouvé de Louis-François Pinagot. Sur les traces d'un inconnu (1798–1876)*. Paris: Flammarion, 1998.
Cott, Nancy F. *Intersection of Work and Family Life: Historical Articles on Women's Lives and Activities*. New York: K.G. Saur, 1992.
Couder, Laurent. "Les Italiens dans la région parisienne." *Publications de l'École Française de Rome*, No. 94 (1986): 501–46.
Crisp, Richard J., ed. *Intergroup Relations*. Thousand Oaks: Sage, 2014.
Cross, William E. *et al.* "Identity work: Enactment of racial-ethnic identity in everyday life." *Identity* 17, No. 1 (2017): 1–12.
Dallier, Gaston. *La Police des étrangers à Paris et dans le département de la Seine*. Paris: Rousseau, 1914.

Bibliography

Darnton, Robert. *The Great Cat Massacre and Other Episodes in French Cultural History*. New York: Vintage, 1984.

Das, Santanu, ed. *Race, Empire and First World War Writing*, Cambridge: Cambridge University Press, 2011.

Daudé-Bancel, Achille. "Une coopérative de consommation, 'La Famille', société coopérative de consommation, d'épargne et de Prévoyance sociale, 104, avenue de Paris, La Plaine-Saint-Denis (Seine)." *L'Action populaire*, No. 88 (1905): 3–28.

De Bock, Jozefien. *Parallel Lives Revisited: Mediterranean Guest Workers and their Families at Work and in the Neighbourhood, 1960–1980*. New York: Berghahn, 2018.

De Gaspari, Olimpia. *Il racconto del piccolo vetraio*. Turin: Paravia, 1903.

Delattre, Simone. *Les Douze heures noires: la nuit à Paris au XIXe*. Paris: Albin Michel, 2000.

Dewerpe, Alain. *Le Monde du travail en France, 1800–1950*. Paris: Armand Colin, 1989.

Diamond, Larry, and Marc F. Plattner, eds. *Nationalism, Ethnic Conflict, and Democracy*. Baltimore, London: Johns Hopkins University Press, 1994.

Diaz, Paola, and Guido Nicolosi. "Corps, identités et technologies 'par les nombres' dans l'imaginaire migratoire." *Socio-anthropologie* 40, No. 1 (2019): 9–28.

Dieckhoff, Alain. *La Nation dans tous ses états. Les identités nationales en mouvement*. Paris: Flammarion, 2000.

Dietlind, Stolle, Stuart Soroka, and Richard Johnston. "When does diversity erode trust? Neighborhood diversity, interpersonal trust and the mediating effect of social interactions." *Political Studies* 56, No. 1 (2008): 57–75.

Donham, David. *Violence in a Time of Liberation: Murder and Ethnicity at a South African Gold Mine, 1994*. Durham: Duke University Press, 2011.

Dornel, Laurent, and Céline Regnard. *Les Chinois dans la Grande Guerre. Des bras au service de la France*. Paris: Les Indes savantes, 2018.

Dornel, Laurent. *La France hostile. Socio-histoire de la xénophobie, 1870–1914*. Paris: Hachette, 2004.

Dornel, Laurent. *Les Étrangers dans la Grande Guerre*. Paris: La Documentation française, 2014.

Douzenel, Pierre. *À Saint-Denis, les rues aussi ont leur histoire*. Saint-Denis: Douzenel, 1981–90.

Duroselle, Jean-Baptiste, and Enrico Serra, eds. *L'Emigrazione italiana in Francia prima del 1914*. Milan: F. Angeli, 1978.

Einaudi, Luigi, and Giuseppe Prato. "La liberazione di ottanta piccoli martiri, una santa crociata nelle vetrerie francesi." *La Riforma Sociale* 11 (1901): 1101–13.

Eleb-Vidal, Monique, and Anne Debarre. *L'Invention de l'habitation moderne: Paris, 1880–1914*. Paris: Hazan, 1995.

Eley, Geoff, and Ronald Suny, eds. *Becoming National*. Oxford: Oxford University Press, 1996.

Elias, Norbert. *The Established and the Outsiders*, edited by John Scotson, Thousand Oaks: Sage, 1994 [1976].

Epple, Angelika. "Lokalität und die Dimensionen des Globalen. Eine Frage der Relationen." *Historische Anthropologie* 21, No. 1 (2013): 4–25.

Esch, Michael. *Parallele Gesellschaften und soziale Räume. Osteuropäische Einwanderer in Paris 1880–1940*. Frankfurt, New York: Campus Verlag, 2012.

Fagnot, François. *Rapport sur le travail de nuit des enfants dans les usines à feu continu*. Paris: Alcan, 1908.
Fahrenthold, Stacy D. *Between the Ottomans and the Entente: The First World War in the Syrian and Lebanese Diaspora, 1908–1925*. Oxford: Oxford University Press, 2019.
Fahrmeir, Andreas, Olivier Faron, and Patrick Weil, eds. *Migration Control in the North Atlantic World: The Evolution of State Practices in Europe and the United States from the French Revolution to the Inter-War Period*. New York, Oxford: Berghahn, 2003.
Farcy, Jean-Claude. *Les Camps de concentration français de la Première guerre mondiale, 1914–1920*. Paris: Anthropos, 1995.
Farge, Arlette. "Les archives du singulier. Quelques réflexions à propos des archives judiciaires comme matériau de l'histoire sociale." In *Histoire sociale, histoire globale*, edited by Christophe Charle (Paris: Éditions de la MSH, 1993), 183–9.
Faure, Alain, and Claire Lévy-Vroelant. *Une chambre en ville. Hôtels meublés et garnis de Paris, 1860–1990*. Paris: Créaphis, 2007.
Faure, Alain. "L'invention des banlieusards. Les déplacements de travail entre Paris et sa banlieue (1880–1914): Première approche." *Villes en parallèles*, No. 10 (1986): 233–48.
Faure, Alain. "Une génération de Parisiens à l'épreuve de la ville." *Bulletin du Centre d'histoire de la France contemporaine*, No. 7 (1986): 157–73.
Faure, Alain, ed. *Les Premiers banlieusards: Aux origines des banlieues de Paris (1860–1940)*. Paris: Créaphis, 1991.
Faure, Alain. "Comment se logeait le peuple parisien à la Belle Époque." *Vingtième siècle*, No. 64 (1999): 41–51.
Faure, Alain. "Aspects de la vie du quartier dans le Paris populaire de la fin du XIXe siècle." *Recherches contemporaines* 6 (2000–2001): 283–97.
Favre-Le Van Ho, Mireille. "Un milieu porteur de modernisation: travailleurs et tirailleurs vietnamiens en France pendant la Première Guerre mondiale." Doctoral diss. in history, École nationale des Chartes, 1986.
Favre-Le Van Ho, Mireille. *Des Vietnamiens dans la Grande Guerre. 50 000 recrues dans les usines françaises*. Paris: Vendémiaire, 2014.
Feld, Jan, Nicolás Salamanca, and Daniel Hamermesh. "Endophilia or exophobia: Beyond discrimination." *The Economic Journal* 126, No. 594 (2016): 1503–27.
Fernández López, Javier, and Carmelo Zaita. *El ferrocarril de la Robla*. Madrid: Agualarga, 1987.
Ferrari, Mario Enrico. "I mercanti di fanciulli nelle campagne e la tratta dei minori, una realtà sociale dell'Italia fra '800 e '900." *Movimento operaio e socialista* 6, No. 1 (1983): 87–108.
Flannery, James. *The Glass House Boys of Pittsburgh: Law, Technology, and Child Labor*. Pittsburgh: University of Pittsburgh Press, 2009.
Fontanon, Claudine. "La banlieue Nord-Est de Paris: structuration des espaces industriels et des zones de résidence." *Villes en parallèles* 1, No. 10 (1986): 14–38.
Foot, John. "Micro-history of a house: Memory and place in a Milanese neighbourhood, 1890–2000." *Urban History* 34, No. 3 (2007): 431–52.
Forbes, Hugh Donald. *Ethnic Conflict. Commerce, Culture, and the Contact Hypothesis*. New Haven: Yale University Press, 1997.

184 Bibliography

Fourcaut, Annie, and Mathieu Flonneau, eds. *Une histoire croisée de Paris et de ses banlieues à l'époque contemporaine. Bibliographie, bilan d'étape.* Paris: Ville de Paris, 2005.

Fourcaut, Annie. *La Banlieue en morceaux: la crise des lotissements défectueux en France dans l'entre-deux-guerres.* Paris: Créaphis, 2000.

Fox, Jon, and Demelza Jones. "Introduction: Migration, everyday life and the ethnicity bias." *Ethnicities* 13, No. 4 (2013): 385–400.

Frader, Laura Levine. "From muscles to nerves: Gender, 'race' and the body at work in France 1919–1939." *International Review of Social History* 44, No. 7 (1999): 123–47.

Francis, Emerich K. *Interethnic Relations: Essay in Sociological Theory.* New York: Elsevier Science, 1976.

Freeman, Susan. *The Pasiegos: Spaniards in No Man's Land.* Chicago: University of Chicago Press, 1979.

Gabaccia, Donna. *From Sicily to Elizabeth Street: Housing and Social Change among Italian Immigrants, 1880–1930.* Albany: SUNY Press, 1984.

Gabaccia, Donna. *From the Other Side: Women, Gender, and Immigrant Life in the U.S., 1820–1990.* Bloomingdon: Indiana University Press, 1994.

Gabaccia, Donna, and Franca Iacovetta, eds. *Women, Gender and Transnational Lives: Italian Workers of the World.* Toronto: University of Toronto Press, 2002.

Gabaccia, Donna, and Fraser M. Ottanelli, eds. *Italian Workers of the World: Labor Migration and the Formation of Multiethnic States.* Urbana: University of Illinois Press, 2001.

Gaillard, Jeanne. "Les migrants à Paris au XIXe siècle. Insertion et marginalité." *Ethnologie française* 10, No. 2 (1980): 129–36.

Galante, John. "Distant loyalties: World War I and the Italian South Atlantic." Doctoral diss. in history, University of Pittsburgh, 2016.

Garden, Maurice. "Mariages parisiens à la fin du XIXe siècle: une micro-analyse quantitative." *Annales de démographie historique* 1998: 111–33.

Garrabou, Ramón, ed. *La crisis agraria europea de finales del siglo XIX.* Barcelona: Crítica, 1988.

Gatrell, Peter, and Liubov Zhvanko, eds. *Europe on the Move: Refugees in the Era of the Great War, 1912–1923.* Manchester: Manchester University Press, 2017.

Gaziel. *Diario de un estudiante: París 1914.* Translated by José Ángel Martos Martín. Barcelona: Diërensis, 2013 [1914].

Gellner, Ernest. *Nations and Nationalism.* Ithaca: Cornell University Press, 1983.

Gerber, David. "Acts of deceiving and withholding in immigrant letters: Personal identity and self-presentation in personal correspondence." *Journal of Social History* 39, No. 2 (2005): 315–30.

Gerber, David. "Epistolary ethics: Personal correspondence and the culture of emigration in the nineteenth century." *Journal of American Ethnic History* 19, No. 4 (2000): 3–23.

Gérôme, Noëlle, Danielle Tartakowsky, and Claude Willard, eds. *La Banlieue en fête: de la marginalité urbaine à l'identité culturelle.* Paris: Presses universitaires de Vincennes, 1988.

Gervaise, Patrick. "Les Passages à Levallois-Perret. Quartier populaire, quartier de la 'Zone' (1826–1972)." Doctoral diss. in history, University of Paris VII, 1986.

Ghobrial, John-Paul. "Moving stories and what they tell us: Early Modern mobility between microhistory and global history." *Past & Present* 242, No. 14 (2019): 243–80.
Girard, Alain, and Jean Stoetzel. *Français et Immigrés. L'attitude française. L'adaptation des Italiens et des Polonais en France.* Paris: PUF/INED, 1953.
Girault, Jacques, ed. *Ouvriers en banlieue XIXe–XXe.* Paris: L'Atelier, 1998.
Glick Schiller, Nina, Linda Basch, and Cristina Blanc-Szanton. "Transnationalism: A new analytic framework for understanding migration." *Annals of the New York Academy of Sciences* 645, No. 1 (1992): 1–24.
Gould, Roger. *Insurgent Identities: Class, Community and Protest in Paris from 1848 to the Commune.* Chicago: University of Chicago Press, 1995.
Gourdon, Vincent. "Les témoins de mariage civil dans les villes européennes du XIXe siècle: quel intérêt pour l'analyse des réseaux familiaux et sociaux?" *Histoire, économie & société* 27, No. 2 (2008): 61–87.
Grancea, Liana, Rogers Brubaker, Jon Fox, and Margit Feischmidt. *Nationalist Politics and Everyday Ethnicity in a Transylvanian Town.* Princeton: Princeton University Press, 2006.
Green, Nancy, and Marie Poinsot, eds. *Histoire de l'immigration et question coloniale en France.* Paris: La Documentation française/CNHI, 2008.
Green, Nancy, and Roger Waldinger, eds. *A Century of Transnationalism: Immigrants and Their Homeland Connections.* Urbana: University of Illinois Press, 2016.
Green, Nancy. *Les Travailleurs immigrés juifs à la Belle Époque. Le "Pletzl" de Paris.* Paris: Fayard, 1984.
Green, Nancy. *Repenser les migrations.* Paris: Presses universitaires de France, 2002.
Grendi, Edoardo. "Microanalisi e storia sociale." *Quaderni Storici* 12, No. 35 (1972): 506–20.
Gribaudi, Maurizio. *Itinéraires ouvriers. Espaces et groupes sociaux à Turin au début du XXe siècle.* Paris: EHESS, 1987.
Guerry Linda. *Le Genre de l'immigration et de la naturalisation. L'exemple de Marseille (1918-1940).* Lyon: ENS, 2013.
Guglielmo, Raymond. "Désindustrialisation et évolution de l'emploi à Saint-Denis." *Villes en parallèle*, No. 11 (1986): 116–33.
Guglielmo, Thomas. *White on Arrival: Italians, Race, Color and Power in Chicago, 1890–1945.* New York: Oxford University Press, 2003.
Guichard, Éric, and Gérard Noiriel, eds. *Constructions des nationalités et immigration dans la France contemporaine.* Paris: Presses de l'ENS, 1997.
Guilbert, Madeleine. *Les Femmes et l'organisation syndicale avant 1914: présentation et commentaires de documents pour une étude du syndicalisme féminin.* Paris: CNRS, 1966.
Guillerme, André, Anne-Cécile Lefort, and Gérard Jigaudon. *Dangereux, insalubres et incommodes. Paysages industriels en banlieue parisienne, XIXe–XXe siècles.* Seyssel: Champ Vallon, 2004.
Gurak, Douglas, and Fe Caces. "Migration networks and the shaping of migration systems." In *International Migration Systems: A Global Approach*, edited by Mary Kritz, Lin Lean Lim, and Hania Zlotnik (Oxford: Clarendon Press, 1992), 150–76.
Guyot, Yves. "Les industries, les salaires et les droits de douane." *Journal de la société statistique de Paris* 45 (1904): 132–44.

Halbwachs, Maurice. *La Classe ouvrière et les niveaux de vie*. Paris: Alcan, 1913.
Hargreaves, Alec G. *Immigration, "Race" and Ethnicity in Contemporary France*. London, New York: Routledge, Psychology Press, 1995.
Haubrichs, Wolfgang, and Reinhard Schneider, eds. *Grenzen und Grenzregionen. Frontières et régions frontalières*. Saarbrücken: SDV, 1993.
Haug, Sonja. "Migration networks and migration decision-making." *Journal of Ethnic and Migration Studies* 34, No. 4 (2008): 585–605.
Haupt, Heinz Gerhard, Michaël M. Müller, and Stuart Woolf. *Regional and National Identities in Europe in the 19th and the 20th centuries*. The Hague, Boston: Kluwer Law International, 1998.
Heywood, Colin. "The market for child labour in nineteenth-century France." *History* 66, No. 216 (1981): 34–49.
Heywood, Colin. *Childhood in Nineteenth-Century France. Work, Health and Education Among the "Classes Populaires."* Cambridge: Cambridge University Press, 1988.
Hobsbawm, Eric, and Terence Ranger. *The Invention of Tradition*. Cambridge: Cambridge University Press, 1983.
Hodes, Martha. *The Sea Captain's Wife: A True Story of Love, Race, and War in the Nineteenth Century*. New York: W. W. Norton, 2006.
Hodson, Gordon, and Miles Hewstone, eds. *Advances in Intergroup Contact*. London, New York: Psychology Press, 2012.
Hoerder, Dirk, and Christine Harzig, eds. *What is Migration History?* Cambridge: Polity Press, 2009.
Hoerder, Dirk, ed. *"Struggle a Hard Battle": Essays on Working-Class Immigrants*. De Kalb: Northern Illinois University Press, 1986.
Hoggart, Richard. *The Uses of Literacy: Aspects of Working-Class Life, with Special References to Publications and Entertainments*. London: Chatto and Windus, 1957.
Hondagneu-Sotelo, Pierrette. *Gendered Transitions: Mexican Experiences of Immigration*. Berkeley: University of California Press, 1994.
Horne, John, ed. *State, Society, and Mobilization in Europe during the First World War*. Cambridge: Cambridge University Press, 1997.
Horne, John. "Immigrant workers during World War I." *French Historical Studies* 14, No. 1 (1985): 57–88.
Horowitz, Donald. *Ethnic Groups in Conflict*. Berkeley: University of California Press, 1985.
Horrall, Andrew. "The 'foreigners' from Broad Street: The Ukrainian sojourners from Ottawa who fought for Canada in the First World War." *Histoire sociale/ Social history* 49, No. 98 (2016): 73–103.
Horton Cooley, Charles. *Social Process*. New York: Scribners, 1918.
Hugo, Victor. *Notre-Dame de Paris*. Translated by Alban Krailsheimer. Oxford: Oxford University Press, 1999.
Jacoby, Karl. *The Strange Career of William Ellis: The Texas Slave Who Became a Mexican Millionaire*. New York: W. W. Norton, 2016.
Jacquemet, Gérard. "Belleville ouvrier à la Belle Époque." *Le Mouvement social*, No. 118 (1982): 61–77.
Jenkins, Richard. *Rethinking Ethnicity: Arguments and Explorations*. London: Sage, 1997.

Jenkinson, Jacqueline, ed. *Belgian Refugees in First World War Britain.* Abingdon: Routledge, 2018.
Jenkinson, Jacqueline. *Colonial, Refugee and Allied Civilians after the First World War: Immigration Restriction and Mass Repatriation.* Abingdon: Routledge, 2020.
Johnson, Paul E. "Reflections: Looking Back at Social History." *Reviews in American History* 39, No. 2 (2011): 379–88.
Justino, Patricia, Tilman Brück, and Philip Verwimp, eds. *A Micro-Level Perspective on the Dynamics of Conflict, Violence, and Development.* Oxford: Oxford University Press, 2013.
Kalifa, Dominique. *L'Encre et le sang. Récits de crimes et société à la Belle Époque.* Paris: Fayard, 1995.
Koikkalainen, Saara, and David Kyle. "Imagining mobility: The prospective cognition question in migration research." *Journal of Ethnic and Migration Studies* 42, No. 5 (2016): 759–76.
König, Mareike. *Deutsche Handwerker, Arbeiter und Dienstmädchen in Paris: Eine vergessene Migration im 19. Jahrhundert.* Munich: Oldenburg, 2003.
Koselleck, Reinhart. *Zeitschichten: Studien zur Historik.* Frankfurt: Suhrkamp, 2000.
Kronenberger, Stéphane. "Des temps de paix aux temps de guerre: les parcours des travailleurs étrangers de l'Est et du Sud-Est de la France (1871–1918)." Doctoral diss. in history, University of Nice, 2014.
Kubat, Daniel, ed. *The Politics of Return. International Return Migration in Europe.* New York: Center for Migration Studies, 1984.
Laffond, Colette. "L'industrie de la chaussure à Izeaux (Bas-Dauphiné)." *Revue de géographie alpine* 34, No. 1 (1946): 69–85.
Lamont, Michèle, and Virág Molnár. "The study of boundaries across the social sciences." *Annual Review of Sociology* 28 (2002): 167–95.
Langrognet, Fabrice. "Accueil et représentations des migrants en temps de guerre: Les étrangers à la Plaine-Saint-Denis, 1914–1919." *Migrance*, Nos. 45–6 (2016): 161–72.
Langrognet, Fabrice. "Contingent minorities: What the Great War meant for the migrant youth of the Plaine-Saint-Denis." *The Journal of the History of Childhood and Youth* 11, No. 2 (2018): 208–26.
Langrognet, Fabrice. "Geodesic distance as metric of cross-group networks in migration history." *Journal of Migration History* 6 (2020): 405–28.
Langrognet, Fabrice. "Interethnic resentment or mundane grudges? A 1900 Paris fight under the microscope." *Immigrants and Minorities. Historical Studies in Ethnicity, Migration and Diaspora* 37, Nos. 1–2 (2019): 24–43.
Langrognet, Fabrice. "The crossings of Luigi Pirolli, a migrant among others (1886–1953)." *Quaderni storici* 54, No. 3 (2019): 831–57.
Langrognet, Fabrice. "Exploitation or public service? The import-export trade of underage glassmakers in Saint-Denis, France (1892–1914)." *The Journal of the History of Childhood and Youth* 15, No. 1 (2022): 112–30.
Lautieri, Monica. *Industrie manifatturiere e mondo tessile nell'antica provincia di Terra di Lavoro.* Villanova di Guidonia: Aletti, 2017.
Le Moal, Marcel. *L'Émigration bretonne,* Spézet: Coop Breizh, 2013.
Le Roy Des Barres, Adrien, and Paul Louis Gastou. *Le Choléra à Saint-Denis en 1892, rôle des différents agents infectieux et des conditions hygiéniques dans l'invasion, la marche et la propagation du choléra.* Paris: Asselin et Houzeau, 1893.

Lecoq, Marcel. *La Crise du logement populaire*. Paris: Société immobilière de la région parisienne, 1912.

Lefèbvre, Henri. *Le Droit à la ville*. Paris: Anthropos, 1968.

Lemercier, Claire. "Analyse de réseaux et histoire de la famille: une rencontre encore à venir?" *Annales de démographie historique* 109, No. 1 (2005): 7–31.

Lemercier, Claire. "Formal network methods in history: Why and how?" In *Social Networks, Political Institutions, and Rural Societies*, edited by Georg Fertig (Turnhout: Brepols, 2015), 281–310.

Lemoine, Jean. "L'émigration bretonne à Paris." *Science sociale* 14, No. 1 (1892): 39–60, 165–84, 239–48, 362–73.

Lémonon, Ernest. *L'Après-guerre et la main-d'œuvre italienne en France*. Paris: Félix Alcan, 1918.

Lepoutre, David. "Histoire d'un immeuble haussmannien. Catégories d'habitants et rapports d'habitation en milieu bourgeois." *Revue française de sociologie* 51, No. 2 (2010): 321–58.

Lequin, Yves, ed. *Histoire des étrangers et de l'immigration en France*. Paris: Larousse, 1992.

Lequin, Yves. "Les citadins et leur vie quotidienne." In *Histoire de la France urbaine*, edited by Georges Duby, vol. 4 (Paris: Seuil, 1983), 275–358.

Lesger, Clé, Leo Lucassen, and Marlou Schrover. "Is there life outside the migrant network? German immigrants in 19th century Netherlands and the need for a more balanced migration typology." *Annales de démographie historique* 104, No. 2 (2002): 29–50.

Levavasseur, Chanoine Fernand. *Saint-Denis à travers l'histoire*. Montrouge: Impr. Ferrey, 1975.

Levine, John M., and Michael A. Hogg, eds. *Encyclopedia of Group Processes and Intergroup Relations*. Thousand Oaks: Sage, 2009.

Levitt, Peggy. "Social remittances: Migration driven local-level forms of cultural diffusion." *International Migration Review* 32, No. 4 (1998): 926–48.

Lewis, Mary D. *The Boundaries of the Republic: Migrant Rights and the Limits of Universalism in France, 1918–1940*. Palo Alto: Stanford University Press, 2007.

Lillo, Natacha, ed. *Histoire des immigrations en Île-de-France de 1830 à nos jours*. Paris: Publibook, 2012.

Lillo, Natacha. "Coexistence des migrants." *Projet*, Special issue, April 2, 2008. Last accessed July 27, 2021. https://www.revue-projet.com/articles/2008-04-lillo-coexistence-des-migrants/8012.

Lillo, Natacha. "Espagnols en 'banlieue rouge'. Histoire comparée des trois principales vagues migratoires à Saint-Denis et dans sa région au XXe siècle." Doctoral diss. in history, IEP Paris, 2001.

Lombard-Jourdan, Anne. *La Plaine Saint-Denis: deux mille ans d'histoire*. Paris: CNRS, 1994.

Lombard-Jourdan, Anne. *Saint-Denis, lieu de mémoire*. Paris: Fédération des sociétés historiques et archéologiques de Paris et de l'Île-de-France, 2000.

Lucassen, Jan, Leo Lucassen, and Patrick Manning. *Migration History in World History: Multidisciplinary Approaches*. Leiden, Boston: Brill, 2010.

Lucassen, Leo, ed. *The Immigrant Threat: The Integration of Old and New Migrants in Western Europe since 1850*. Urbana: University of Illinois Press, 2005.

Luconi, Stefano. "Becoming Italian in the US: Through the lens of life narratives." *MELUS* 29, Nos. 3–4 (2004): 151–64.
Ma, Li, ed. *Les Travailleurs chinois en France dans la Première Guerre mondiale.* Paris: CNRS, 2012.
MacMaster, Neil. *Colonial Migrants and Racism: Algerians in France, 1900–1962.* New York: St. Martin's Press, 1997.
Madoz, Pascual. *Diccionario geográfico, estadístico y histórico de España y de sus posesiones de Ultramar.* Madrid: Madoz & Sagasti, 1984 (1st ed. 1849).
Magnússon, Sigurður Gylfi, and István M. Szíjártó. *What is Microhistory? Theory and Practice.* Abingdon: Routledge, 2013.
Maitte, Corine. *Les Chemins de verre: Les migrations des verriers d'Altare et de Venise (XVIe–XIXe siècles).* Rennes: Presses universitaires de Rennes, 2009.
Manz, Stefan, Panikos Panayi, and Matthew Stibbe, eds. *Internment During the First World War: A Mass Global Phenomenon.* Abingdon: Routledge, 2018.
Maruani, Margaret and Monique Meron. "Le travail des femmes dans la France du XXe siècle." *Regards croisés sur l'économie*, No. 13 (2013): 177–93.
McNeill, William H., and Ruth S. Adams. *Human Migrations.* Bloomington: Indiana University Press, 1978.
Menjot, Denis, and Jean-Luc Pinol, eds. *Les Immigrants et la ville. Insertion, intégration, discrimination (XIIe-XX^{e}siècles).* Paris: L'Harmattan, 1996.
Merriman, John M. *The Margins of City Life: Explorations on the French Urban Frontier, 1815–1851.* New York, Oxford: Oxford University Press, 1991.
Meynier, Gilbert. *L'Algérie révélée. La guerre de 1914–1918 et le premier quart du XX^{e}siècle.* Saint-Denis: Bouchène, 2015 (1st ed. 1981).
Michel, Marc. "'Immigrés malgré eux': soldats et travailleurs coloniaux en France pendant la Première Guerre mondiale." *Historiens & Géographes*, No. 384 (2003): 333–44.
Michel, Marc. *Les Africains dans la Grande Guerre.* Paris: Karthala, 2003.
Milza, Pierre, Antonio Bechelloni, and Michel Dreyfus, eds. *L'Intégration italienne en France: un siècle de présence italienne dans trois régions françaises: 1880–1980.* Brussels: Complexe, 1995.
Mitchell, Brian. *International Historical Statistics: Europe, 1750–1988.* New York: Stockton Press, 1992.
Moretti, Enrico. "Social networks and migrations: Italy 1876–1913." *International Migration Review* 33, No. 3 (1999): 640–57.
Moriceau, Caroline. "L'hygiène à la Cristallerie de Baccarat dans la seconde moitié du XIXe siècle. La santé ouvrière au cœur de la gouvernance industrielle." *Le Mouvement Social* 213, No. 4 (2005): 53–70.
Moriceau, Caroline. *Les douleurs de l'industrie, L'hygiénisme industriel en France, 1860–1914.* Paris: EHESS, 2009.
Morrissey, Robert Michael. "Archives of Connection." *Historical Methods: A Journal of Quantitative and Interdisciplinary History* 48, No. 2 (2015): 67–79.
Moulin, Brigitte, ed. *La Ville et ses frontières. De la ségrégation sociale à l'ethnicisation des rapports sociaux.* Paris: Karthala, 2001.
Musée d'art et d'histoire de Saint Denis. *Des cheminées dans la Plaine, cent ans d'industrie à Saint-Denis, 1830–1930.* Paris: Créaphis, 1998.
Nathans, Sydney. *To Free a Family: The Journey of Mary Walker.* Cambridge: Harvard University Press, 2012.

Nelli, Humbert. "The Italian padrone system in the United States." *Labor History* 2 (1964): 153–67.
Ngai, Mae. *Impossible Subjects: Illegal Aliens and the Making of Modern America*. Princeton: Princeton University Press, 2004.
Ngai, Mae. *The Lucky Ones: One Family and the Extraordinary Invention of Chinese America*. Princeton: Princeton University Press, 2012.
Nogaro, Bertrand, and Lucien Weil. *La Main-d'œuvre étrangère et coloniale pendant la guerre*. Paris, New Haven: PUF, Yale University Press, 1926.
Noguer, Narciso. "Desventuras del emigrante español." *Razón y fe* 23, No. 1 (1912): 4–20.
Noiriel, Gérard. *État, nation et immigration: vers une histoire du pouvoir*. Paris: Belin, 2001.
Noiriel, Gérard. *Le Creuset français*. Paris: Seuil, 1988. Translated by Geoffroy de Laforcade as *The French Melting Pot: Immigration, Citizenship, and National Identity*. Minneapolis: University of Minnesota Press, 1996.
Noiriel, Gérard. *Le Massacre des Italiens. Aigues-Mortes, 17 août 1893*. Paris: Fayard, 2009.
Olmos, Rosa. "Mémoire de l'immigration algérienne, Oued Souf (Algérie) – Hauts-de-Seine (France): Projet de collecte, conservation et traitement de sources orales." *Bulletin de l'AFAS*, No. 38 (2012): 16–7.
Oltmer, Jochen, ed. *Migrationsforschung und interkulturelle Studien*. Osnabrück: University of Osnabrück, 2002.
Olzak, Susan. *The Dynamics of Ethnic Competition and Conflict*. Palo Alto: Stanford University Press, 1992.
Page Moch, Leslie. *Moving Europeans. Migration in Western Europe since 1650*. Bloomington: Indiana University Press, 1992.
Page Moch, Leslie. *The Pariahs of Yesterday: Breton Migrants in Paris*. Durham: Duke University Press, 2012.
Panayi, Panikos, ed. *Minorities in Wartime: National and Racial Groupings in Europe, America and Australia during the Two World Wars*. Oxford: Berg, 1993.
Papanikolas, Zeese. "To a Greek bootblack." *Journal of the Hellenic Diaspora* 20, No. 1 (1994): 65–85.
Passeron, Jean-Claude, and Jacques Revel, eds. *Penser par cas*. Paris: EHESS, 2005.
Paulucci di Calboli, Raniero. "La traite des petits Italiens en France." *La Revue des Revues* (1897), 1.07.1897: 393–408.
Paulucci di Calboli, Raniero. *Parigi 1898. Con Zola, per Dreyfus. Diario di un diplomatico*. Edited by Giovanni Tassani, Bologna: CLUEB, 1998.
Peretti, Pierre de. *Saint-Denis 1870/1920. Les Témoins parlent*. Saint-Denis: Saint-Denis Municipal Archives, 1981.
Perrot, Michelle. "Les rapports des ouvriers français et des ouvriers étrangers (1871–1893)." *Bulletin de la société d'histoire moderne* 58, No. 12 (1960): 4–9.
Perrot, Michelle. "De la manufacture à l'usine en miettes." *Le Mouvement social*, No. 125 (1983): 3–12.
Perrot, Michelle. "Fait divers et histoire au XIXe siècle." *Annales. Économies, sociétés, civilisations* 38, No. 4 (1983): 911–8.
Perrot, Michelle. "Dans le Paris de la Belle Époque, les 'Apaches,' premières bandes de jeunes." *La Lettre de l'enfance et de l'adolescence*, No. 1 (2007): 71–8.

Picoche, Philippe. "Une entreprise vosgienne. La verrerie de Portieux (1850–1950)." Doctoral diss. in history, University of Lyon II, 2000.
Pinchard, Benoît. "L'étude socio-généalogique des verriers. Problématiques, méthodes et perspectives." *Éclats de verres*, No. 18 (2011): 53–9.
Pinol, Jean-Luc. *Les Mobilités de la grande ville. Lyon, fin XIXe–début XXe*. Paris: FNSP, 1991.
Piselli, Fortunata. *Parentela ed emigrazione. Mutamenti e continuità in una comunità calabrese*. Turin: Einaudi, 1981.
Pistilli, Emilio. *Acquafondata e Casalcassinese*. Acquafondata: Comune di Acquafondata, 2004.
Poitrineau, Abel. *Remues d'hommes: les migrations montagnardes en France au XVIIe–XVIIIe siècles*. Paris: Aubier, 1983.
Prezioso, Stéfanie. "Les Italiens en France au prisme de l'engagement volontaire: les raisons de l'enrôlement dans la Grande Guerre (1914–1915)." *Cahiers de la Méditerranée*, No. 81 (2010): 147–63.
Protasi, Maria Rosa. *Emigrazione ed immigrazione nella storia del Lazio*. Viterbo: Sette Città, 2010.
Protasi, Maria Rosa. *I fanciulli nell'emigrazione italiana. Una storia minore (1861–1920)*. Isernia: Cosmo Iannone, 2010.
Pullan, Wendy, and Britt Baillie, eds. *Locating Urban Conflicts: Ethnicity, Nationalism and the Everyday*. Basingstoke: Palgrave Macmillan, 2013.
Putnam, Lara. *The Company They Kept: Migrants and the Politics of Gender in Caribbean Costa Rica, 1870–1960*. Chapel Hill: University of North Carolina Press, 2002.
Radouan, Sébastien. "La rénovation du centre-ville de Saint-Denis aux abords de la basilique, de la Libération au Mondial 98: une modernité à la française." Doctoral diss. in art history, University of Paris IV, 2008.
Raffaelli, Enzo, and Lorenzo Cadeddu, eds. *I ragazzi del '99: Il racconto dei diciottenni al fronte*. Udine: Gaspari, 2016.
Rahikainen, Marjatta. *Centuries of Child Labour: European Experiences from the Seventeenth to the Twentieth Century*. Aldershot: Ashgate, 2004.
Rainhorn, Judith, and Didier Terrier, eds. *Étranges voisins. Altérité et relations de proximité dans la ville depuis le XVIIIe siècle*. Rennes: Presses universitaires de Rennes, 2010.
Redono Cardeñoso, Jesús-Ángel. "El turno de los campesinos: protesta social en la España rural del cambio de siglo (1898–1923)." *Revista de História da Sociedade e da Cultura* 12 (2012): 393–415.
Remotti, Francesco. *Contro l'identità*. Rome, Bari: Laterza, 1996.
Revel, Jacques, ed. *Jeux d'échelles*. Paris: Gallimard/Seuil, 1996.
Robert, Jean-Louis, and Danielle Tartakowsky. *Paris le peuple, XVIIIe–XXe siècles*. Paris: Publications de la Sorbonne, 1999.
Robert, Jean-Louis. *Les Ouvriers, la Patrie et la Révolution: Paris 1914–1919*. Besançon: Presses universitaires de Franche-Comté, 1995.
Roediger, David. *Wages of Whiteness: Race and the Making of the American Working Class*. New York: Verso, 1991.
Romains, Jules. *Paris des hommes de bonne volonté*. Paris: Flammarion, 1949.
Romano, Sergio. *Histoire de l'Italie du Risorgimento à nos jours*. Paris: Le Seuil, 1977.

Rosenberg, Clifford. *Policing Paris. The Origins of Modern Immigration Control between the Wars*. Ithaca, London: Cornell University Press, 2006.
Rosental, Paul-André. "Between macro and micro: Theorizing agency in nineteenth-century French migrations." *French Historical Studies* 20, No. 3 (2006): 457–81.
Rosental, Paul-André. *Les Sentiers invisibles. Espaces, familles et migrations dans la France du XIXe siècle*. Paris: Éditions de l'EHESS, 1999.
Rothschild, Emma. *An Infinite History: The Story of a Family in France over Three Centuries*. Princeton: Princeton University Press, 2021.
Ruane, Joseph, and Jennifer Todd. "The roots of intense ethnic conflict may not in fact be ethnic: Categories, communities and path dependence." *Archives européenes de sociologie* 45, No. 2 (2004): 209–32.
Rubio, Javier. *La emigración española a Francia*. Barcelona: Ariel, 1974.
Ruiz, Vicki L., and Ellen Carol DuBois, eds. *Unequal Sisters: A Multicultural Reader in U.S. Women's History*. New York: Routledge, 1990.
Rygiel, Philippe, ed. *Le Bon grain et l'ivraie. La sélection des migrants en Occident, 1880–1939*. Paris: Presses de l'ENS, 2004.
Rygiel, Philippe. "Archives et historiographie de l'immigration." *Migrance*, No. 33 (2009): 50–9.
Saada, Emmanuelle. *Empire's Children: Race, Filiation, and Citizenship in the French Colonies*. Chicago: The University of Chicago Press, 2012.
Sachs, Miranda. "'A sad and... odious industry': The problem of child begging in late nineteenth-century Paris." *The Journal of the History of Childhood and Youth* 10, No. 2 (2017): 188–205.
Saillard, Auguste, and Henri Fougerol. *Les Allocations aux familles des mobilisés, réfugiés et victimes civiles de la guerre*. Paris: Berger-Levrault, 1917.
Saíz, Julián. *Olvido o recuerdo. Un médico español en Aubervilliers*. Aubervilliers: J. Saíz, 2001.
Sánchez Alonso, Blanca. *Las causas de la emigración española, 1880–1930*. Madrid: Alianza, 1995.
Santelli Emmanuelle, and Beate Collet. "Couples endogames, couples mixtes: Options conjugales et parcours de vie de descendants d'immigrés en France." *Migrations Société* 145, No. 1 (2013): 107–20.
Sauvaire-Jourdan, François. "La crise du change en Espagne." *Bulletin hispanique* 7, No. 3 (1905): 293–304.
Savoye, André. "La vie quotidienne dans la banlieue Nord et Nord-Ouest de Paris pendant la Grande Guerre." Doctoral diss., University of Paris IV, 2007.
Savoye, André. *Guerre et après-guerre en banlieue nord parisienne, 1914–1922*. Paris: Soteca, 2010.
Schaub, Jean-Frédéric. *Race Is about Politics: Lessons from History*. Translated by Lara Vergnaud. Princeton: Princeton University Press, 2019.
Schneider, Dorothee. *Crossing Borders: Migration and Citizenship in the Twentieth-Century United States*. Cambridge: Harvard University Press, 2011.
Schontz, André, and Arsène Felten. *Le Chemin de fer en Lorraine*, Metz: Serpenoise, 1999.
Schor, Ralph. *Histoire de l'immigration en France de la fin du XIXe siècle à nos jours*. Paris: Armand Colin, 1996.

Scott Divita, David. "Acquisition as becoming: An ethnographic study of multilingual style in la Petite Espagne." Doctoral diss. in romance languages and literatures, University of California, Berkeley, 2010.
Scott, Rebecca, and Jean Hébrard. *Freedom Papers: An Atlantic Odyssey in the Age of Emancipation*. Cambridge: Harvard University Press, 2012.
Scott, Rebecca. "Microhistory set in motion: A nineteenth-century Atlantic creole itinerary." In *Empirical Futures: Anthropologists and Historians Engage the Work of Sidney W. Mintz*, edited by George Baca et al. (Chapel Hill: University of North Carolina Press, 2009), 84–111.
Silverman, Maxim. *Deconstructing the Nation: Immigration, Racism and Citizenship in Modern France*. London: Routledge, 1992.
Simon, Pierre-Jean. *Pour une sociologie des relations interethniques et des minorités*. Rennes: Presses universitaires de Rennes, 2006.
Simonton, Deborah. *A History of European Women's Work: 1700 to the Present*. Abingdon: Routledge, 1998.
Singer-Kérel, Jeanne. *Le Coût de la vie à Paris de 1840 à 1954*. Paris: Armand Colin, 1954.
Sinke, Suzanne. "Gender and Migration: Historical Perspectives." *International Migration Review* 40, No. 1 (2006): 82–103.
Sommi-Picenardi, Galeazzo. "La tratta dei piccoli italiani in Francia." *Nuova antologia* 37, No. 723 (1902): 460–83.
Song, Miri. "Is intermarriage a good indicator of integration?" *Journal of Ethnic and Migration Studies* 35, No. 2 (2009): 331–48.
Sori, Ercole, and Anna Treves, eds. *L'Italia in movimento: Due secoli di migrazioni*. Udine: Forum, 2008.
Sori, Ercole. *L'emigrazione italiana dall'Unità alla Seconda guerra mondiale*. Bologna: Il Mulino, 1979.
Spire, Alexis. *Étrangers à la carte. L'administration de l'immigration en France (1945–1975)*. Paris: Grasset, 2005.
Stamberger, Janiv. "The 'Belgian' Jewish experience of World War One." *Les Cahiers de la Mémoire Contemporaine* 13 (2018): 95–124.
Stibbe, Matthew, ed. *Captivity, Forced Labor and Forced Migration in Europe during the First World War*. Abingdon: Routledge, 2009.
Stoler, Ann Laura, and Frederick Cooper, eds. *Tensions of Empire: Colonial Cultures in a Bourgeois World*. Berkeley: University of California Press, 1997.
Stovall, Tyler. "Colour-blind France? Colonial workers during the First World War." *Race and Class* 35, No. 2 (1993): 35–55.
Thébaud, Françoise. *Les Femmes au temps de la guerre de 14*. Paris: Payot, 1980.
Thiesse, Anne-Marie. *La Création des identités nationales*. Paris: Seuil, 2001.
Tombs, Robert P., ed. *Nationhood and Nationalism in France*. London: Routledge, 1992.
Torpey, John. *The Invention of the Passport Surveillance, Citizenship, and the State*. Cambridge: Cambridge University Press, 2000.
Trivellato, Francesca. "Microstoria/Microhistoire/Microhistory." *French Politics, Culture & Society* 33, No. 1 (2015): 122–34.
Vaillot, Benoît. "L'exil des Alsaciens-Lorrains. Option et famille dans les années 1870." *Revue d'histoire du XIXe siècle. Société d'histoire de la révolution de 1848 et des révolutions du XIXe siècle* 61 (2020): 103–22.

Vajda, Joanne. *Paris, Ville Lumière: Une transformation urbaine et sociale, 1855–1937*. Paris: L'Harmattan, 2015.

Vandamme, Tobit. "The rise of nationalism in a cosmopolitan port city: The foreign communities of Shanghai during the First World War." *Journal of World History* 29, No. 1 (2018): 37–64.

Vecoli, Rudolph, and Francesco Durante. *Oh Capitano! Celso Cesare Moreno-Adventurer, Cheater, and Scoundrel on Four Continents*. New York: Fordham University Press, 2018.

Vecoli, Rudolph, and Suzanne Sinke, eds. *A Century of European Migrations, 1830–1930*. Urbana: University of Illinois Press, 1991.

Vecoli, Rudolph. "An inter-ethnic perspective on American immigration history." *Mid America* 75, No. 2 (1993): 223–35.

Vecoli, Rudolph. "Contadini in Chicago: A critique of *The Uprooted*." *The Journal of American History* 51, No. 3 (1964): 404–17.

Vegliante, Jean-Charles, ed. *Gli Italiani all'estero*. Paris: Publications de la Sorbonne nouvelle, 1990.

Vegliante, Jean-Charles, ed. *La Traduction-migration. Déplacements et transferts culturels Italie-France*. Paris: L'Harmattan, 2000.

Vertovec, Steven. "Super-diversity and its implications." *Ethnic and Racial Studies* 30, No. 6 (2007): 1024–54.

Vial, Éric. "Les Italiens en France." *Historiens et Géographes*, No. 383 (2003): 251–65.

Viet, Vincent. *La France immigrée. Construction d'une politique (1914–1997)*. Paris: Fayard, 1998.

Vilar, Juan Bautista, and María José Vilar. *La emigración española a Europa en el siglo XX*. Madrid: Arco, 1999.

Vu-Hill, Kimloan. *Coolies into Rebels: Impact of World War I on French Indochina*. Paris: Les Indes savantes, 2011.

Wahl, Alfred, and Jean-Claude Richez. *La Vie quotidienne en Alsace entre France et Allemagne, 1850–1950*. Paris: Hachette, 1993.

Wahl, Alfred. *L'Option et l'émigration des Alsaciens-Lorrains (1871–1872)*. Strasbourg: Presses universitaires de Strasbourg, 1973.

Waldinger, Roger. *The Cross-Border Connection*. Cambridge: Harvard University Press, 2015.

Weber, Eugen. *Peasants into Frenchmen: The Modernization of Rural France, 1870–1914*. Palo Alto: Stanford University Press, 1976.

Weil, Patrick. *Qu'est-ce qu'un Français? Histoire de la nationalité française depuis la Révolution*. Paris: Gallimard, 2002.

Weissbach, Lee Shai. *Child Labor Reform in Nineteenth-Century France: Assuring the Future Harvest*. Baton Rouge: Louisiana State University Press, 1989.

Wessendorf, Susanne. "Settling in a super-diverse context: Recent migrants' experiences of conviviality." *Journal of Intercultural Studies* 37, No. 5 (2016): 449–63.

Whalen, Philip, and Patrick Young, eds. *Place and Locality in Modern France*. London, New York: Bloomsbury Academic, 2014.

White, Jerry. *Rothschild Buildings: Life in an East-End Tenement Block, 1887–1920*. London: Pimlico, 2003 (1st ed. 1980).

Wimmer, Andreas, and Nina Glick Schiller. "Methodological nationalism and beyond: Nation-state building, migration and the social sciences." *Global Networks* 2, No. 4 (2002): 301–34.
Wimmer, Andreas. "Does ethnicity matter? Everyday group formation in three Swiss immigrant neighbourhoods." *Ethnic and Racial Studies* 27, No. 1 (2004): 1–36.
Wimmer, Andreas. *Ethnic Boundary Making: Institutions, Power, Networks.* Oxford: Oxford University Press, 2013.
Winter, Jay, and Jean-Louis Robert, eds. *Capital Cities at War: Paris, London, Berlin, 1914–1919.* Cambridge: Cambridge University Press, 1997.
Winter, Jay, ed. *The Cambridge History of the First World War.* Cambridge: Cambridge University Press, 2014.
Wyman, Mark. *Round-Trip to America: The Immigrants Return to Europe, 1880–1930.* Ithaca: Cornell University Press, 1993.
Yans-McLaughlin, Virginia, ed. *Immigration Reconsidered: History, Sociology, and Politics.* Oxford, New York: Oxford University Press, 1990.
Yazbak, Mahmoud, and Yfaat Weiss, eds. *Haifa before and after 1948: Narratives of a Mixed City.* Dordrecht, St. Louis: IHJR, 2011.
Zalc, Claire, and Nicolas Mariot. *Face à la persécution. 991 Juifs dans la guerre.* Paris: Odile Jacob, 2010.
Zalc, Claire, and Tal Bruttmann, eds. *Microhistories of The Holocaust.* New York: Berghahn, 2017.
Zalc, Claire. *Melting shops. Une histoire des commerçants étrangers en France.* Paris: Perrin, 2010.
Zalc, Claire. *Denaturalised: How Thousands Lost Their Citizenship and Lives in Vichy France.* Translated by Catherine Porter. Cambridge: Harvard University Press, 2020.
Zanou, Konstantina. *Transnational Patriotism in the Mediterranean, 1800–1850: Stammering the Nation.* Oxford: Oxford University Press, 2018.
Zerubavel, Eviatar. *Hidden Rhythms: Schedule and Calendars in Social Life.* Berkeley: University of California Press, 1985.
Zittoun, Tania. "Imagination in people and societies on the move: A sociocultural psychology perspective." *Culture & Psychology* 26, No. 4 (2020): 654–75.
Zucchi, John. *The Little Slaves of the Harp: Italian Child Street Musicians in Nineteenth-Century Paris, London and New York.* Montreal: McGill-Queen's University Press, 1992.
Zunz, Olivier. *The Changing Face of Inequality: Urbanization, Industrial Development, and Immigrants in Detroit, 1880–1920.* Chicago: University of Chicago Press, 1983.

Glossary

Apache(-s)   A reference to the native American tribe whose supposed ferocity had been popularised by French novels in the second half of the 19th century, the term appeared in the national press around 1900 to designate gangs of young bandits in Paris, especially in outlying neighbourhoods and near the fortifications. Its use receded after the First World War.

Bureau de bienfaisance   The expression refers to the local charity institution which municipalities were enboldd to set up, by virtue of a law adopted during the French Revolution. The *Bureaux* could hand out food (bread, flour, oil, meat), coal, and cover medical fees (orthopedic protheses, in particular). Financial handouts were rare. Their budget was made up of municipal subsidies, a special tax on balls, theatres, concerts and cinemas (called *droit des pauvres*) and the returns of estates donated to the town.

Certificat de coutume   To this day, this legal document written by a foreign lawyer and translated into French by a certified translator is delivered by diplomatic missions to be produced before French officials (notaries, mayors, judges). Its function is to certify the existence and interpretation of one particular provision of law in the country of origin of the person presenting the certificate. In the context of marriages at the beginning of the 20th century, the *certificat de coutume* was meant to prove that in certain countries, major citizens were not required to prove parental consent to be able to marry.

Conseil de révision   In every *canton* (Saint-Denis was the main town of one such administrative division), this institution created under the French Revolution was the military recruiting board. Every year, it would decide whether or not conscripts were fit to accomplish their service. Based on a variety of legal motives, the *conseil de révision* could grant exemptions, discharges and postings outside of active military duty. Annual sessions of the *conseil de révision* took place in the spring at the city hall of the canton's main town–usually in mid-April in Saint-Denis– and were composed of the *préfet* (or the *sous-préfet*), superior military officers and other personalities.

Débit (de boissons) Dating to the first decades of the 19th century, the term *débit* initially referred to different kinds of retail shops, in particular those selling tobacco (*débit de tabac*) and liquors (*débit de boissons*). By the end of the century, the noun *débit* without further precision came to designate any bar or restaurant serving alcohol. The term long remained more popular than its equivalent *bistro* (also spelled *bistrot*).

Employé, employée In census registers of the late 19th and early 20th century, this French term designated people employed in white-collar jobs (clerks, secretary, typists), and who often enjoyed permanent contracts, as opposed to *journaliers*, blue-collar workers paid on a daily basis.

Feuille d'immatriculation In 1893, the possession of this certificate, legally called *extrait du registre d'immatriculation*, became compulsory for foreigners who intended to work or run a business (law of 8.08.1893). They received it upon compliance with the requirement to register within eight days of their arrival to a new town. Failure to register could result in fines ranging from 50 to 200 francs, and employers who hired non-registered foreigners were also liable to financial sanctions.

Garni The adjective *garni*, which in the context of housing meant "furnished" – the equivalent of today's *meublé*– became a noun in the 19th century and came to designate a room rented with furniture, in either a hotel or a private apartment. People who wished to run a garni in the Seine had to file a declaration at the Préfecture de police and were subject to a number of occupancy and hygiene requirements.

Journalier, journalière At the glassworks as elsewhere in the Plaine, most positions were based on daily employment until the 1930s. From a legal standpoint, job contacts were renewed every day (hence the term *journalier*). Nevertheless, customs of each industrial sector usually mandated short periods of notice before any termination of the contract by one of the parties. Workers were paid every other Friday, based on the number of days they had worked over a two-week period. After the First World War, an informal practice took hold at the glass factory as well as other factories in the Plaine, consisting in giving workers daily advances on their salaries.

Justice de paix Present in every *canton* (Saint-Denis was the main town of one such administrative division), the *justice de paix* was the local court in charge of minor civil lawsuits and execution procedures (such as seizures of salaries and assets after the inexecution of a previous ruling) until 1958. Free of charge for plaintiffs, it generally encouraged settlement through conciliation before scheduling a hearing before a judge. In Saint-Denis, the building of the *justice de paix* also hosted a criminal court, the *tribunal de* *simple police*, which was in charge of minor offenses and could only sentence people to fines.

Livret de travail The first version of this document (lit. "work booklet") was created in 1803 to control the movements of adult workers and were compulsory until 1890. The factory management had custody of the *livret*, and the worker could not leave without it. It also had to be signed by the local authorities and indicate the town of destination. Laws on child work (19.05.1874, Art. 10; 2.11.1892, Art. 10) prescribed the establishment of a different sort of *livret*, this time for every worker under the age of 18 (see chapter 4, figure 4.1). Bearing the name, date of birth and hiring dates of its holder, the children's *livret* was not so much an instrument of mobility control as an identity document, created with the purpose of enforcing the legal requirement on the minimum age.

Locataire principal This expression (lit. "main tenant") designated tenants who signed a rental agreement for an entire property divisible into smaller units and on which subleasing was not prohibited. The *locataires principaux* had the same obligations towards their subtenants as regular landlords. They also remained responsible for all damages to the property (Civil code, Art. 1735).

Padrone (-i), padrón (-es) In the late 19th century, the Italian words *padrone* and *incettatore (di fanciulli)* referred to intermediaries who were entrusted with children in Italy to make them work as street peddlers and later as factory workers. The feminine *padrona* was used for *padroni's* wives, as well as independent female child-suppliers. Castilian-speakers used the equivalents *padrón, padrones*. The French press would sometimes use the word *comprachico,* coined by Victor Hugo in 1869 in *L'Homme qui rit*.

Terra di Lavoro Literally meaning "Land of Labour" in Italian, *Terra di Lavoro* was the name of a historical province of the Kingdom of Two Sicilies and then of Italy after unification. Its northernmost subdivision (*circondario*) corresponded to the area around Sora and Arpino, which bordered Molise (administrative centre, Campobasso) to the west. The administrative centre of *Terra di Lavoro* was Caserta. This province was abolished in 1927.

Tirage au sort Literally meaning the "draw" or the "lottery," the *tirage au sort* happened in every French *canton* in winter, in order to establish the list of conscripts who would then be subject to the final decisions of the *conseil de révision*. Initially meant to divide annual levies into two groups – one that had to serve and the other that did not– the distinction between "good" and "bad numbers" shifted to the duration of service after 1873 (one or five years). From 1889 to 1905, everyone had to serve for three years, and the draw only determined whether the conscripts would be enrolled in the Navy or the Army. The draw was abolished in 1905.

Index

Alsatians and Lorrainers 2, 40, 53–6, 58, 61–2, 66n12, 67n32, 73, 93, 97, 99, 101–2, 104–6, 107n12, 113, 117, 126–8, 131–5, 148, 150
animals: cows 19, 25; dogs 25, 56; horses 19, 25, 29, 55, 159
apaches 110, 118–9, 122n56, 150
assistance, benefits, handouts 44, 62, 125, 129–31, 135–6, 144

bars, *débits* 9, 21–3, 26, 29–30, 34n60, 46–7, 51n67, 62, 64, 71, 80, 98, 110, 112, 114, 117, 119, 151–2, 162
Basque Country 56, 67n34–5, 71, 74–5, 85n31
Belgians 56, 62, 112, 144, 147, 149, 156n32
benefit societies 10, 76, 131, 138n31
bombings 26, 159–61, 164n3
borders 2, 52, 56, 59–60, 64, 81, 136, 146–7, 154
Bretons 6, 40, 49n25, 53, 62, 66n27, 97, 102, 105

census 9, 16n46, 37–43, 48n18, 55, 78, 104, 125–6, 136, 137n5
Chemin de fer du Nord (railway company) 73, 149, 157n44
children 1–2, 27–9, 37–9, 45, 55, 60–2, 67n32, 69n57, 72, 74–83, 88n68, 88n77, 98, 102, 104–6, 111, 114, 116, 118, 128, 130–1, 135, 142n97, 145, 153, 160–2
Chinese workers 63–4, 151
citizenship 4, 8, 53, 60, 74, 120, 125–37, 149–54, 158n73, 161, 163

class 8, 22, 27, 36, 62–3, 65, 93, 101–2, 112, 115, 125, 163
colonial workers: from Indochina 63, 117, 151–3, 158n70; from North Africa 63, 112–3, 117, 151–2, 159, 161
crime 53, 77, 110–20, 127, 130

diplomatic missions and personnel: French 138n23, 145; Italian 47n2, 77, 128, 144, 148, 155n22; Spanish 128, 132, 144

elections 22, 60, 125, 130, 154
ethnicity 2–8, 12, 15n42, 22, 36, 40, 62, 72, 76, 83, 93–4, 98–101, 104–6, 110–3, 115–7, 119–20, 131, 143, 161, 163

festivals, fairs 23, 30, 114, 116, 118–9
Feuille d'immatriculation 127, 144
First World War 6, 9, 22, 41, 47, 61–3, 72–3, 75–6, 112, 117, 125, 127, 131, 137, 143–54, 161
food 28, 30, 44, 56, 76, 79, 114, 125
friendship 29, 71, 83, 93, 97–101, 104–5, 114, 117–9, 134, 151, 154

gender 3, 8, 22, 36, 44, 47, 65, 72, 82, 97, 99, 105, 119, 125, 143, 150–4, 163
German Empire 26, 53–5, 59, 93, 96, 128, 138n25
glassworkers: men 1, 21, 23–4, 41–3, 49n35–6, 54–5, 59, 73, 93, 101–2, 104, 114–20, 135; women 38, 42, 44, 49n40, 50n49, 82–4; children 72, 75, 78–84, 105
Greeks 62, 103, 151

Index

health 37–9, 46–7, 77, 83, 129, 135, 144, 158n70
hygiene 9, 28, 30, 35n85, 38, 57, 149

identity papers 127–7, 144
income, salaries, wages 32n33, 36, 39, 41–7, 51n65, 51n67, 53–4, 59, 63, 66n19, 76, 79, 83, 115–6, 133, 141n69, 142n89, 150, 153
Italians: Casertans and Molisans 5, 28, 39, 53–5, 58–9, 61–2, 65n2, 67n34, 68n41, 73–83, 96–7, 100–2, 104–5, 110–2, 114–19, 121n16, 128–31, 133, 135–6, 145, 147–8, 150; from other regions 24, 40, 62, 76–7, 100, 126, 130–1, 144, 146–7, 149, 151, 155n22

judicial institutions: Saint-Denis *justice de paix* 7, 23, 33n53, 81, 120n15; Seine criminal courts 33n55, 77, 79–80, 118–9, 121n29, 122n56, 123n57, 124n80, 127, 130, 137n14

La Villette 73–4, 87n67
labour inspectors 77–9, 82, 89n90, 118
language 55, 101–3, 104–6, 133, 152
Legras–owner 1, 31n3, 73, 82, 89n94, 134; glass factory 23, 32n30, 38, 41–4, 46–7, 50n49, 54, 62, 66n20, 73–82, 89n89, 93, 101–2, 105, 107n28, 110, 115–8, 128, 131, 134, 145, 149, 161, 164n12
Lyon 61, 77, 118

market 23, 80, 119
marriage 10, 62, 64, 74, 93–100, 102–3, 105, 127, 152–3
Marseilles 67n34, 118
masculinity 81, 119, 150
memory 22, 25–6, 28, 44, 161–2
military service 60–1, 63, 74, 128–9, 134, 136, 147, 149, 150
Mouton (factory) 42–4, 54, 102, 112, 145, 160
municipal authorities 21, 27, 33n56, 45, 60, 81, 129–30, 145, 147
music 26, 52, 56, 58, 65n2, 74, 76, 82

Naples 52, 67n34, 77
naturalisation 7, 9–10, 39, 45, 56, 126–7, 130, 132–6, 138n25, 141n86, 147, 153–4, 156n29
New York 40, 52, 67n34

newspapers 9–10, 28, 105, 111, 113–20, 144, 147
Normandy 1, 52, 54, 58, 65n2, 74, 88n77

Padrón (pl. *padrones*) 79–82, 88n87, 131
Padrone (pl. *padroni*) 76–82, 104, 131
passports 87n55, 125, 127–8, 136, 145–6, 150, 154
Patronato español 102–3, 132
Pirolli family (from Pozzilli): Giacinto 55, 58, 77–8; Giustino 78, 128, 134, 145–6; Luigi/Louis 10, 52–3, 55, 57, 60, 62–4, 74, 76, 78, 83, 131, 134, 136, 145, 159; Maria (née Rodi) 57–8, 60, 136, 159
police and gendarmerie 6–7, 10, 22, 28, 32n28, 49n24, 53, 60, 80, 89n90, 104, 111, 113, 115–6, 120n15, 125, 127, 133–5, 144, 149, 154, 161
politics: local 5, 81, 129–30; national 115, 134
Portuguese 103, 151
Préfecture de police 87n50, 127, 133

race and racism 3–4, 64, 110–3, 115–8, 143, 151–4, 158n73, 163–4
refugees 39, 62–3, 125, 143, 149, 150
religion 3, 10, 23, 93, 101–3, 106, 132
remittances 22, 73
rent 19–20, 24–7, 33n53, 37, 40, 44–6, 57, 140n64
return trips 52, 55, 58–61, 65, 68n50, 72, 128, 134, 136, 140n64, 145–7, 153

Santol, Joseph 78–9, 81
sex workers 63, 82, 149, 151
shops 9, 21–2, 26, 41, 45–6, 54, 76, 125, 129–30, 134, 148, 151, 159
smells 24, 28, 163
soldiers: Americans 64, 159; British 151; French 125, 133, 135, 143, 149, 151; Italian 118, 147, 150
sounds 24–5, 163
Spaniards: from Cantabria and Burgos 27–8, 39–43, 55, 58, 62, 73–4, 79–83, 100; from Extremadura 40, 97, 100, 111, 128, 161; from other regions 5–6, 40, 56, 71, 74–5, 97, 99, 101–6, 112, 126, 131–2, 143–7, 151–2, 163
Spanish Mission (rue de la Pompe, Paris) 102–3, 132

theft 26, 29, 111, 118–9, 123n57, 130

transport: metro 23, 103; trains 19, 23–4, 56, 67n34, 131, 144–5; tram 19, 23, 29; ships 67n34, 83
trees 19, 29

unemployment 41, 49n30, 129, 147

Versigny, Louise 19, 22–6, 45–6
Vozza, Donato 77, 81, 104

walls of Paris 23, 29, 151

wandering trades: musicians 52, 58, 65n2, 74, 76, 82; strolling peddlers 2, 76, 79–80, 46
weapons: guns 68n50, 111, 114–9; knives 110, 114–6, 119, 143
women 22, 29–30, 37–8, 41–4, 47, 51n65, 55, 60–4, 72, 74, 80, 82–4, 99, 102, 104–5, 108n55, 111–2, 116, 118, 121n32, 125–7, 151–4, 159–60

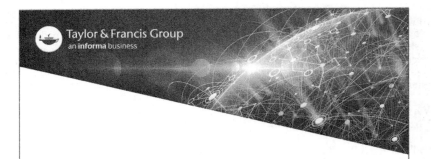